Great Hostesses

By the same author

Molière (1969)
Sartre (1969)
Saint-Exupéry (1970)
Rabelais (1971)
Camus—A Study (1973)
Wynyard Hall and the Londonderry Family (1974)
Dreams about H.M. The Queen (1974)
The Dukes (1975)
Now Barabbas Was a Rotter:
the Extraordinary Life of Marie Corelli (1978)
The Mistresses of Charles II (1980)
Georgiana, Duchess of Devonshire (1981)

BRIAN MASTERS

Great Hostesses

CONSTABLE
LONDON

First published in Great Britain 1982
by Constable and Company Ltd
10 Orange Street London WC2H 7EG
Copyright © 1982 by Brian Masters
ISBN 0 09 464000 9
Set in Monophoto Ehrhardt 11pt by
Servis Filmsetting Ltd, Manchester
Printed in Great Britain by
St Edmundsbury Press
Bury St Edmunds, Suffolk

Dedicated to

NATALIA MAKAROVA

Contents

Illustrations

Acknowledgements

This book has not been written by one man alone in a library. I have spent as much time bothering people to dredge their memories as I have going through published works which deal with the period and unpublished papers not previously consulted. My debts of gratitude are not therefore scanty, and I acknowledge them eagerly.

Mr Valentine Lawford allowed me the use of part of his diary and some personal letters. Mary, Countess of Pembroke gave me a long letter addressed to her late husband, and the late Lord Gage gave me pages of his own reminiscences. Miss Ann Pegrum and Mr Anthony Palmer guided me through the Desborough Papers at Hertfordshire County Record Office, and Mr Hutton of Pembroke College, Cambridge helped me sift the diaries of Sir Ronald Storrs. Mr Ramon R. Hernandez was most helpful in sending material in the possession of the McMillan Memorial Library at Wisconsin Rapids, and the staffs of the Western Reserve Historical Society and the Cleveland *Plain Dealer* responded generously to my request for material. The gentlemen who run the *Evening Standard* newspaper library were always most welcoming. *Fortune* magazine have kindly permitted the use of an article. Miss Susana San Sanchez typed part of the early manuscript, and Miss Monica Kendall made a fine job of the finished product.

Mr Michael Colefax devoted much time and energy to pointing

me in the right direction and correcting errors which I made along the way. I am grateful also to Mr Michael Bloch for many valuable hints and constant encouragement. Mrs Hoogterp never tired of my questions and gave me a great deal of information.

Others who have given information or have been helpful in different ways include Mr Stuart Preston; the Dowager Duchess of Buccleuch; the Countess of Sutherland; Lady Sudeley; Lady Mairi Bury; Lord Olivier; Lady Gladwyn; Lady Selina Hastings; Lady Diana Cooper; Mr James Lees-Milne; Mr Patrick Leigh-Fermor; Baron Radowitz; Hon. Sonia Cubitt; Lord Boothby; Mr Michael Hornby; Hon. David Herbert; the Duke of Portland; Mr George Dix; Lord David Cecil; Mr Henry McIlhenny; Dame Rebecca West; Mr Peter Quennell; Sir Harold Acton; the late Hon. James Smith; Mr Nigel Nicolson; Miss Joan Haslip; Mr Peter Coats; Nancy Lancaster; Rosamund Lehmann; Mr Julian Jeffs; Hon. Mrs B.H. Burns; Sir John Leslie, Bart; Mr Ronald E. Bassett; Mrs Win Rothman; Mr Thomas Carr Howe; Mr Robert Heber-Percy; Baroness Elliot of Harewood. Should there be more whom I have unwittingly omitted, I pray they may believe my gratitude is no less real for being unexpressed.

Dr H. Montgomery Hyde deserves my special thanks for having suggested the subject in the first place.

I have given no references for the various quotations which appear in the course of the text. Some are from private conversations, others from sources published and unpublished. A full bibliography is appended for those readers who may wish to pursue the subject further.

The printed sources that have been most useful to me include *Julian Grenfell* by Nicholas Mosley, *The Londonderrys* by H. Montgomery Hyde, *Emerald and Nancy* by Daphne Fielding, *Queen of the Golden Age* by Cornelius Vanderbilt, and the diaries of Sir Harold Nicolson, Sir Henry Channon and Sir Cecil Beaton. I am happy to acknowledge my debt to the authors and publishers of these.

B.M.

London, 1982

Introduction

'A great hostess and creator of a salon needs an unflagging curiosity about other people, a flair for making them feel at home, or at least stimulated in her circle, almost unlimited time to organize her entertainments and to devote herself to the pursuit and domestication of those rising celebrities her shrewdly selective eye has marked down; and plenty of money.'

So wrote John Lehmann in his autobiography, and since he knew a number of the women who are the subjects of subsequent chapters, and had watched them at work, his observations are the fruit of experience. To his almost comprehensive list of requirements one might add that a hostess needs to be bossy, to control conversation and mobilize friendships by shifting people around the room, preferably in so subtle a manner that her guests do not realize they are being manipulated; and she must ruthlessly exclude all bores from her table, or, if one is inadvertently admitted, stifle his excesses with dispatch.

These necessary talents may occasionally be at variance with one another, as, for example, when you find a first-rate celebrity who is also a colossal bore, and the hostess must decide if the light of his name is bright enough to obliterate the tedium of his company. Or, indeed, if your desire to twist the kaleidoscope and have guests interrupt a well-launched conversation in order to begin a new one with someone else conflicts with your duty to place everyone at his ease. It is by no means a straightforward job, and only a handful of women in each generation are skilful enough to meet all the demands it makes upon their energies. While there are hundreds of would-be hostesses who failed, all those mentioned in the ensuing pages stayed the course long enough to be recognized as hostesses by their contemporaries, as experts in the art of entertaining, as prime agents of social mobility in their time. What is more, and really quite astonishing, they all appear to have enjoyed it.

Making one's guest feel comfortable, or rather, avoiding a situation in which he might feel uncomfortable, is not nearly so simple as it sounds. Its most obvious manifestation lies in giving your guest the wonderfully enhancing impression that he is the *one* person you have been waiting to speak to all week. Ettie Desborough was the most accomplished in this art. On the other hand, Mrs Ogden Mills gave the equally firm impression that she could not care less if she never saw you again, and still contrived to be reasonably successful as a hostess; which shows, perhaps, that you do not need to possess *all* the required attributes in equal measure. Lady Diana Cooper was altogether brilliant in putting guests at their ease, as is attested by Alan Pryce-Jones's memory of her at lunch one day in France. One of her guests, a princess over whom the shadow of poverty had fallen, enjoyed herself so much with the food and wine that she gradually slid under the table. Lady Diana promptly fell to her hands and knees and joined her, saying that it was much more comfortable to have one's coffee at ground level. Not many hostesses would have had the wit to cope so well.

It is difficult to conceive anything quite so inimical to the comfort of one's guests as open hostility between host and hostess. This rarely arises because most of the husbands of really determined hostesses are quiescent, or absent, or dead. But Mr and Mrs Bernal Osborne (grandparents of the 12th Duke of St Albans) did entertain regularly without ever exchanging a word with each other during the meal. They do not figure elsewhere in this book.

A hostess should also ideally possess antennae sensitive enough to draw out the particular talent, characteristic, or interest of every guest, a task made difficult in England by inbred reticence, and unrewarding in America by social pressures towards conformity. In London, Lady Cunard was especially adept in discovering, with an uncanny knack and remarkable speed, unsuspected brightness in the most unlikely people.

One way of sparking hidden talents is to mix a disparate selection of guests from different professions and see what happens. The best hostesses bring together politicians, writers, musicians, and artists, for their mutual enjoyment and interest, choosing the most distinguished men and women in each field, and throwing in some younger persons who might prove their distinction later. The dining-list *chez* Lady Cunard, Lady Colefax, or Lady Desborough might well represent a horizontal slice through English society with every area of interest personified by its most celebrated exponent. A novelist, a philosopher, a general, might find themselves sitting opposite an ambassador, a member of the Cabinet and a painter. There was nothing haphazard about this. Hostesses consciously strove to bring the great to their tables, and their gatherings could with justification be called demonstrably and purposefully *élitist*. This is quite different from implying that hostesses were snobs (though of course some, like Laura Corrigan, certainly were, and detractors of Lady Colefax constantly claim that she was snobbish without understanding the distinction to be made between snobbery and élitism). It was important that each guest be remarkable for some quality or other; the ordinary was abhorrent. It has been written of Lady de Grey, the flamboyantly beautiful hostess of a period slightly before Lady Desborough's, that 'everyone interested her, provided he was first-class. A brilliant politician, a sensational beauty, an inspired artist, and an astonishing fortune-teller interested her equally. She was so far removed from any prejudice that she did not even know the meaning of the word "snobbism".' One of the few ladies who today continue the tradition of entertaining in the proper spirit, planning her guest-list with care, is Joseph Duveen's daughter, Mrs B.H. Burns. 'I invite people I admire,' she says, 'and I enjoy hearing them talk, either to me or to each other.' A Burns dinner-party for sixteen might include the American Secretary of State for Defence, the writer Kingsley Amis, a member of the Habsburg family, a duke or two, a reviewer on the *Times Literary Supplement*, a designer of shoes, a surgeon. It is more or less certain that none of them would have been offered the opportunity of meeting the others without the thought and foresight of Mrs Burns. Hence the difference between a hostess and a lady who has dinner-parties.

It is also important to remember that the best at their job always contrived to introduce some young tyro into the assembly and allow him or her to mix with the great and the distinguished in the land. This was a delightful education, the benefits of which are still prized by those men, now much older, who learnt some of the lessons of life at the table of Emerald Cunard or Sibyl Colefax. Some still recall vividly the intense pleasure and privilege of being present at dinner with a clutch of adults all recognized for their experience and achievement, when they were schoolboys. That kind of education is now sorely missed.

The need to control the tedious or pedantic guest was paramount, for the most illustrious must be made to enjoy themselves and relax to the extent that they would want to repeat the experience. Poor Lady Colefax had the most unenviable task in this respect, for it was generally agreed that the most boring man one could hope to encounter was her husband. If Lady Cunard thought a guest was being too expansive, she would yell out, 'Shut up, dear', and turn the attention to someone else. Mme Geoffrin in the eighteenth century would interrupt a discursive speaker with the simple remark, 'Voilà qui est bien', indicating that enough was enough. With the successful hostesses, a guest really had to be on his toes. The *salons* of Lady Cunard and Lady Londonderry were no place for the slow-witted or the shy. To be invited to their table was an honour bestowed upon a trembling knight, for one knew one's nerves would be taut with the fear of having the attention of the whole table turned upon one by the hostess. Mediocrity was banished. Sensitivity was out of place. Dullness was unspeakable. One had to shine, or else. Or else one was not invited again. It seemed cruel and ruthless, but it was essential if the hostess was to maintain the brittle tenor of her entertainments. She was, after all, a professional.

And she was vain enough to realize that though she might be

feared, she would not be ignored. She organized the conversation at her table with the deft experience of a stage director, and ever kept a watchful eye upon the eddies of guests at her larger parties, flitting from group to group with unobtrusive concern. The best 'stage manager' of large luxurious parties was not a hostess but a host, Sir Philip Sassoon. Sadly, he does not have a chapter in this book, but his magnificent receptions at Port Lympne, his manifold attentions to every guest, his extraordinary ability to make everyone feel completely relaxed though they were under his invisible subtle control, the sheer glow of pleasure one left with, all give him the right to be remembered as the greatest host in England in the twentieth century.

Acting as impresario with one's guests can lead an aspiring hostess into fatal mistakes. It is emphatically not a good idea, for example, to announce a subject of conversation in advance of the dinner and ask guests to prepare themselves accordingly. One who actually did this was Mme Aubernon in the 1890s. On an evening when the topic was 'adultery' a flustered guest had to explain that she had prepared 'incest' by mistake. The Italian poet Gabriele d'Annunzio was at her table when the subject in question was 'love'. He refused to be drawn. 'Read my books, madam,' he said, 'and let me get on with my food.' Spontaneity has ever been the first essential of dinner-table conversation, and the hostess who offends against this rule will not attract the guest who has an alert mind.

Surprisingly, there have been long periods when spontaneity was considered improper by society hostesses. The French hostesses of the 1650s and 1660s actually thought it far more elegant to use artificial conceits wrapped up in pretentious, elaborate language. You were not invited to sit down, you were asked to accept the embrace of the chair. If you had something to say about love, you were obliged to follow the precise map of the art of tenderness charted by Mademoiselle de Scudéry, or else you were out of line. Such hostesses and their female guests were soon termed '*précieuses*', and Molière was wickedly to point out their absurdities and lampoon their intellectual pretensions in a number of plays, notably *Les Femmes Savantes*. The Précieuses had an influence on French language and manners which has not yet entirely evaporated.

Hostesses are more than happy to think that they have exerted some influence, though most will deny that their intention was ever more than to offer good food to good company. Their influence may be of many kinds. On social habits in New York Mrs Stuyvesant Fish left her mark by introducing the revolutionary concept of a meal consumed in under an hour. More importantly, artistic taste in London was profoundly influenced by the energies of two successive hostesses, Lady de Grey and Lady Cunard, who between them were responsible for the resurgence of opera. Lady de Grey spread her influence to the ballet as well. It was she who first brought Diaghilev's company to London in 1911, to participate in a gala season which marked the coronation of George V. Lady de Grey made it possible for Londoners to see Nijinsky dance. As far as the opera was concerned, she and Lady Cunard virtually educated the British public by forcing society to patronize fine performances if they wanted to be 'in', thus enabling the best orchestras and singers to come to London and gradually appeal to all levels of the theatre-going public. Until Lady de Grey set to work on Covent Garden, the repertoire had been shabby and second-rate, the singers poor, the orchestras abysmal. It should be admitted, of course, that Gladys de Grey knew nothing of music; her regeneration of the opera had social motives. Yet all London benefited. Lady Cunard, on the other hand, she who supported Beecham in a later age, was genuinely fond of good music.

Far more difficult to ascertain is the degree to which hostesses exerted political influence. The use of the dining-table as the forum for frank exchange of ideas in an atmosphere free from inhibition, even for mild negotiation, has long been acknowledged unofficially. In the 1780s, the French Ambassador used regularly to corner Charles James Fox after dinner at Devonshire House and learn from him the intentions of the British Government in foreign affairs; it was, he said, the only time he could get any satisfactory answers out of Fox. A little later, Talleyrand used to dine at Holland House three times a week, when he was informed of Cabinet discussions. Dr Leslie Mitchell has pointed out, 'in a very real sense, Holland House for a moment became the Foreign Office'.

This kind of negotiation-by-catering is extremely hard to define, for it is of its nature evanescent and undocumented, and probably all the more important as a result. Politicians talked in the secure knowledge that no one was writing down their every word, though they hoped that the purport of their remarks would be brought home in the right quarters. In such circumstances, the hostess had a significant role to play, not only choosing who should meet whom on a particular occasion, but by making sure that certain views should be aired in the presence of certain ambassadors. It has been known for a dispatch to be written immediately following a dinner-party in 'Society'. Louise von Alten, the 'double' Duchess (first of Manchester, then of Devonshire) openly used entertainments and dinners at Chatsworth to bring pressure upon the representatives of foreign countries to report back the opinions they encountered while having a good time as her guests.

Using the dining-table for influence became especially dangerous in the period covered by this book, for hostesses had a real responsibility when entertaining the German Ambassador to make known the level of true feeling in England. This is not to say that their own opinions were of such weight, but that they were in a very strong position to see that opinions of which they approved were heard at their table, simply by inviting the right (or wrong) people. Mrs Greville was at fault in this regard, for she gave the impression that England would never resist Germany. Lady Colefax, on the other hand, was helpful in presenting the contrary view. Harold Nicolson was well aware of what he called the 'subversive' influence of hostesses like Mrs Greville and Lady Astor. 'They dine and wine our younger politicians and they create an atmosphere of authority and responsibility and grandeur, whereas the whole thing is mere flatulence of the spirit. That is always what happens with us. The silly people are regarded as representative of British opinion and the informed people are dismissed as "intellectuals".'

On another level, Lady Desborough must have had some small influence upon her close friend the Prime Minister Arthur Balfour, and Lady Londonderry certainly did have a profound and damaging influence upon another Prime Minister, Ramsay MacDonald (though she would have been horrified to know that it was damaging). The Abdication crisis also saw influence of a sort exerted by Lady Cunard and Lady Colefax, if only because it was at their tables that the King and Mrs Simpson met frequently and could relax their guard and their tongues. Mrs Simpson went so far as to seek Lady Colefax's advice; she would never even have known her had she not been a hostess.

Entertaining on a prodigious scale has been rendered impossible by many convergent social pressures. In the first place, there is no longer the money available to be squandered (for it was, one must admit, wasteful) on food, drink, orchestras, decorations and all the paraphernalia of an 'entertainment'. With the notable exception of Sibyl Colefax, all the ladies who are the subjects of this book were rich well beyond the normal scope of the word. It is no longer possible to find armies of poor people ready to enter into service, and one cannot easily cater for two hundred, or even twenty, guests without servants. Nor does anyone have the space to receive society *en masse*. Devonshire House and Dudley House in London have disappeared, as have the mansions at 640 and 477 Fifth Avenue, and the descendants of those who lived in them now inhabit houses and flats so small in comparison that the old 'double' Duchess of Devonshire and Mrs Cornelius Vanderbilt could never have imagined existence in such cramped and squalid conditions. Gone, too, is the formality which was always thought an integral part of real entertaining, the questions of precedence, of etiquette, of fine manners.

Moreover, one has to recognize that the quality of guests available is in decline. Certainly in the political field there are none of those large personalities who could delight a dinner table with inspired chatter, and were Lady Cunard alive now she might have difficulty in finding anyone in Westminster who was interesting as well as earnest. Today's political leaders are by comparison mundane. One cannot imagine Margaret Thatcher, James Callaghan, Edward Heath either enjoying or bestowing scintillating conversation, and faced with such guests a modern hostess may well give up in despair. It is to her credit that the late Pamela Hartwell went on entertaining political people in spite of the paucity of material. Newspaper proprietors, too, are less colourful than their giant predecessors, and literary folk are far less social than they were. American men of power talk like hesitant schoolboys, painfully choosing their words so as to obscure rather than enlighten.

The result of these various social upheavals is that the grand hostess cannot flourish in the modern world. Perhaps the last of the truly professional hostesses was the late Ann Fleming, although everyone can no doubt think of two or three candidates alive now who might qualify. Dollie Burns, already mentioned, would be on my personal list, as would Henry McIlhenny, the Philadelphian art collector who lives for five months every year in a romantic castle in Ireland, and has anything from fourteen to twenty-four people to lunch and dinner every day throughout that period. He also possesses those other necessary qualifications for a host, charm, invisible organization, and a large and varied acquaintance. Lord Weidenfeld entertains on a large scale, and Michael Heseltine to a less grandiose degree. An American living in London, Marguerite Littman, specializes in guests from the world of fine art and painting. In America there have been a number of women established as hostesses in their own cities, notably Mrs John Work Garrett of Baltimore, Mrs Stotesbury of Philadelphia (who had so many clothes she had to refer her maid to the inventory—'I'll wear page 248 with shoes 492 today'), Mrs Jack Gardner in Boston, and in Washington the three B's—Mrs Beale, Mrs Bliss, and Mrs Bacon. Probably the most distinguished hostess in Los Angeles today is Ruth Lesserman, whose guests quite naturally spring from the film world.

It must be obvious that the ladies celebrated in this book belong to a personal list, chosen with a mixture of whim and reason. I have omitted Margot Asquith, Nancy Astor and Lady Ottoline Morrell because they have all been the subject of extensive study in the past, and need no further biography. Emerald Cunard has also been written about often enough, but as she is, for my taste, the greatest and most irresistible of them all, she had to be included. Laura Corrigan has been hitherto virtually unknown except in footnotes. Some are professional hostesses in the sense that the art of receiving guests night after night became their overriding purpose in life;

others are hostesses because they occupied a position in society which demanded they should be.

There is a clear division between the grand hostesses of the old school, who entertained as naturally as they breathed, because they were born to it, and the new crop of ambitious women who grasped their way up the social ladder until they became a force which could not be ignored. The division is marked, not entirely artificially, by the First World War.

Into the first group fall Lady Desborough, the last Whig hostess, and in America Mrs Vanderbilt. There was another important lady in England who ought not to be forgotten and has already made a passing appearance, Gladys de Grey. Lady Gladys Herbert, subsequently Lady de Grey and even later the Marchioness of Ripon, was (and this cannot truly be said of any of the ladies who are accorded whole chapters) one of the most beautiful women of her day. When she entered a room, the eyes were so dazzled that one saw green afterwards, as if one had been looking at the sun. E.F. Benson said she made everyone else appear a shade shabby, wanting a touch of the sponge or duster. She was unusually tall, but such were her grace and manner that other women merely seemed squat. Politics bored her, so Lady de Grey entertained the artistic and bohemian set and became, as we have said, a serious patron of the arts. Her manner was consciously theatrical, one might nowadays say 'camp', and her talk was fluid and agitated. She seemed to be in a perpetual state of excitement. She was also a *grande amoureuse*, whereas her contemporary Lady Desborough was only a fairly innocent flirt.

Others of the period were Mrs Charles Hunter, who specialized in the musical world, and Mrs Arthur James, rather mean for a hostess; she would pass a note to her butler with 'D.C.S.C.' scribbled on it, which meant 'Don't cut second chicken'. Guests often had to make do with a thin chop.

The second group, the successful 'upstarts', includes Lady Cunard, Mrs Greville, Lady Colefax and Mrs Corrigan, struggling novices by comparison and pale imitations of the real thing. Lytton Strachey was typically scathing about them; 'shorn beings' he called them, 'for whom the wind is not tempered—powerless, out of place, and slightly ridiculous'. None the less he accepted their invitations, fascinated, hallucinated as in a trance, inexorably drawn to see how they functioned. Virginia Woolf, too, pretended to sneer, and one can sympathize with her frustrated cry, 'Surely in our time something better than this "seeing" people might be contrived.' She was drawn by the novelist's need to observe and listen, to satisfy her insatiable curiosity about people. 'I might pick up a crumb perhaps', she told Ethel Smyth.

One need not take Bloomsbury sniping too seriously. The best hostesses were not mere caterers, filling the bellies of the famous, they were impresarios who knew how to enhance that intangible pleasure gregarious man feels in social life. They made dining at their tables a positive event. And moreover they were the linesmen of history. For a *salon* is as good as its *habitués*, and the catalogue of interesting prominent people who again and again accepted the invitations of society hostesses is sufficient indication of their value. Whether they be politicians and poets at Lady Desborough's, noblemen at Mrs Corrigan's, musicians and writers at Lady Cunard's, the 'best families' of America at Mrs Vanderbilt's, royalty at Mrs Greville's, Mrs Vanderbilt's and Mrs Corrigan's, or absolutely everyone at Lady Colefax's, the men and women who are the dramatis personae of our recent history spent their leisure evenings at the houses of these women. It is most improbable we shall see their like again. That is our misfortune.

CHAPTER ONE

Lady Desborough

Not since the captivating Georgiana, Duchess of Devonshire, a hundred years before, had there been any grand lady in society so universally loved as Ettie Desborough, 'the most perfect type of womanhood that has been evolved out of modern times' in the words of Constance Wenlock. Margot Asquith, not an easy one to please, told her, 'You make me cover my face with my hands and thank God I have such a friend.' Lord Revelstoke called her 'so golden and so strong', while the Duke of Portland wrote, 'her charm is magnetic; her friendship is constant and true; her kindness is unfailing. It is no wonder that, men and women alike, all love and adore her.' George Curzon found her 'always gentle, always thoughtful of others, always well equipped for any call either of brain or heart; always incomparably dressed and an epicure's feast for the eye.' One besotted admirer told her she was 'far above the meannesses and pettinesses which enter into most people's lives', and Betty Ponsonby reflected 'what a quantity of both flash and stodge are devoted to you'. The 'flash' were her own brilliant coterie of friends, who came to be known as 'The Souls', and the 'stodge' were mostly the friends of her admirable but rather heavy husband. Upon both she bestowed the benefits of what some one called her 'stubborn gospel of joy', bringing more happiness to more people than any of her contemporaries, which, in view of her own abysmally tragic life, was nothing short of an awesome accomplishment. Lady Desborough defeated unpleasantness by refusing to countenance it. She was one of fate's victors, not victims, and those who gathered around her, for more than sixty years, were immeasurably cheered by her spirit. 'Her genius lay in a penetrating understanding of the human heart and a determination to redress the balance of life's unhappiness . . . she was a woman of genius who, if subtly and accurately described, either in her mode of life, her charm, wits or character, would have made the fortune of any novelist.' Her own son, the soldier-poet Julian Grenfell, was as much dazzled by his mother's unusual gifts as his seniors. When a schoolboy, he told her that her wonder was inexhaustible, and came upon him with the shock of newness every time. 'Everyone else is like flat soda water after you.'

Such a fulsome introduction would be difficult to justify were it not for the many who survive to this day and raise their eyes to the ceiling, spread their hands wide in a gesture of amazement, as they remember the pleasure of her company. One of Lord David Cecil's keenest moments of nostalgia is to recall visiting Lady Desborough when he was a boy of fifteen, self-consciously imagining himself gauche and *de trop* amid a splendid company of elders, when the hostess interrupted her conversation with an eminent statesman to devote twenty minutes talking solely to him; he was made to feel older, wiser, more interesting than perhaps he was. That was her remarkable gift. She made everyone else feel, for a moment, that he was brilliant. Another young man who was eventually to become her son-in-law, Lord Gage, remembers being alarmed at their first encounter by her disconcerting habit of concentrating her attention upon him. But before long he found that, in spite of his alarm, she made him laugh, and this was quickly followed by the astonished realization that he, too, was amusing and entertaining. A hostess could not possibly aspire to do better than that.

Not that Lady Desborough needed to aspire at all. Unlike some other ladies who decorate subsequent chapters in this book, and who strove to establish themselves as hostesses, who made of the art almost a profession, Lady Desborough was a hostess by nature and upbringing. The habit was in her bones and in her genes. She entertained Prime Ministers because she was brought up so to do. The comparison with Duchess Georgiana is instructive and serves to illustrate the vast gulf which separates Lady Desborough from an amiable hostess like Sybil Colefax, a witty one like Lady Cunard, or a brittle woman such as Mrs Greville. Just as Georgiana dominated Whig society at the end of the eighteenth century, entertaining by aristocratic right and unforced inclination, so Lady Desborough dominated the descendants of that same society at the end of the nineteenth and beginning of the twentieth centuries for the same reasons. She was, in short, the last of the great Whig hostesses, the last woman to bring the tradition of aristocratic entertaining to within living memory. By her mode of life, she was a link with centuries past. By comparison, the Ladies Colefax and Cunard, Mrs Greville and Mrs Corrigan, counterparts in the United States like Mrs Stuyvesant Fish and Mrs Potter Palmer, all had to learn the art from scratch and try to emulate the graces of the past.

Also like Georgiana, Ettie Desborough achieved little, but deserved to be remembered for her charm. It is the most ephemeral of attributes, it leaves no visible or tangible legacy, but it is among the most valuable human gifts and should not be buried with the bones of its possessor. Ettie had charm. It radiated through her parties at Taplow and it brightened the lives of those who were fortunate to be invited there. To record how this charm manifested itself is to understand why this untalented but beguiling woman earned such extravagant praise from her friends.

She was born Ethel Priscilla Fane ('Ettie' for short), daughter of Julian Fane and granddaughter of the 11th Earl of Westmorland. Her antecedents on her mother's side were even more illustrious, and more significant in the light of her subsequent fame as a hostess. Ettie's great-grandmother was Emily, Lady Palmerston, who was a daughter of the clever and cynical Lady Melbourne. Thus Ettie was a direct descendant of two formidable Whig hostesses. She inherited the tradition.

Ettie's childhood was stalked by grief. When she was only a year old, her mother died after giving birth to her baby brother. A year after that, her father died, leaving Ettie and brother Johnnie orphans before their childhood even started. They were brought up by grandparents, aunts and uncles, with due love and care, though Ettie remembered the pervading sense of gloom which overhung the nursery. She did not wear anything but black, she said, until she was five, and one of her first memories was sitting in a dark room in Portman Square surrounded by grown-ups who were crying. More was to come. Her beloved brother died after an illness which lingered throughout one winter when Ettie was eight years old. Thereafter she was brought up at Panshanger, the vast seat of the Earls Cowper in Hertfordshire, but she did not easily recover from the loss of her infant companion. She felt 'desperately forlorn without Nanny and Johnnie, from whom I had never before been separated'. At Panshanger she came into contact with the great and powerful men of England, though she was herself still a little girl. Her uncle Henry Cowper was a Liberal M.P., and it was through him that Ettie first met Arthur Balfour and various other prominent gentlemen. She was trained early in the art of charm.

Ettie's resilience was further tried when her favourite grandmother, Lady Cowper, who had been 'my refuge and stength ever since I could remember', also died. Ettie was then thirteen. The very foundations of her emotional existence seemed one by one to be chopped away. She later recalled 'the wretched embarrassment of a child in grief; the shame of tears, the utter impossibility of expression'. Death was by now familiar to her, but no less dreadful for that. It left a mark which few people were ever permitted to see. While her 'stubborn gospel of joy' brightened the lives of those around her, its essential primary purpose was to protect herself from further hurt. She was privately pessimistic and stoical, as her tiny pocket diaries show. She formed the habit in adulthood of jotting down her favourite quotations at the back of the otherwise uncommunicative diaries. '*Equanimitas, magnanimitas*' closes one volume, '*Vivre c'est survivre*' is at the end of another. From Robert Louis Stevenson she noted, 'We but attain qualities to lose them, life is a series of farewells', and from another source she approved the maxim that gladness was a 'plain duty'.

Added to the doleful series of emotional shocks she suffered in her earliest years, Ettie also inherited a natural propensity to melancholia, congenital in many aristocratic families and spread, probably, by the habit of intermarriage. Once the gene of melancholy is introduced into a family, it is extremely difficult to dislodge and assumes all the power of a persistent illness. In one frank letter written in 1921, Ettie confessed she had been prey to 'the most insidious temptation to despair that old morbid Satan has to offer. I still have such *appalling* bouts of it, such attacks of nausea about myself,—but I believe one must treat and ignore them just like bouts of physical sickness, even though of course they contain *sub-strata* of truth. But they would paralyse not only effort but Faith if we let them prevail.' It was Ettie's triumph never to let them prevail. The gospel of joy was no affectation, as some have since implied; it was wholly necessary to maintain her sanity. Turning her back upon misery was not to pretend it was not there; it was to rob it of the power to annihilate positive impulses. Lord Gage discerned in her 'the face of an ascetic, relieved by frequent and happy laughter, but I have never seen a face so indicative of self-control'. She conquered unhappiness by will-power. She would need to draw heavily upon her reserves in later life.

Ettie Fane married Willy Grenfell on 17 February 1887, when she was nineteen and he thirty. It was a perfect union, destined to give her the security which had previously been so elusive. She enjoyed the simple pleasures of home life and adored her husband. Five years after the wedding Lord Pembroke was able to write, 'I congratulate you heartily on your marriage and hope to see you when the honeymoon's over.' Willy was proud of his marriage, and so certain of it that he was able, fifty years later, to joke about it. He told the story of the little girl who asked her mother, 'Why did you marry Daddy?' and received the reply, 'So you have begun to wonder, too!' He told the story because he knew it was so completely foreign to his own experience. Ettie never wondered; she always admired her husband, who possessed those qualities of solidity and reliability which a woman in her position most needed. Grenfell lived at Taplow Court, a fine Victorian house and estate in Buckinghamshire, on the Thames, which he had inherited at the age of nine. He had won a scholarship to Balliol, and was later to be a Liberal M.P. until the dispute with Gladstone over Home Rule for Ireland upset allegiances, and Grenfell moved over to the

Conservatives. A die-hard Conservative anyway, by inclination, he sat as Tory M.P. from 1900 to 1905, until he was elevated to the peerage as Baron Desborough. It is henceforth as Lord and Lady Desborough that Willy and Ettie will be mentioned.

As a sportsman, Lord Desborough was more accomplished in more separate fields than any Englishman before or since. At Harrow he had run a mile in 4 min. 37 sec., a record unbeaten for sixty years. He had been a member of the victorious Oxford crew in the Boat Race of 1878, and seven years later had rowed from Oxford to Putney, with two other men, in one day. He had climbed the Matterhorn three times by three different routes, won the punting championship of the Thames in three successive years, represented England in fencing at the Olympic Games, was an expert wrestler, swimmer and cricketer. There was no challenge in sport which Desborough would not accept, and none that he could not meet. He was also better than anyone else at killing things—fish, elephants, stags, pheasants. When he was not punting, swimming, or climbing mountains, he was stopping fish from swimming, animals from running, birds from flying. Margot Asquith called him 'a British gladiator' and Lytton Strachey grudgingly recognized that he was 'a huge old rock of an athlete'.

His most amazing feat was to swim across the foot of Niagara Falls in 1884, and then, to satisfy an American who bet him, he did it again in 1888 in stormy, turbulent conditions. Asked if it was difficult, Willy said it was all right if you were a strong swimmer, had a cool head, and kept your legs as near the surface as possible, to avoid the pull of the undercurrent. The second time, he was pulled back towards the Falls, and saw a vast mass of water above his head. 'Just for a minute or two, I really did think something might go wrong,' he said.

Something nearly did go wrong when he was on an expedition in the Rocky Mountains. Again to satisfy a bet, Willy went out alone before breakfast to shoot something. He lost his way, and wandered alone high in the mountains for two days and two nights, until he was spotted by a trapper and rescued. Even so, such was the belief in Willy's strength that no one supposed he would have perished if left to his own devices.

Of course, with all this, it would have been extravagant had Willy also been a scintillating conversationalist. He was not. A fine education had failed to interest him in the activities of the mind. Even before he and Ettie married, Mabell Airlie had told her, 'he may be a little dull, but after all what a comfort it is to be cleverer than one's husband!' The dullness encroached to such an extent that he became a perfect committee member, at one time sitting on no less than 117 different committees, and as if to consolidate his reputation, he conceived a deep passion for bimetallism, the proposal to introduce both gold and silver currencies into the economy. His other great interest was the Thames Conservancy Board, of which he was Chairman. These were not subjects likely to be an asset in conversation, or to enthrall weekend guests, but at least it was attractive to be punted on the Thames after lunch at Taplow by the champion punter himself. To his credit, Willy was perfectly aware that he was tedious. 'I sometimes wonder that I have a friend left', he said, 'as I am apt to bore my acquaintances with the number of gallons which go over Teddington Weir.'

Nicholas Mosley has written that, as Lord Desborough grew older, he almost gave up speech altogether. He was a man 'who had renounced all pretensions to imagination or enquiry. As a young man Willy had seemed to try to exercise his mind as he exercised his body; but then he and those like him had handed over processes of mind to women. Willy now moved from committee to committee, from the killing of birds to the killing of stags, without much more mental originality being required of him than that to deal with railway timetables.' To be fair, Lord Desborough was fine and honest as well as brave. More than one person said he was the best man they ever knew, or that there had never been a greater Englishman. His exquisite manners, if not his conversation, made him the perfect consort for a hostess. His behaviour, like Ettie's interested concern, made people feel the better for having been with him. One wrote, 'He was the only man whose actual appearance had the quality of ennobling those with him', an achievement far more subtle and valuable than the hundreds of stags he could claim to have shot. He was fashioned in the masculine style; to Ettie were left the gentler virtues of a feminine sensibility.

Indeed they made a splendid couple to preside over the best *salon* of the first years of the twentieth century.

Ettie had by now grown into a woman of arresting elegance. Tall and slim, with a back always perfectly straight, she carried what some one called 'an evident air of authority, almost of divinity'. Harold Nicolson thought she was one of the most patrician women of her age; 'her distinction might have seemed alarming had it not been that her fastidiousness was accompanied by an artistic perfection of courtesy.' Ettie's standards of elegance and courtesy were of the highest, and were inviolable. With her heavy eyelids and downward glance, she seemed at first grander than royalty, but as she turned the smallest encounter with another person into a ritualized treat, all who met her were enchanted. She was a woman who could have had as many slaves as she desired, and indeed she did. She lisped beguilingly, and screwed up her eyes in ready laughter. When she witnessed a minor collision involving a bus in Oxford Street, the driver having swerved to avoid a negligent pedestrian, she saw the poor man was in a state of nervous agitation, and got out of her car to talk to him and calm him down. The proprieties were observed, the British obsession with class was undisturbed, yet the man showed every sign of being bewitched by Ettie's sheer niceness. She elevated courtesy to the highest peak of civilized behaviour.

Elegance was likewise refined by Ettie into a positive enhancement of life. No one who spotted her erect figure 'in a tangle of greyhounds and their leashes' was ever likely to forget the vision.

Lord and Lady Desborough had five children: Julian, born in 1888, Billy in 1890, Monica in 1893, a third son, Ivo, in 1898, and Imogen in 1905. The two eldest boys, Julian and Billy, were blessed with remarkable beauty. A photograph of mother and sons, taken about 1900, shows them blond and curly-headed, perfectly angelic. Ettie's life, after a muddled beginning, appeared at last to have settled with marriage and motherhood into blissful contentment. The house-parties made her known far beyond the family circle, but any impression that she lived only for entertaining, as did Laura Corrigan for example, and to an increasing extent Lady Colefax, would be mistaken. Ettie never lost sight of the reality of home life.

The décor to this reality, Taplow Court, though not an especially attractive house (one visitor called it 'an ugly, overgrown villa furnished like a hotel') was comfortable and well situated. Apart from the butler, footman, valet, housekeeper and cook, there were six maids and a shifting number of men looking after the gardens and stables. It was certainly the most important house in the area, and, with the presence of all the great in the land at weekends, it quickly became the best-known. It was said that if you hired a horse at Windsor, it automatically turned its head towards Taplow. H.G. Wells found the idyllic life there quite intoxicating. 'Taplow Court shall be sacred,' he wrote, 'and one delightful family at least secure from the guillotine.' With every conceivable comfort provided for, a couple of days at Taplow were, as John Morley remarked, 'most blighting to one's democracy'. One's aesthetic antennae, however, suffered a peculiar assault. Ettie had a poor idea of interior decoration, and in this particular at least was far outclassed by the exquisite taste of Sibyl Colefax. Ettie's taste was for vivid reds and oranges and yellows, with curtains and cushions apparently made from old evening dresses. A solitary vase might contain sham poinsettias. The guest bedrooms were named according to their dominant colour after a flower, which was not (and still is not) unusual, but the total effect was a hotch-potch because Ettie lacked a sense of harmony. There was a Tulip Room, a Magnolia Room, a Poppy Room, Rosemary Room, Lilac Room, Buttercup Room, Daisy Room, Bluebell Room, and so on. Small wonder that Tommy Lascelles was reminded of an hotel. The house was sometimes known as 'Honeymoon Hall' owing to Ettie's constant eagerness to let it to newly-wed couples.

Ettie's day at Taplow was severely organized as part of her deep need to remain in control. Not only were breakfast, lunch, tea and dinner at punctual hours, but precisely one and a half hours were set aside to read *The Times*, another one and a half hours for writing letters, and an hour's rest after lunch was followed by two hours' walk. She wrote notes to herself—'No nerves. No hurry. *Eat.* Spare eyes when tired.'

Her day was considerably more frenetic when, at weekends, the twenty or more guests would appear, but she contrived never to

Lady Desborough with her sons, Julian and Billy Grenfell, *circa* 1900. Of Julian it was said that merely to see him in the street made one's eyes fill with tears

Lord Desborough, 'a huge old rock of an athlete'

Lady Desborough at the races

Taplow Court, the Grenfell family home and
scene of many a gathering of the 'Souls'

allow 'busyness' to show. 'Her social keenness is beyond doubt and she works very hard', wrote her friend and fellow 'Soul' Mary Elcho. Ambition cannot have been her motive, but having accepted that it was her place and role in life to entertain on a large scale, Ettie played the part to perfection, making sure that she was seen always to advantage and having the list of her guests published in the *Morning Post* on Monday. If she was in London, she was careful to be observed in the right place at the right time. There was no point in being a hostess unless you took the matter seriously. Lady Desborough was not without her own degree of self-consciousness. She certainly knew who she was.

The group of friends who came to be known collectively as 'The Souls' was the nucleus of Lady Desborough's weekend parties at Taplow and their fame eventually confirmed her reputation as a hostess. Among aristocratic circles at the end of the nineteenth century they represented a rebellious innovation. The norm of upper-class behaviour was typified by the Marlborough House set which clustered round the Prince of Wales; they were aggressively masculine, graceless, boorish, proudly philistine, and contemptuous of all intelligence. Marlborough House people hunted, gambled and seduced, all with singular lack of style. Their aims were entirely hedonistic, their manner frankly rough. The Souls could not have been more different. To no degree did they purposefully rise in opposition to the Marlborough House set, but they made little secret that they despised its philistinism. The Souls cultivated the more feminine qualities of sensitivity, art, courtesy and good manners. They read and wrote poetry. They talked about life and its meaning, about metaphysical things, about the mysteries of destiny and of the human character, all matters far beyond the understanding of the Prince of Wales and his friends. They were like a mini-university, constantly holding seminars and discussions on important questions relating to the mind or the emotions. They read everything they could lay their hands on.

Besides Ettie Desborough, the group included the Duke and Duchess of Rutland (Diana Cooper's parents), the Duke and Duchess of Sutherland, Lord and Lady Elcho, Lord and Lady Ribblesdale, Lord and Lady Pembroke, Margot Tennant (later

Margot Asquith), George Wyndham, Harry Cust, George Curzon, Evan Charteris, the Brownlows, the Cowpers and the Horners. A glance at the Visitors' Book at Taplow reveals that most of these were present virtually every weekend. Of course, the numbers were swollen by 'outsiders' as the Souls were by no means insular. Occasional guests included the Duke of Portland, Churchill, Gladstone, Asquith, Rosebery, Hartington, Salisbury and Chamberlain, five of whom were Prime Ministers, and a sixth— Lord Hartington—could have been Prime Minister three times, but declined. Then there was every ambassador of note at some time or other, and four reigning monarchs of England.

The 'star' of the group not so far mentioned was yet another Prime Minister, Arthur Balfour, who visited Taplow Court more often probably than any other individual. All the Souls admired, even worshipped him, and when he came to form his Cabinet it was observed how large a proportion of its members were regular Taplovites (Willy and Ettie Desborough were nicknamed 'the Taplovite Winnies'). Balfour's pre-eminence at the centre of the circle is made manifest by the list of rooms at Taplow; between the Tulip dressing-room and the Buttercup Room was, simply, 'Mr Balfour's Room'. There has scarcely been a more overt example of influence-by-entertainment. Balfour's closeness to the Souls would one day tarnish his reputation, just as Ramsay Macdonald's friendship with Lady Londonderry would permit others to question his independence.

The Souls were not founded as a group in any organized manner. They came together in mourning for the untimely death of Laura Lyttelton (a sister of Margot Asquith, and incidentally, of two ladies still alive in 1982—Dame Margaret Wakehurst and Baroness Elliot of Harewood), and gradually their meetings became regular. It was Lord Charles Beresford who in 1887 gave them the name of Souls; they spent so much time talking about their souls, he said, that that was what they should be called. The name stuck. Ettie professed to detest the name, as it sounded so contrived. 'How I always disliked the word and the classification,' she wrote some forty years later. Nevertheless, some of her letters show just how appropriate the term was. 'If we don't encourage our souls, so *little* of us can live,' runs one such, 'and we cannot permanently affect anyone but our own husbands lovers friends or sisters except through their souls. *What* can we do for each other except love . . . all the rest is scaffolding, the soul is the spire.'

The Souls spent their time playing games like charades, or more demanding games based on literary knowledge, taking long pleasant walks, even bicycling. They were known to go for long rides on their bicycles, the servants taking the train to meet them at a pre-determined spot. They played tennis, they punted on the Thames—never a moment in the day was wasted in idleness. Even the walks were meant to be instructive, with talks about the birds, the lime trees, the 'wide expanse of fertile country', 'the beauty and delight of life'. All of them wrote verse at one time or another. George Wyndham had the especial fame of having written a long poem with complex rhymes and metre while resting for an hour between bouts of tennis. James Barrie scribbled in the Visitor's Book in 1922,

At Taplow all the clever ones are bards
'Tis but the rubbish who sit down to cards.

Apart from Barrie, other writers who found their way to Taplow were Edmund Gosse ('Gossekins'), H.G. Wells, John Morley and Oscar Wilde.

Meals were naturally the most important events of the day, for it was then that conversation, an art highly prized by the Souls, could simmer and bubble comfortably for an hour or two. Even breakfast was considered a communal event. Ettie would stay at the breakfast table sometimes until eleven o'clock, engaging her guests successively in interesting banter about the news or a reflection suggested by the previous night's topic. In every case it was the guest who was allowed to shine; Ettie was merely the Mistress of Ceremonies, the impresario. Conversation was sophisticated and witty, with the kind of wit which is evanescent, of the moment, and difficult to record. At Cliveden you would reach for your notebook to jot down the wisdom of Shaw, for example, but at Taplow the feathers of wit, delicious as caviare, would blow away within seconds. Ettie herself said that conversation at her table was characterized by 'an extreme lightness of touch'.

Not everyone was impressed. Mrs Sidney Webb was far too earnest a figure to enjoy a gathering of Souls. 'The conversation was easy and pleasant, but it was all froth', she wrote. 'No one said what they thought, and every one said what they thought to be clever.' Constantine Benckendorff, son of the Russian Ambassador, was another unflattering witness:

> a sort of intellectual carouse would begin, consisting of a series of sharp skirmishes where no subject, even the most outrageous, was barred, so long as it led to an argument . . . the strange thing was that the ring of bystanders . . . seemed to have no strong conviction one way or the other, and were more impressed by the ingenuity of an argument than by its factual merit.

Ettie advised one to 'do all the dodges on earth for preserving a cold steel brain and iced concentration', which would suggest she thought the activity of the mind was more important than any conclusions such activity might promote. Hence the accusation of frivolity. Balfour was wise enough not to be upset by such accusations, for he appreciated the value of intellectual frivolity. At least Ettie was no hypocrite. She claimed no grand purpose for her gatherings, no higher aim than enjoyment. She was not in any measure pompous.

Nor was she bitchy. Margot Asquith later claimed that they never thought it amusing or distinguished to make people feel uncomfortable. 'The modern habit of pursuing, detecting and exposing what was ridiculous in simple people and the unkind and irreverent manner in which slips were made material for epigram were unbearable to me.' Forgetting for a moment Margot Asquith's own propensity towards epigram, and not always a gentle one—she meant that the Souls were polite and sophisticated, never malevolent. Hence guests would feel at ease in their company, free from the fear that whatever they said might be reported elsewhere. This meant that they were able to cross political and ideological barriers to an unusual degree. Although they were mostly solid

Conservative supporters, differences of opinion were welcomed and explored at Taplow without personal friendship ever being sacrificed.

Harold Nicolson's diary sketch of Margot Asquith is among the most perceptive, and serves also to illustrate some of the qualities which characterized the Souls. 'It is curious to think how posterity will misunderstand Margot,' he writes,

They will think her a vulgar and disagreeable advertiser. She is nothing of the sort. She is vain of course, but it is no common vanity. She is observant rather than intelligent. Above all, she is brave, affectionate, loyal. Her zest is like champagne. Her generosity of thought and action is like a fresh wind. The love which hangs above her house gives it a spirituality which is different from the ghoulish intellectualism of other circles.

All of which might apply with equal felicity to Ettie Desborough. Affection, loyalty, enthusiasm were all hers. She was no intellectual. Her reading was wide rather than profound. When Balfour published *The Foundations of Belief* in 1895, the book inevitably came up for discussion at Taplow, and Balfour confided in Lady Elcho that Ettie 'had got stuck in some very unexpected places'. Lord Esher suggested that, as no one would be likely to trouble Ettie and her friends about the details of their hero's book, they could 'pretend to know all about it'.

She could be witty but not original. An essay for her sons' school magazine, 'Hints to Eton Parents', gives an idea of the measure of her humour. When you are introduced to your boy's friends, she wrote, 'do not be sprightly, knowing, hearty, youthful, slangy, arch, sporting, or witty. Humility is the only wear for parents. Apologise for your existence, and explain it as far as you can.'

Ettie had no real interest in painting, and positively hated music. In appreciation of the arts, she bore no comparison with the genuinely intelligent Lady Cunard. But none of this mattered, for the first requirement of a hostess is that she know how to handle people. Her real expertise was in human beings, meeting them, understanding them, talking to them, reading about them.

Thus, like Margot Asquith, she was observant rather than intelligent.

She was also curiously formal, in a cool, distant way. She was certainly not tactile. 'I don't like Harry Cust,' she said, 'I cannot bear people who finger one's sleeve and hold one's bread at dinner.' Even her daughter Monica recalled how surprised she had been to see other siblings embracing, as they had never been so demonstrative at Taplow as to throw their arms about each other's necks, however affectionate they in fact were. A Grenfell arm on your shoulder had as much warmth as a stick. Endearments toppled over one another in letters and in conversation, but a friendly press on the elbow was considered vulgar.

Where Ettie and her friends definitely strayed into extravagance was in the language they used, and in their harmless but ultimately artificial romantic flirtations.

The language of the Souls reminds one, in its full-blown and self-conscious hyperbole, of the *Précieux* in seventeenth-century France. Had Ettie ever read, one wonders, Molière's *Précieuses Ridicules* or *Les Femmes Savantes* before she wrote of the weather that it was 'wholly blissfully ideally delicious'. Her son Julian caught the habit early. Pamela Lytton, he said, was so miserable she was 'utterly utterly'. Rather arch euphemisms were employed to hide (why?) certain words. 'Spangle' was to flirt, 'relever' to gossip, 'dewdrop' a compliment, 'heygate' conventional,* and 'brahms' was condescending. Letters to Ettie are replete with endearing nicknames. She is 'Angel', 'Etsy', 'Etts', 'Beloved', or 'Darling' according to the fulsomeness of the writer and his mood.

No one understood this fulsome mood better than the Taplow butler, who had been familiar with its nuances and emphases for years. One day he was asked by Lady Desborough to dispatch a telegram accepting an invitation. Though not an excitable man himself, he could imitate an effusive style when called upon. The

---

* The man who is thus unfortunately immortalized was Arthur Heygate (1862–1935), a clever and learned schoolmaster at Eton between 1887 and 1918. He apparently lacked the gift of enthusiasm, and his lessons were notoriously pedestrian and boring. His name was used by some of the Souls to denote conventionality or want of excitement.

text of the message he sent read YES HOW PERFECTLY WONDERFUL
LOVE LOVE LOVE. Unfortunately, it was later discovered that the
invitation had come from a senior official at the Thames
Conservancy Board.

In his short story 'Maltby and Braxton' Max Beerbohm satirized
Lady Desborough as the Duchess of Hertfordshire, a woman given
to saying that everything was *too* splendid, *too* wonderful, or
perfectly divine. 'If she hadn't been a Duchess, I might have
thought her slightly hysterical.' Beerbohm also remarked that,
while her husband was reputed to have climbed trees on every
continent, the 'Duchess of Hertfordshire' had a simpler hobby: she
sat aloft and beckoned desirable specimens up.

The apparently flippant tone of this language gave rise to a
suspicion of hypocrisy among the Taplovites and caused a hostile
reaction from the new generation who formed themselves into a
rival group known as the 'Corrupt Coterie'. They included mildly
adventurous beauties like Diana Manners and fierce anarchists like
Nancy Cunard. While Ettie never smoke or drank (her only
aberration was a White Lady one evening which made her so tipsy
she had to be helped downstairs), the Corrupt Coterie took tobacco
and drugs, drank champagne to violent excess. Ettie never used a
gross word, but the Coterie would say 'fuck' if it suited them. Ettie
valued courtesy above all else, even if it meant a quiet deception
(she told enough white lies to ice a cake, said Margot Asquith), but
the Corrupt Coterie prized honesty whether or not it offended. The
young mistook Ettie. The flippancy they detected existed only in
style, not in substance. Her frivolous manner is misleading to
modern ears, which notice its elegant coating and ignore its centre
of genuine feeling.

More than anything else, however, it was the excess of romantic
attachments, ritualized and unconsummated, expressed in lush
marshmallow language, that antagonized the new generation who
not only called a spade a spade but did not hesitate to use it. In
contrast, Ettie Desborough's succession of *amitiés amoureuses*
appeared to them silly, smug and hypocritical. Again, they were
wrong. Falling in love was never central to Ettie's existence. She
had many strong emotional ties of friendship to which she gave

expression with an extravagance of tone we should nowdays reserve
for a declaration of lust. The Souls were victims of their own
hyperbole.

Snatches from various letters sent to Ettie by 'admirers' who
were intimate members of the set suggest that she inspired the most
abject devotion. Lord Revelstoke spoke of her in the third person
when addressing her in case his outpourings should be discovered.
'I have never known or even dared to dream what happiness could
be till she came to make my life one bright undivided joy', he wrote.
And again, 'she realizes how completely she has possession of every
part of me and what a terrible power of happiness or misery she
wields in her dear, dear heart.' Revelstoke never married; his
commitment to Ettie was total. Evan Charteris, who has been
described as 'inexhaustibly attentive' to Ettie, told her, 'I hunger
for you there—to share the same sunshine—the same stars—to be
touched by the same winds under the same forest trees . . . there is
none of me that is not every hour of life ascending to you in
adoration and worship.' Another swain, Archie Gordon, wrote, 'my
love precedes me from here, warm from the sun and the joy that
there is here.'

Was this merely the 'double distilled honey of flattery'? Were
these refined protestations empty at the core? Some of Ettie's
glamour has been tarnished by the relentless modern investigation
into these romantic attachments. Had she given herself bodily to all
these beaux, we should rejoice in saying, Ah, there's the hypocrisy
of the age, double standards which allow the appearance to conceal
the truth. But if she did not give herself, we still feel able
to condemn: Ah, there's the hypocrisy of the age, we say, all
appearance concealing no truth at all; what is the point of lasting
devotion without substance? It is our attitudes which are confused,
however, not Lady Desborough's. The point of such friendships
was to awaken and nourish fine feelings; the mistake, in modern
eyes, was simply to express such feelings in exorbitant language.

'There was a ritual to such relationships which ensured that
words, in certain circumstances, were merely inconsequential
froth', wrote Max Egremont in his biography of Balfour. Nicholas
Mosley, who has written the biography of Ettie's son, Julian

Grenfell, said that her special accomplishment seemed to be the making of conquests without making enemies. Indeed it was. When George Wyndham wrote to her, 'you are probably pursuing some wild animal somewhere, or Willy is and somebody else is pursuing you', he was not reprimanding her, but celebrating her. 'Lucky dog whoever he be' Wyndham added in postscript, and the point was that all Ettie's admirers considered themselves lucky to be able to serenade her. There was a refinement about the friendships among the Souls which seems foreign to us, and was certainly odd compared with the clumsy promiscuity of the Marlborough House set. Ettie could not have maintained her role as a magnificent hostess had she been fair game for seduction. The hostess must cover everyone with the glow of her favour, not a chosen two or three. Lady Cunard lavished affection upon young men, but that, too, was a ritual. Mrs Corrigan had no interest in sex, nor had Mrs Greville. Lady Colefax was completely loyal to her husband, and Lady Londonderry's only digression into *amitié amoureuse* was with Ramsay MacDonald. The hostess may be depicted as a siren, but everyone must know the depiction is fantasy. This was harmless and agreeable enough.

Ettie Desborough, tall, slim, elegant, languid, was adored by all her guests, but was not at all interested in serious philandering. Henry Chaplin, Lady Londonderry's father, said that the Soul creed was 'each woman shall have her man, but no man shall have his woman', and one of the chief lady Souls, Mary Elcho (afterwards Lady Wemyss) confirmed that 'nearly all of the group were married women with husbands whom they loved and by whom they had children, but each had her friend who was a friend only'. It may be said that Ettie was possessive of her 'friends' and not at all pleased if they diverted their declarations elsewhere, but that was because the ultimate sin was disloyalty, not the satisfaction of passion. It was not such a dreadful ethic.

But, of course, to Ettie's adolescent sons all this aimless adoration may not have appeared so innocent. Julian, the eldest, a boy of whom one of the Eton masters said he was so beautiful merely to see him in the street made one's eyes fill with tears, could not bring himself to indulge in declarations of affection. His 'affectionateness', he told his mother, either was not there or had 'got into the hell of a dark corner'. He loved Ettie as a mother, but grew gradually to dislike her as a hostess. Perhaps the alienation of one's children, who are naturally emotionally selfish, is one of the penalties a successful hostess must pay. Certainly they began to quarrel violently ('scarlet arguments', Julian called them) and would often both end in tears. Julian berated his mother for her love of society, even going so far as to accuse the Souls of conventionality and stupidity, the very faults they prided themselves on avoiding. 'You like the smart set,' he told her. 'I like the solitary life—or few people at a time . . . I *do* like you; and that is why it grieves me to see you always surrounded by 101 princes of the blood royal.'

Maurice Baring, in a letter to Ethel Smyth, confirms that Julian and Billy hated the 'social' life, preferring to romp around at whim. For a while they crusaded violently against social customs and conventions, and used to walk about London hatless and in tennis shoes 'to show they didn't care'. The arguments with his mother invariably concerned the face one shows the world. Ettie's point of view, according to Baring, was *'Ne savez-vous pas qu'il faut s'habiller comme tout le monde et peindre comme personne.'* Julian thought this hypocritical.

Julian's own friends were the more down-to-earth youngsters of the Corrupt Coterie, and more particularly the Manners sisters, Marjorie, Diana and Letty, girls who earned Lady Desborough's disapproval for their 'fast' ways. They were collectively known as the Hothouse owing to their exotic and undisciplined behaviour. Ettie found them and their like far too wild and unpredictable to be allowed on the graceful lawn at Taplow.

The temporary rift between mother and son drove Julian into morose depression, in which he even pondered on suicide. Ettie's sufferings, which must have been as intense, were as usual controlled and concealed. Her iron resilience would shortly be submitted to its severest test. Julian Grenfell welcomed the coming of war as an escape from introspection. He and his brother Billy eagerly embraced the opportunity to go to Europe and fight. They had no fear, no vestige of apprehension. In Julian's case, there was a

strong hint of wilful enjoyment of danger and open acknowledge-
ment of the possibility of death. (There was an atavistic side to his
nature which disconcerted the queasy; he was said to have sucked
the wound of a buffalo he had shot.) One of Ettie's friends had once
said that Julian reminded her of the Greek epigram of the boy who
was so beautiful he died. Did she recall this cruel reflection as her
son went off to the Front? She would not say. But the maxims she
quoted from Goethe, Dante, Renan, Whitman at the end of her
pocket diaries were ever more stoical. At a previous parting five
years before, Ettie had admitted she was 'cut in half and bled to
death'.

On 12 May 1915, at Ypres, a German shell landed a few yards
from Julian, and a splinter of shell lodged in his skull. The wound
was not thought to be serious enough for his return to England, so
he was taken to the Casualty Clearing Station, whence he wrote a
blood-stained letter to his mother, telling her his skull was 'slightly
cracked'. On his arrival at the hospital in Boulogne, it was
discovered the splinter had entered deep and damaged the brain.
An operation was performed. Ettie and Willy came from England,
and took lodgings in the town. Nicholas Mosley has movingly
described her state of mind. 'Ettie found herself in the position that
she had been in before', he wrote, 'and would be in again, of having
to wait a number of days before she knew whether or not someone
she loved was dying.'

The period of waiting extended to almost two weeks. Julian knew
he was lost. To his sister Monica he said, on May 25, 'Goodbye
Casie', and to his mother, 'Hold my hand till I go'. Then, as
sunlight from the window cast across his feet, he said 'Phoebus
Apollo' and smiled. The only other time he spoke was to utter his
father's name.

Julian lingered another night and day, his parents and sister
beside him. On 26 May, at 3.40 p.m., he moved his mother's hand
to his lips, opened his eyes slightly, smiled again, and was gone. The
agony of those last days was recorded by Ettie in a few reticent
words in the tiny diary, far more eloquent than all the extravagant
expressions of the Souls: 'we thought Julian was dying at 7.30 a.m.,

but he lived to 20 mins to 4 p.m. We thought he knew us to the very end.'

Lady Cynthia Asquith claimed she was forever haunted by the thought of Ettie seeing her glorious son die by inches. Julian was buried in the soldiers' cemetery outside Boulogne, his grave covered by wild flowers strewn by Ettie. Afterwards, Ettie scribbled a quotation from Shakespeare in the diary: 'If it be now, 'tis not to come; if it be not to come, it will be now; if it be not now, yet it will come; the readiness is all.'

On 29 May, Billy Grenfell joined his family in Boulogne for one day, before returning to the trenches. He found his mother summoning her strength. An extraordinary number of tributes poured in to Ettie and Willy, and *The Times* published Julian's celebrated poem 'Into Battle'. Lord Londonderry said he was a 'fine creature and brave as a lion'. Patrick Shaw Stewart, who would himself fall victim to the war in 1917, said 'his physical splendour was so great . . . He was the most magnificent human thing I have ever seen.' Winston Churchill said that he lived and died as he would have wished, which was quite true, and was 'all that our race needs to keep its honour fair and bright'. Evan Charteris talked loftily of the things the Souls cherished so much, the spirit which was greater than death, 'of a beauty that cannot be touched by death', and voiced a hope for Ettie Desborough which everyone shared. 'God grant you strength to be with this sorrow as you are with all else in life,' he wrote, 'gentle in thought and in courage supreme.'

She was to need more courage than ever should be asked of one woman. On 30 July, two months after Julian's death, Billy was killed heading a charge near Hooge, only a mile from the spot where his brother had been wounded by the shell. His body was buried amid hundreds, and never rediscovered.

The strain on Ettie was almost invisible. She admitted to pain in her eyes, but managed to continue with life, and with entertaining, in a bold and warm spirit. Some thought her apparent recovery callous, but she was secretly heart-broken to an extent which her detractors could not imagine. She was inured to tragedy, and knew from cruel experience the way to conquer death. She wrote a *Family*

Journal* as a monument to her dead sons, privately printed and circulated; Lady Wemyss, who also lost two sons in the war, did the same. Though the weekend parties at Taplow continued, with, among the guests, George V and Queen Mary, Sibyl Colefax in 1922, and the loyal Balfour until his death in 1926, there was a noticeably subdued accent to the erstwhile lush conversation, though the courtesy and dignity were never compromised.

Lady Cynthia Asquith saw a great deal of Ettie during this time, and recorded her admiration for her apparent immunity to grief. There seemed to be nothing strained or artificial about Ettie's marvellous courage, just a sort of alchemy which translated tragedy to the exclusion of all gloom. Surrounded by her friends and guests she made every show of an unimpaired zest for life, behaving quite normally in company. 'But directly she is alone with one,' said Lady Cynthia, 'she is just a simple, effortless woman with a bleeding heart. Tears pour down her cheeks . . . she told me she found the complete, sudden disappearance of Billy harder to bear than the long, loving farewell to Julian.' To suggest that she was a poor mother is cruel and unworthy. As for Lord Desborough, he looked to Lady Cynthia 'like some great animal who has been struck on the brow'.

In 1926, the Desboroughs' third son, Ivo, was driving home late one night when the steering of his car appeared to fail. He leaned over the side, still moving, to look at the front wheels, and his head was struck by a wall. For two weeks he lay in hospital surrounded by his family, but eventually died of the injury. Ettie said it was just like the vigil in Boulogne eleven years before, 'every wound torn upon and bleeding together'. It was a wonder she retained her sanity. 'A less magnificent woman would have been shattered by the violent deaths of her three almost legendary sons,' wrote Harold

---

* Maurice Baring, at the front, borrowed a copy from Philip Sassoon and then wrote eulogistically to Ettie: 'It is to me much more than a record of Billy and Julian . . . It is the reflection of the soul and spirit and the CORE of England. It sums up all that is best of England, and English things, like a Constable landscape, or a speech in Shakespeare. It is a wonderful PAGEANT, too, of youth, courage and gaiety . . . nobody can ever see it without feeling a ray of light upon them. I can't read anything of it without crying.'

Nicolson in *The Spectator*. A less sagacious woman, too, would have surrendered to self-pity.

The great joyful days of entertaining at Taplow were smothered by the heavy foot of sorrow. Ettie and Willy were now in their fifties and had little desire for games. Yet visitors continued to the very eve of the Second World War. While frolics transferred to the houses of more *arriviste* hostesses, quiet wit and gentle pleasantness continued at Taplow. The Visitors' Book comes to a sudden halt in August 1939. Among the last guests in the final week before war was declared are the Duke and Duchess of Portland, Lord Londonderry, Mr Baldwin, and Winston Churchill.

Taplow was immediately handed over to the country, and Ettie prepared to evacuate to make way for 190 babies brought up from London, and 40 attendants. 'One's whole life for 52 years packed up in 3 days,' she wrote. Her other house, Panshanger, was likewise given over to homeless families. She and Willy retained an apartment at Taplow.

There were to be no more happy days. No sooner had this second war ended than Lord Desborough died, in 1945, at the age of 89. Ettie herself was now crippled, confined to a wheelchair. She moved to the vast Hertfordshire house of Panshanger, which she had inherited from her Cowper relations, and lived her last years there virtually in one room, while in the rest of the deserted house, like a battleship, 'all life seemed to have stopped'. Her dreadful illness and her enveloping loneliness she faced with 'statuesque endurance. She gave to illness itself a calm and lovely elegance . . . she retained her splendid curiosity in the varied doings of the outside world . . . [and was] just as interested in the younger generation as in the old.' (Harold Nicolson) Few who saw her in these last years could have imagined the exalted position she held in the world of fashion fifty years before, the divine centre of a self-confident and self-conscious *salon*. With the ghost of a smile which could touch the heart, she would say, 'We did have fun, didn't we?'

Lady Desborough died in 1952, aged 84.

Two Lady Londonderrys

Just as Lady Desborough enabled the art of the Whig hostess to survive into the twentieth century, so the tradition of the Tory political hostess was maintained right up to the Second World War by two successive inhabitants of Londonderry House in Park Lane: Theresa, wife of the 6th Marquess of Londonderry, who reigned in the great house until the First War; and Edith, wife of the 7th Marquess, who took her place at the top of that famous staircase in the twenties and thirties.

Both women were solidly aristocratic, Theresa the daughter of the Premier Earl of England, Lord Shrewsbury, and Edith the daughter of Henry Chaplin and granddaughter of the Duke of Sutherland (she was actually brought up by her aunt, Millicent Duchess of Sutherland). They were both intensely political even before they married into the Londonderry family, which, to say the least, was a considerable advantage in the pre-eminent role they were destined to play. They both aspired to real power, and won it, and they both used beauty as a tool in their respective careers. They differed from the nascent crop of 'professional' hostesses (the Cunards, Colefaxes and Corrigans) as smoked salmon does from minced beef, because they did not have to learn the art of entertaining—they inherited it in their genes along with lofty manners and a back straight enough to support the weight of the most famous tiara in London, which Theresa called the 'family fender'. Moreover, whereas Bache Cunard, Arthur Colefax, Ronald Greville and James Corrigan were all nondescript, the Lords Londonderry were men of distinction and accomplishment in the world of politics, men who were not accustomed to taking a back seat while their wives presided. The ambitions of Theresa and Edith were in support of, not in spite of, their husbands, and so far did they achieve their aim of exercising influence that one suspected Cabinet lists were drawn up in the boudoir at Londonderry House. Junior Cabinet Ministers deferred to them, flattered them, went in fear of incurring their displeasure. They dominated the social life of the Conservative party from the elegant eighteenth-century Park Lane house, where traditionally on the eve of every Parliamentary session a huge reception was given, with Lord and Lady Londonderry and the Prime Minister of the day artfully positioned at the top of the magnificent staircase, which it might well take twenty minutes to climb, with a dense throng before you, before you were received by the hostess, whom you had perceived on high long before you reached her. The Londonderrys appreciated the stage-management necessary to wring out the dramatic aspects of hierarchy.

For generations this had been the scene of glittering political gatherings. Prime Ministers from Disraeli to Macmillan, monarchs from William IV to Elizabeth II, mounted those stairs before their eventual demolition in 1962. Sometimes they held so many people that scaffolding had to be erected to give them added strength. The most incongruous figure to appear there, one who delighted in these extravagant parties more than was good for him, was the first Labour Prime Minister, Ramsay Macdonald. The trouble caused by his friendship with the senior Tory hostess offers a lesson in the perils of confusing social pleasures and political principles; as we shall see, both the aristocrat and the Labour hero paid a heavy price for succumbing to this confusion.

Though not spectacularly ancient (Edith's husband once said he was a 'peer of mushroom growth'), the Londonderry title, dating from 1816, was supremely political. The second Marquess, better known to history under his courtesy title of Lord Castlereagh, was the architect of the Treaty of Vienna and the Act of Union with Ireland. The third Marquess, his brother, fought with Wellington in the Peninsular War and had been Ambassador in Vienna. He had been dead two years when Lady Theresa Chetwynd-Talbot was born in 1856.

'I began liking politics when I was only ten years old,' Theresa later recalled. Like her father, she was a staunch Tory, considering Mr Gladstone 'a horrible wretch', though she grew to tolerate the Liberals so far as to invite Gladstone and Sir William Harcourt to her Londonderry House parties in later years. Still, her Toryism no doubt weighed in her favour when the Londonderrys were looking for a consort for their son and heir. She married Lord Castlereagh in 1875, and nine years later, when he succeeded as 6th Marquess of Londonderry, she moved into Londonderry House as well as Wynyard (in County Durham), Mount Stewart in Ireland, and Seaham Hall. It quickly became apparent that the new Lady Londonderry would relish her role as hostess. She brought to the task qualities of nerve and cold determination. 'There was nothing wistful, reflective or retiring about Lady Londonderry,' said her rival Margot Asquith. 'She was keen and vivid, but crude and impenitent.' Consuelo Vanderbilt, the American Duchess of Marlborough, noticed the same ruthlessness, what she called her material obsession with success in social and political life.

Margot Asquith was even less circumspect in private communications which she did not expect ever to be published. One such has turned up among the Desborough Papers, and in it Margot gives a quite merciless picture of Lady Londonderry:

She has rather a vulgar foundation upon which is heaped a very luxurious aristocratic habit of living and thinking. She has a clear head for figures and facts such as race-horse pedigrees etc., a great deal of energy and ambition and competitive qualities, terrific complacency, and a very 'surface soul' as the new book says. She has not a very sensitive mind and never sees the rubbish she talks, she has *no* imagination or reflective power whatever and very little critical faculty. Her remarks upon books are paralysing. Her nature has not been watered by good hard work or feeling or responsibilities. It has been scented by contact with a certain world, invigorated by vanity, and encouraged by success. One could never love her, but I don't mind her. She is not happy and never will be.

Lady Londonderry was also possessed of rich, luscious beauty, which could certainly be an asset in advancing her husband's career, as well as a liability in securing his serenity at home. She gave him two children, Charles, who would eventually succeed as 7th Marquess, and Helen ('Birdie'), who became Countess of Ilchester. There was another son, too, a winsomely handsome boy called Reginald, whose father was Theresa's brother-in-law, Lord Helmsley. Reginald inherited the weak constitution of Helmsley's family, the Duncombes, many of whom had been carried off with consumption in their twenties. Reginald, with his cough and his limp, was a tragic figure destined to die at nineteen and then to be forgotten for over seventy years. Only recently were the sad colours of his life rediscovered with the revelation of his dark-room at Wynyard, still stocked with his photographic plates and his chemicals, where Reginald and his mother pursued their secret hobby of photography. Some of his photographs have since been published and received much praise. The present Lord Londonderry's second son is named Reginald in memory of the forlorn boy.

Reginald was Lady Londonderry's only love-child, though by no means her only indiscretion. She was rumoured to have been a mistress of Edward VII (but so was virtually everyone else who entertained him), and was further said to leave the window of her bedroom unlocked so that the gamekeeper could jump in when the mood took him. As Theresa was an uncommonly imperious woman, it is more likely that he paid his visits on command, when the mood took *her*.

The most notorious of her liaisons, one which has passed down already into the pseudo-certainty of folklore, was with the philanderer Harry Cust, a man of infinite charm, astonishing good looks, and blatant lack of moral scruple. There was scarcely a beautiful aristocratic lady in England whom he had not wooed and won, including the ravishing Duchess of Rutland; Harry Cust was the father of her daughter Lady Diana Manners (Diana Cooper). Harry was editor of the *Pall Mall Gazette* and would soon be an M.P. He was a hereditary aristocrat himself, being a member of the Brownlow family. Reckless, libidinous and hedonistic, Cust was able quite neatly to carry on affairs with more than one woman at a time. This he did with Lady Londonderry and Lady de Grey, both sexually attractive and socially challenging, as they both had reputations as leading hostesses, Theresa Londonderry in the political field, and Gladys de Grey in the artistic. Lady Londonderry made the cardinal error of writing him love letters.

When Lady de Grey suspected that Cust's attentions were not reserved exclusively for her, she rummaged around among his things in his bachelor apartment, and found Theresa's letters, all of them indiscreet, some actually disparaging in their remarks about Lord Londonderry. She took them. In the weeks that followed, Lady de Grey entertained her friends by reading out choice passages from Lady Londonderry's letters, and when the delights of this mischief palled, she gave them to a servant and bade him deliver them into Lord Londonderry's hands at Wynyard. A more wicked ruse it would be difficult to imagine, or a more telling comment on the lengths to which social rivalries would impel behaviour in the Edwardian period.

After this, rumour and gossip take the place of truth. It has been said, and published, that Lord Londonderry never forgave his wife her treachery, and refused ever to speak to her again, except in public. Another story has it that she sent him a note on his deathbed, some thirty years later, and he declined to see her. In fact, though these stories make dramatic anecdotes, the ability of Edwardian society to withstand any amount of fraying at the edges was remarkable, and the reconciliation between the couple, though frosty at first, was eventually affectionate and enduring. Theresa's most spectacular mistake was forgiven. The beguiling version of the rumpus which has husband and wife eating in silence for a quarter of a century found its way into Vita Sackville-West's fine novel *The Edwardians*, where Theresa's fictional immortality is incarnated in the personage of Lady Roehampton.

Theresa was so large, so dominant a personality that she hardly needed a fictional gloss. E.F. Benson describes her vividly in *As We Were*:

> She revelled in personal splendour, she frankly and un-mitigatedly enjoyed standing at the head of her stairs when some big party was in progress, . . . hugging the fact that this was her house, and that she was a marchioness from top to toe and was playing the part to perfection. . . . She liked violence and strong colour, and sweeping along with her head in the air, vibrant with vitality. She did not plot or plan or devise, and 'went for' life, hammer and tongs, she collared it and scragged it and rooked it like a highwaywoman in a tiara, trampling on her enemies, as if they had been a bed of nettles—and occasionally getting stung about the ankles in the process—incapable of leniency towards them, or of disloyalty to her friends.

The personal splendour of which Benson speaks was apparent every time Theresa acted her role as Marchioness. When a tenant was ill on the estate at Wynyard, Lady Londonderry would dress in full panoply, diamonds agleam, before visiting the invalid with a tot of her own medicament. She knew perfectly well that tenants expected to be dazzled, and she was not about to disappoint them. Personal splendour, in such an instance, was employed as a solace, an aid to recovery. It could also be used quite openly as an instrument of intimidation. She belonged to a generation which still believed that the trappings of power were their own eloquence. When her son was canvassing for election to Parliament, she sent down her barouche with four horses and postillions. 'This paraded the constituency and duly impressed those whom such display influences', wrote Edward Hills, Chairman of the Conservative Association. 'I should think it was almost the last time when such an argument was brought to bear on an English electorate.'

To Theresa, it seemed perfectly natural that she should seek to impress. In middle-age she was an austere, formidable woman, with what Daisy Fingall called 'the proudest face I have ever seen'. The Sargent portrait of her, looking imperiously down her nose at the portraitist, supports this view. Sargent caught the character of the woman with insolent panache.

Of course, had she been merely a *grande dame*, Theresa would have been a somewhat flat personality. She was 'one of the most striking and dominating feminine personalities of our time,' wrote Colonel Repington, 'terrifying to some, but endeared to many friends by her notable and excellent qualities. She was unsurpassed as a hostess, clear-headed, witty, and large-hearted, with unrivalled experience of men and things social and political, and with a most retentive memory and immense vivacity and *joie de vivre*.'

There are many accounts of the extraordinary parties she gave at Londonderry House, of which Sir Almeric Fitzroy's recollection of the reception in honour of the King's birthday in 1903 may serve as an example. 'The crowd at Londonderry House was the densest I had ever seen at a London party', he wrote. 'The rooms upstairs were never full because a large section of the company had to remain in the hall, and a still larger body was collected in Park Lane and never entered the house. On his return from conducting Princess Christian to her carriage, Lord Londonderry was very nearly torn in pieces, and the struggle to get out of the house was one of superhuman difficulty. One girl fainted in the street and had to be laid out on the pavement, and one or two others collapsed inside the building.' In terms of numbers, Londonderry receptions were unbeatable.

In terms of gastronomic excellence, which all guests agree is an essential concern of the hostess, Lady Londonderry's parties were more haphazard. Of course, with twenty-eight people in the kitchens, and obviously unlimited financial resources, the food was more than merely acceptable, but getting to the table and getting from it were more urgent considerations than eating. Indeed, the Londonderry House receptions were more often than not after-dinner events rather than dinner-parties, as Lady Londonderry wanted to entertain as many people as possible, and Lord Londonderry did not believe in wasting time with knife and fork. When he was Viceroy of Ireland, he instituted frantically short meals instead of the usual mammoth banquets which had become the norm. Daisy Fingall recalled,

I believe half an hour was the time allowed for dinner and the occasion was a poor one for a gourmet. A footman stood behind nearly every chair and plates were often whipped away from the guests before they had finished. If you stopped to talk, you would get nothing to eat at all. Lord Londonderry must have cut down the number of dishes. He also instituted cold entrées and it was a new idea to be offered cold ham at dinner.

One night I sat beside a Lord Mayor at a State Banquet. The Lord Mayor who, no doubt, had been looking forward to his Viceregal meal, was a slow eater and talker and while his head was turned towards me the footman took away his plate and he was left looking in some surprise at the empty one put before him for the next course. When he was offered cold ham his endurance gave out and he expressed his feelings to me: 'I don't call this a dinner at all,' he said, 'I call it a rush,' and, eyeing the ham disdainfully, 'cheap, too!'

The evidence is that when royalty was present the cold ham was left in the pantry. Londonderry was the very opposite of mean, but his sense of priorities led him to avoid wasting time eating when important political business claimed his attention. The Prince and Princess of Wales, later Edward VII and Queen Alexandra, were however to be treated without frugality. The royal couple were particular friends of the Londonderrys, being entertained in state no less than eight times between 1890 and 1903, in addition to the countless functions at Londonderry House. Usually the ostensible reason for a royal visit extending over several days was a shooting party, a pastime of which the King was especially fond, and if it could be combined with a romantic weekend, so much the better. On one such occasion, the King was not accompanied to Wynyard by Queen Alexandra, nor was Mrs Keppel accompanied by her husband. Theresa much enjoyed encouraging these arrangements.

On this same occasion, a footnote to history was made when the King held a Privy Council at Wynyard in order to appoint Lord Londonderry President of the Council. It was the first time a Privy Council had been held in the country house of a subject since the time of Charles I, the last having been at Wilton in 1625; moreover, this very unusual event has not recurred since. The documents recording the business of the Council were headed 'At the Court at Wynyard', a unique reversal to the old style which gave Theresa intense pleasure.

The King's favour also gave undisguised pleasure to the Londonderry servants. Once, Theresa went to her drawing-room earlier than she was expected, and found a housemaid, duster in hand, busily sitting in all the chairs in turn. Theresa immediately guessed her purpose. 'That's the chair the King sat in,' she said. 'Now sit in it.'

At Edward VII's coronation, Theresa Londonderry was one of the select party of special women friends who were accorded a section of the public gallery screened off from the remainder. It was wittily referred to as 'The King's Loose Box' and contained, besides Theresa, Sarah Bernhardt, Alice Keppel and Mrs Arthur Paget. Theresa's attendance at the coronation had been preceded by unfortunate incidents which tested all her breeding and sang-froid. On the way down Park Lane in the Londonderry coach, Theresa grew impatient as the horses reared and neighed. Leaning out of the window, she motioned the *hoi polloi* to get out of the way. A cab-driver within earshot was insufficiently cowed. 'Go and fuck yourself, you and your fucking Coronation,' he shouted. It was almost certainly the first time she had ever been addressed in quite that manner.

By the time she arrived at the Abbey, Theresa was under-standably a trifle agitated. She decided that she ought to go first to the lavatories which had been especially installed for peeresses, to compose herself. She was in the cubicle so long that a queue of other robed and tiara'd peeresses formed outside, and their growing discomfort occasioned some unladylike murmurings. Suddenly Theresa's voice was heard from within; she was calling for some forceps! Now irritation gave way to amazement on the faces of the ladies in line. Surely not! The scandal would be unprecedented! An urgent message was sent for the nearest doctor, who shortly appeared with the required forceps. When Theresa emerged, she explained that while she had been adjusting her dress, the Londonderry tiara, with its precious diamonds and rubies, had fallen down the lavatory pan, and she could not possibly risk anything but the most delicate instrument to retrieve it.

Though Lady Londonderry mostly entertained political men, her receptions having the practical function of serving her husband's career, she could legitimately boast friendly acquaintance with some of the erudite men of her day. Edmund Gosse and Thomas Hardy were among her friends, and neither would suffer for long a woman with merely social graces. Once her literary knowledge got her into trouble with the woman who was to be, as Margot Asquith, her staunch political rival (and who, as we have already seen, found Theresa's literary talk 'paralysing'). Then she was just Margot Tennant, a woman some years junior to Theresa, who asked her whether she admired the style of John Addington Symonds, whose *Studies in Italy* she had been reading. Margot said that she did not like the style, though she liked some of the books. Lady Londonderry then assumed her most imperious air. 'I should be curious to know, Miss Tennant, what you have read by Symonds.'

'Oh, the usual sort of thing,' replied Margot, fully conscious that a game was about to be played, and deliberately feigning a nonchalant approach.

'Have you by any chance looked at *Essays, Suggestive and Speculative*?' enquired Theresa.

'Yes, I've read them all.'

'Really! Do you not approve of them?'

'Approve?' said Margot. 'I don't know what you mean.'

'Do you not think the writing beautiful? The style, I mean.'

'I think they are all very bad,' replied Margot with confidence, 'but then I don't admire Symonds's style.'

Lady Londonderry then went in for the kill. 'I am afraid you have not read the book,' she declared, raising herself some inches. 'I am afraid, Lady Londonderry, that you have not read the preface,' said the pert young woman. 'The book is dedicated to me.'

In fairness one should point out that the only version of this encounter is Margot's, who was certainly sure to accord herself the ultimate triumph. Such risks have ever attended the life of the social hostess. It is doubtful whether Theresa would have allowed herself to be deflected by risks. Once when dining with Queen Alexandra she whisked a coffee cup from the hands of an astonished butler and sank in a curtsy to serve the Queen herself, claiming that it had been the ancient right of her family to honour the monarchy in this way. Others present may have tittered behind their fans, but Lady Londonderry was undaunted.

Her most serious energies were reserved for the encouragement of Lord Londonderry's political career. Apart from his post in Ireland, he had been Postmaster-General in 1900, and President of the Board of Education in 1902. When he was appointed Lord President of the Council in 1903 he contrived to combine his duties in this office with those of the Education department, being overtly assisted in both by his wife. She took more than just a keen interest, as is attested by an occasion when she presided over a departmental meeting in the Lord President's room, questioning the Permanent Secretary and his staff while Lord Londonderry sat in 'isolated dignity' at the head of the table. Almeric Fitzroy recorded the incident, paying due tribute to Lady Londonderry's 'quickness and mastery of detail in handling the subject, and a power of apprehension of principles that astonished the officials', but he felt bound to reflect on the oddness of the situation. 'It is certainly a new departure when a Minister's wife undertakes to look into matters of departmental administration in the very seat of her husband's authority, and leaves to him the simple functions of an interested listener.'

Successive Marquesses of Londonderry have indeed been fortunate in finding wives who would not only support them, but push them forward in their careers, and their use of the role of hostess to further these ends was well known. Guests invited to Wynyard and Mount Stewart would be selected according to their value as supporters. Left to themselves, the Londonderry men would not have been so pushy. They are not by nature ambitious or self-seeking. The one overriding quality they have had, independently of any encouragement by their consorts, is a profound sense of honour. The Londonderrys are loyal, brave and proud; they are incapable of a dishonourable act. This conflict between inherent principle and the ambitions of a well-meaning wife would sometimes cause embarrassment, but when a Londonderry stood by what he felt to be right, his wife would cease her positioning and recognize the overwhelming authority of a good heart. Theresa's husband was advised by Edward Carson to have nothing to do with the establishment of an Ulster Provisional Government, as his family had so much to lose and would inevitably be placed in a position of danger. Londonderry would hear nothing of it. With teras streaming down his face, he clasped Carson's hands and said he would never stand aside while his friends went into peril. 'My dear Edward,' he said, 'if I was to lose everything in the world, I will go through with you to the end.' After his death, Carson was to pay him the finest tribute, calling him 'a great leader, a great and devoted public servant, a great patriot, a great gentleman, and above all the greatest of great friends'. Daisy Fingall had said much the same when she described him as a man who always 'did the right thing by instinct'.

The 6th Marquess died in 1915, his wife four years later. In the manner of long-established monarchy, the 7th Marquess and his wife assumed the responsibilities of their name without a moment's pause for transition. The parties at Londonderry House continued as before, and Edith Marchioness of Londonderry came gradually to dominate the social aspects of the London political scene even more triumphantly than her mother-in-law had done.

Theresa Londonderry had been called 'Nellie' by her friends, and a most unlikely nickname, 'Guy', by her immediate family. Edith was to adopt a name far more suggestive in its implications— 'Circe'. Her great friend Ramsay MacDonald teased her about this:

nay, nay, surely not Circe. Was she not a *wicked* witch? Witches I love, but they should be good and romantic, and of the family of that delightful creature Diana . . . But Circe! Circe is uncanny. Circe's mother was met by Macbeth. Circe cannot dance, Circe cannot sing, Circe has no quaint humours . . . No, it must not be Circe. Circe is on the films, in the night clubs. She is a vulgar jade, a bad egg, a snare *and* a delusion. Circe is not a lassie of the hills and the heather, of our sunsets and our east winds. Only drunken men write verse to Circe. She is, in short, a hussie.

Nevertheless, Circe it was, and many were the cynics who thought she had bewitched the Labour Prime Minister, enticing him into a life of luxury and privilege which he enjoyed so much that he forgot the poor folk he was supposed to represent. The nickname began with the foundation at Londonderry House of an élite club the members of which were identified by the name of a magical creature or an animal. Lord Londonderry was 'Charley the Cheetah', Carson was 'Edward the Eagle', Churchill was 'Winston the Warlock', Sir John Simon was 'Simon the Silkworm', and so on. All were members of 'The Ark' and were invested with the Order of the Rainbow. It may sound silly in cold print, but 'The Ark' gained in prestige until some of those who were excluded lived in hope of an invitation to join.

The first step was to be on the list for an invitation to one of the splendid parties at Londonderry House. Circe continued the tradition of receiving the Conservative Party on the eve of a Parliamentary session, on a scale intended to dazzle. Nobody refused. Birkenhead rather contemptuously said that Lord Londonderry was 'catering his way to the Cabinet', but Neville Chamberlain thought the parties did a great deal of good. Londonderry himself was aware of their shortcomings. 'We get the smug-faced citizens of London with their wives and daughters who vote Conservative anyway,' he wrote. 'I always wish that we could touch the other strata where the bulk of the votes lie.'

The new Lady Londonderry had one considerable advantage over her predecessor. She thoroughly enjoyed electioneering, and she was good at it. Whereas Theresa had behaved like a *grande dame*, bullying the electorate into obedience with her lofty scowl, Edith possessed what is sometimes called 'the common touch'; she had a more accessible charm than Theresa, and was thereby more persuasive. She needed to be, for her husband was not often at ease with ordinary folk. He himself admitted, 'I don't look sympathetic like a great many others do', and Harold Nicolson, while he appreciated that Londonderry was 'a real gent', commented that he contrived to look 1760 in 1936. He was aloof, rather touchy, and obviously patrician. Those who did not know him tended not to speak unless spoken to. His beguiling wife was therefore more than an asset, she was his salvation, and the love she inspired in him was real and profound. 'I just want you to know that I love and adore you,' he wrote to her, 'that you have been everything that a wife of a loving friend should be or could possibly be to me.'

Edith never missed an opportunity to impel her husband forward, a task she accomplished with great subtlety. Her own endeavours, her entire energies, were at his service, and even when she founded the Women's Legion in the First World War, harnessing the abundance of feminine drive which had been dissipated on the suffragette movement, there was a sense in which she did it as the wife of Lord Londonderry, rather than as the Marchioness with her own initiative. For this pioneer work she was invested a Dame Commander of the British Empire, and gradually became known as 'the great Lady Londonderry'. Thus, despite her efforts to remain a consort, she grew to enjoy a reputation at least as celebrated as her husband's.

Some measure of her value behind the scenes may be gleaned from the meeting she instigated between her husband, then Minister of Education in Northern Ireland, and the republican Michael Collins. Churchill it was who arranged the meeting, Lady Londonderry who inspired it. That it should even be suggested the man who bore the hated Castlereagh's name might encounter the republican rebel without their hurling themselves at each other's throats was temerity itself. In the event, 'I can say at once that I spent three of the most delightful hours that I ever spent in my life', recalled Lord Londonderry, whose opinion of Collins was completely overturned by the interview, distrust giving way to full and warm respect for his integrity. As for the fierce Michael Collins, he wrote afterwards to Lady Londonderry a pencilled note which indicated that, in different circumstances, he, too, would have been her slave. 'Try to imagine what it means to be a man like myself,' he said, 'entirely self-made, self-educated, without background and trying to cope with a man like Lord L., a man who has every advantage I lack . . . I contrast myself with him, my uncouthness with his distinction, my rough speech with his unconscious breeding and the worst of it is I *like* and admire him, and feel that he is brave and honest.' Lord L., meanwhile, spoke of Collins's enthusiasm and stirring phraseology. Small wonder that Lady Londonderry took her nickname from a sorceress. It is not too fanciful to imagine that she was genuinely upset when Collins was killed in an ambush a few months later.

Circe's greatest conquest was, of course, the Prime Minister, Ramsay MacDonald. That the Prime Minister of the day should take his place at the top of the stairs in Londonderry House was perfectly natural; the surprise in this case was that he was the first Labour Prime Minister, and had fought all his life' against everything that the Londonderrys stood for. Yet Lady Londonderry was eventually his closest, most devoted, most affectionate friend.

They met at MacDonald's first dinner at Buckingham Palace, when he was asked to take Lady Londonderry into the dining-room. They were at ease immediately, largely because they shared a love for the Scottish Highlands. The Londonderrys are the first to have their signatures in the Visitors' Book at Chequers under the premiership of MacDonald. Within a short time they were writing to each other regularly, he addressing her as 'My dearest Ladye', or 'My dearest Friend of all', and signing off 'Ever devotedly Hamish'. Their letters were touched with the lightest feather of flirtation and the deepest flow of affection. 'What generous archangel ever patted me on the back', he said, 'and arranged that amongst the many great rewards that this poor unwelcome stranger to this world was to receive was that he should be permitted, before he returned to his dust, to feel devotion to *you*.' He admitted that he was so terribly fond of her that 'I ought not to tell you how much', and wondered, 'What potion did you put in my wine that night at Buckingham Palace?'

They were neither of them so foolish as not to realize that their open friendship would cause gossip. She reminded him that he would not be popular among his followers if he continued to dine at Londonderry House. 'Promise to let me judge whether accepting invitations from you damages me or not', he told her; it was his worry that she might sacrifice some of her popularity among the Tories. Rumours began to circulate. The Prime Minister and the hostess were lovers, it was said. Her influence over him protected the country from the worst excesses of Socialism, it was whispered. His devotion to her amounted to a public scandal, said Beatrice Webb, not because she thought there was a love affair beneath the friendship (few took that *canard* seriously), but because 'he *ought* not to be more at home in the castles of the great than in the homes of his followers. It argues a perverted taste and a vanished faith.'

In spite of MacDonald's attempts to allay Circe's fears, it soon became clear that the friendship was harmful to his reputation. A Labour M.P. was overheard in the lobby of the House of Commons to say 'A few months ago he sang the Red Flag. Now he whistles the Londonderry Air.' Labour Party supporters felt let down by their leader. What they did not pause to wonder was why he should react so warmly to the offer of friendship from the 'enemy'. Ramsay MacDonald was a profoundly lonely man, a child of the Highlands, and a man of culture who appreciated the benefits of civilized life; he was not a brutish or crude table-thumper. Quite simply, when few others even sought to understand him, Lady Londonderry became his best friend. It was unfortunate, but it was not calculated or artificial; the friendship was spontaneous and wholly natural. For her part, Lady Londonderry was touchingly proud of his achievements.

The dangers were reciprocal. Lord Londonderry was appointed Minister for Air, and ever afterwards thought to be 'Ramsay's man'. Baldwin's friend John Davidson wrote, 'he owed his preferment really to the fact that Ramsay MacDonald greatly enjoyed standing at the top of the staircase in Londonderry House as the first Minister of the Crown in full evening dress', and Baldwin himself told Londonderry's son Lord Castlereagh that ninety per cent of the people did not understand MacDonald's closeness to the Londonderrys. 'To them your Mother's friendship with Ramsay is an act of political expediency to help your Father's political career.'

This turned out to be a tragic misreading of the truth, for Londonderry's tenure of office was one of the most valuable in those dark deluded years preceding the Second World War. He, more than anyone else, was responsible for the maintenance of the Spitfires which would one day save the country. But he was distrusted and disbelieved, and even today has not received full credit for his foresight. This is not the place to examine Londonderry's career, which has been told in detail by H. Montgomery Hyde, but Lady Londonderry's role in the public careers of both her husband and the Prime Minister demonstrates the unseen power of a hostess, especially one who moves in the political world. Had she not been the leading Tory hostess of the day, her acquaintance with Ramsay MacDonald would not have been so publicly displayed and would not have occasioned such anger. Nor would Lord Londonderry's promotion have been questioned, and his ultimate demise applauded. It was supposed, on all sides, that Lady Londonderry had meddled too much in the country's affairs. As Baldwin said, again in his letter to Lord Castlereagh:

> I do not think your Mother has been a very happy influence on your Father in politics. She is a very remarkable person. She was a creative genius in the war. It was she who first set the women at work . . . She has great charm, vitality and courage . . . Your Mother certainly provided a refuge for Ramsay for which your Father paid a high price.

The price was undeserved neglect under Baldwin, and improper reflections on Londonderry's record, which left him bitter and racked with feelings of failure. To make matters worse, he was thought by some to be 'Hitler's friend' (as Harold Nicolson refers to him in his *Diaries*), not so much because he visited Germany, as did others, and sought to make the real intentions of the German Chancellor clear to those in the British government who would not see and would not hear, but because, once again, Lady Londonderry was observed to play hostess to prominent Germans. Never did she attempt to influence their view of the British mood, as did Mrs Greville, but the fact that the Ambassador, Herr von Ribbentrop, dined at Londonderry House and stayed at Wynyard was thought proof positive of Nazi sympathies. The truth was that the Londonderrys did not like Ribbentrop at all, but thought the business of entertaining was to enable all kinds of views to be aired informally. Lady Londonderry took her role as hostess if anything too seriously, and she was chastised for her generosity far more than lesser hostesses who wanted only to have a famous guest at their tables.

Circe played only a subsidiary role in the Abdication crisis. She was not one of the _arrivistes_ who fluttered around Mrs Simpson—indeed she had no need to be—but she did correspond with her, and on one occasion told her frankly that the British people would never tolerate a marriage between their King and a twice-divorced American woman. It was typical of Edith Londonderry that, instead of asking Mrs Simpson what she intended to do, like other women terrified of incurring her displeasure and being out of favour with the King, she told Mrs Simpson what she _should_ do.

After the Second World War, the Londonderrys spent most of their time in Ireland. Lord Londonderry died in 1949, a disappointed man, pouring out his frustration in heartfelt letters to Lady Desborough which reflected his fear that he had not lived up to the reputation of his ancestors. Lady Londonderry, now universally recognized as 'the greatest political hostess of her day', gave her last reception at Londonderry House in 1958, with Prime Minister Harold Macmillan her Guest of Honour. Four months later she was dead, the last of her breed and the last to dominate that famous staircase. Conservative Party receptions are now a much more prosaic affair; the Londonderry tiara and rubies are in a bank, wrapped in velvet; Londonderry House was demolished in 1962 to make way for an hotel.

Theresa, Marchioness of Londonderry. 'A highwaywoman in a tiara'

Edith, Marchioness of Londonderry, arriving with her husband for the State Opening of Parliament

Edith, Lady Londonderry, at a dinner-party with the Hungarian Minister

Mrs Stuyvesant Fish
and Mrs Vanderbilt

It comes as a shock to discover that the most rigid society in the twentieth century was not to be found in England, with its hierarchical nobility, its centuries of practice, and its traditions, but in America. Before the First World War, and to a considerable extent even after it, New York hostesses presided over the grandest set of privileged people on the face of the earth. They made Lady Desborough, for all her inherited elegance and grace, seem an amateur at the game and would never have understood her relaxed attitude. Lady Cunard was an *arriviste* by comparison, and Lady Colefax a mere housewife. Mrs Corrigan would have been banished as the worst sort of vulgarian (indeed, she tried to nudge her foot inside the door of New York society, and failed). The only British hostess who might have gained entry was Mrs Greville, since her stuffiness and ostentation were traits they would have recognized and applauded. The arbiters of New York dinner parties based their test of social acceptability on nothing less than total exclusiveness, and if you were excluded, no amount of money, or influence, or talent could hope to alter your lowly status. New York made a positive fetish of the social list, and one of the tiny group of hostesses who controlled it, Mrs Belmont, said, 'I know of no art, profession, or work for women more taxing in mental resources than being a leader of society.'

Mrs Belmont's mental resources, such as they were, concentrated on one overwhelming purpose—to maintain her position as one of the cream of the élite. To be at the top of the pyramid she had to entertain, rather than be entertained, and to do so more lavishly than anyone else. Dinner parties and balls were given not for fun—they were rarely enjoyable and then only by accident—but as an essential strategy in the battle for supremacy which had to be fought in dire earnest.

The proudest set of all was the Fifth Avenue set in New York, composed of Astors, Vanderbilts, Belmonts and their various clans, immensely rich families who had made their money in the nineteenth century in railroads, tobacco and banking. They looked down with contempt upon the Park Avenue set, barely a hundred yards away, *nouveaux riches* who had acquired their yachts only in the twentieth century. A Fifth Avenue lady *never* accepted an invitation from a Park Avenue hostess, and if a Park Avenue lady was rash enough to drop her card upon a Fifth Avenue house, she would be told, as sure as day was day, that 'Mrs X regrets Mrs Y is not on her calling list this afternoon', and that was that. No argument or appeal was possible. Social climbing was infinitely more difficult in New York than it had ever been in London.

Throughout America similar games were played in the effort to construct social strata where none were supposed to exist. There were sets in Boston, Chicago, Cleveland, San Francisco, even Detroit, each under the sway and dominion of a particular hostess whose favour had to be cherished above every other aim in life. A man from Boston refused to be introduced to two young ladies who found themselves at the same reception as he in Rome, because they did not move in the same society in their native Boston. The Burlinghame set in San Francisco were virtually paralysed by their own stodginess. So solemn and pompous were they that a guest caught using the wrong fork would be banished for ever into nonentity, and they even went so far as to snub Queen Marie of Rumania, leaving word that though Her Majesty might be admitted, she could not be 'received'. To this day, San Francisco high society is quite the most strained and formal in America.

Still, to reach the pinnacle one had to be a Fifth Avenue hostess;

there was no other way. Attention to protocol and the consciousness that they were part of a select few occupied most of their energies. Far from encouraging 'society', in its correct meaning, they were bitter enemies of all social flexibility, with the result that they only met each other, again and again, at their dinner parties. As one who observed from a distance remarked, 'one is either born knowing those extraordinary people or dies without meeting them'. Fifth Avenue obsessions with exclusiveness made the mild preoccupations of an English duchess seem a quixotic fancy. Cornelius Vanderbilt, son of the Mrs Vanderbilt who will form the subject of this chapter, looked back with a severely disgruntled yawn upon the world which had shaped his youth. The business of a hostess, he said, was 'to gather together people who have known each other since infancy and who dislike each other cordially'. The purpose of it all? To make one's friends miserable. And, with the bright exception of one hostess who sported the lyrical name of Mrs Stuyvesant Fish, they succeeded.

Giving large dinner parties in sumptuous Fifth Avenue palaces (and some exceeded the Italian Renaissance in their ornament), with footmen lining the stairs at regulation intervals, and gold dinner plates, was a way of displaying wealth, and thereby drawing attention to the worldly success of the husbands who had created it. For what could be the point of being rich unless you could be seen to be rich? Thus, while the menfolk usually found entertaining a bore, they were grateful to their wives for showing off in their place, and to this end acquiesced in their extravagance. When Mrs Stuyvesant Fish showed signs of a mild cough, her solicitous husband enquired whether he might get anything for her throat. 'Yes, dear,' she said. 'That nice diamond and pearl necklace I saw in Tiffany's this morning.' He bought it the next day. Fifth Avenue ladies packaged themselves in diamonds, millions of dollars worth at a time, and Mrs Frederick Vanderbilt touched the summit of nonchalant wealth when she took on the habit of wearing a huge uncut sapphire or ruby attached to her waist by a rope of pearls and hanging so low that she kicked it with her feet as she walked along.

Another Vanderbilt, Reginald, married Gloria Morgan and took his new bride to lunch with the matriarch of the family, known as

Alice of the Breakers (we shall see why later). Alice asked if Gloria had received her pearls yet. Reginald explained that he could not yet afford good ones (not being the senior male in the family) and would not consider buying cheap ones. Alice of the Breakers called for a pair of scissors, then snipped off about a third from the rope around her neck, worth $70,000. 'There you are, Gloria', she said. 'All Vanderbilt women have pearls.'

This ostentation was carried to many absurd extremes. Mrs Henry Sloane sent back the gloves she had ordered from Paris because the glover had not paid sufficient attention to the contour of her fingernails. No one thought her silly. After all, ladies regularly spent $40,000 a year on clothes, equivalent in spending power to several millions today. Mrs Leeds, known as the 'richest widow in the world', exceeded even this, and Mrs Vanderbilt the Kingfisher had five hundred pairs of shoes with five hundred handbags to match, and some of her dresses were so heavy with jewellery and embroidery that they could not be hung, but had to be laid flat, each one in its own cupboard.

The most awe-inspiring display was to be seen at the opera, when the thirty-five boxes of what was called the 'Diamond Horseshoe' were filled by their glittering owners. For fifty years these boxes were occupied by only twenty families, and when they were all there, more than 175 million dollars' worth of jewellery was on show. That, indeed, was the real purpose of the opera, to which the enjoyment of music played a distinctly subordinate role. How the Metropolitan Opera House in New York came into being is a story which perfectly illustrates the determination of millionaire hostesses to manage the social world for their own benefit.

Since 1854 the home of opera had been the Academy of Music, on 14th Street, supported and financed by the 'old' families of New York (Phelpses, Kanes, Hamiltons, Van Rensselaers, Beekmans, Varicks and so on), who naturally, society being what it is, expended much energy and nervous strain upon the supreme goal of excluding the 'new' families, who included Astors, Bakers, Rockefellers, Richard T. Wilson, Ogden Mills, and above all the Vanderbilts. Unfortunately for the Academy of Music, these new millionaires who appeared to have sprung up from nowhere in one generation from poverty to plenty, were far, far richer than the 'old' families. So they all gathered in colloquy and proposed to build a new opera house at 39th Street and Broadway, grander, finer, more splendid than anything hitherto seen in New York, which would render the Academy of Music obsolete. The old families scorned the idea that anyone who was anyone should migrate so far uptown to visit the opera—it was absurd; so they dismissed the proposal and decided to stay put. (It is at the very least ironical that 14th Street should now be so sleazy and woebegone.)

Construction of the new opera house went ahead, largely underwritten by Vanderbilts but with handsome contributions from the other families, while the old guard at 14th Street glowered. When it was complete, the Diamond Horseshoe contained thirty-five boxes, which were sold off at $65,000 each for life. The Vanderbilts took five—no other family took more than two. The total cost of the building was nearly two million dollars, and the name of Metropolitan Opera House was bestowed upon it.

The inaugural production was fixed to open on 22 October 1883, with a performance of *Faust*. Intending no doubt to teach the newcomers a lesson, the old guard chose the very same evening to open their new season at the Academy of Music, with *La Sonnambula*. Open battle for social supremacy was joined that evening, causing consternation among the uncertain, who were faced with a stark choice upon which their future acceptability at the 'right' dinners would depend. One ambitious hostess bent on climbing to the stars solved the problem by shuttling her daughter up and down Manhattan all evening so that she was seen at both events and could maintain her status in both camps. The hostess was Mrs Stevens, and the lucky daughter Minnie Stevens, who later became Lady Paget and was among the most popular Americans in the Prince of Wales's set in London. Victory went to the millionaires and their new Metropolitan Opera House, which was immediately established as the showplace for the Fifth Avenue set. Thenceforth they were free to concentrate on their far more important internecine warfare, as the matriarch of each Fifth Avenue mansion struggled to achieve superiority over all others.

Entertaining was the means by which ascendance was gained,

and thus the business of being a hostess required as much attention and determination as a military campaign. It is a measure both of the difficulties encountered and the prizes in status to be won that for sixty or seventy years only half a dozen women could claim to have reached the pinnacle. Like Roman Emperors, they succeeded each other with teeth bared and blood spattered.

They spent inconceivable amounts of money in waging the campaign; their age became known, with reason, as the Gilded Age. There was gold everywhere, tiaras on every head, visible glittering signs of financial success in every drawing-room—paintings from Paris, frescoes from Florence, tapestries from Touraine. As one young lady in the midst of it all pointed out, they were often bewildered by their own magnificence. Hostesses were quite simply judged by the jewels they wore.

The first in the line was Mrs Belmont the elder. (Just to confuse matters, there was another Mrs Belmont whom we shall meet later.) Her husband, August Belmont, virtually taught New York society the art of entertaining as it was understood in Europe. Mrs Belmont was succeeded by two Mrs Astors who lived side by side in two houses which occupied the whole block between 33rd and 34th Street on Fifth Avenue, with a ballroom behind which they shared. The senior was Mrs John Jacob Astor, an imposing cultivated lady every bit as much a *grande dame* as the austere Marchioness of Londonderry. Mrs John Jacob Astor possessed the most famous diamonds in America. When her husband died in 1887, her throne was taken by her sister-in-law, Mrs William Astor, who set the standards by which all subsequent hostesses have been judged. She annoyed all other Astors by having her cards printed simply 'Mrs Astor' with the impudent implication that there was only one worth considering, but most of New York eventually allowed her this right. She became *the* Mrs Astor, the undisputed regulator of Society, the sovereign whose crown every aspiring hostess in years to come would seek to inherit. There are those even today who maintain that the tradition of Mrs Astor stands alone.

Mrs Astor ruled Society with remorseless control and little tolerance of newcomers. She regarded it as her sacred duty to make sure that the upper classes of New York remained very upper indeed. With awesome dignity and calm, she dictated what would happen and who would be allowed to witness it. Her decision on social matters was final—there was no appeal. Society was known then as 'the 400', as her ballroom could comfortably contain only that number, and no one who was excluded from Mrs Astor's ballroom could claim any pretence of being in Society. Hence good families were limited, by her decree, to that number. The greatest social event of the year was the annual ball at the Astor mansion. For weeks beforehand she would pore over the lists with her henchman Harry Lehr, an effete and feckless young man-about-town who assumed an impregnable position as arbiter of who was 'in' and who was to be kept 'out', and would be found at the right hand of other hostesses in later years; between them they would decide the destinies of the young and the aspiring. Those whose fathers or husbands were too obviously involved in trade stood no chance of inclusion. Invitations were hand-written by a curious woman of Inca descent called Maria de Baril, social secretary to many of the 400, who never deigned to give her services to any but the very greatest. When a letter arrived with her distinctive Gothic script on the envelope, sighs of relief were uttered as one knew one was safe for another year. If the letter failed to arrive, floods of unconsolable tears were shed. This was no exaggeration. Those to whom it mattered would go to Europe and be out of town at the time of the ball rather than allow it to be inferred that they had not been invited. The power of a hostess had never been greater.

The social secretary, incidentally, was a power in her own right. She not only arranged dinners and balls, but advised on behaviour and etiquette, on rank and precedence, and on tactics. In order to emulate European society which had evolved rules over centuries, the new millionaires' wives often needed a crash course in protocol.

As Mrs Astor's health and stamina showed signs of waning, after nearly twenty years at the helm, various crown princesses jostled in the ante-room. Speculation as to who would succeed dominated the social columns in the newspapers. There certainly did not want contenders. High on the list was Mrs Ogden Mills, a lady of supercilious manners and unimpeachable discrimination. Mrs Mills was, however, even more selective than Mrs Astor, and her wish to reduce the number of people allowed to sit at her table ultimately defeated her. She limited the stable from which her guests could be chosen to two hundred, and would say, in a drawling, self-consciously aloof voice, 'There are really only twenty families in New York.' Her circle was too small to be representative, a disadvantage which in no manner prevented the ambitious from dropping their cards upon her, to no avail of course. The few that were admitted had to withstand the most astonishing rudeness. Mrs Mills was cold and sarcastic, and treated her guests with the most high-handed disdain. She would extend a limp hand to a guest, stare over his shoulder and forget his existence. Still, people courted her favours. 'They were chilled but impressed', wrote Elizabeth Drexel. 'Only a woman who was supremely sure of herself could be so ill-mannered. The ambitious preferred snubs from her to kindness from more human hostesses.'

Another possibility was Mrs Belmont, not the lady already mentioned, but Mrs O. Belmont of the next generation, who had previously been the wife of W.K. Vanderbilt and had forced her poor daughter Consuelo to marry the Duke of Marlborough. Mrs Belmont's trouble was not that she had too few friends, like Mrs Mills, but too many enemies. She simply never mastered the art of diplomacy.

Mrs Stuyvesant Fish was disqualified from assuming the supreme crown owing to her maverick behaviour. She wanted to 'liven things up' with amusing pranks, such as the dinner she gave for her friends' dogs, and she wanted to dispense with rules made by others, to feel unfettered, unrestrained. For many years she was a bright and cheerful figure in an otherwise conventional scene, and we shall hear more of her. But the sparkle of Mrs Fish was a trifle too quixotic for the austere matriarchs of New York, who wanted a leader, not a revolutionary. It is doubtful whether Mrs Fish cared very much. In any case, she was already one of the undisputed rulers of Newport, the millionaires' summer playground.

Newport, on Rhode Island, was the scene where preliminary skirmishes were fought, prior to the main battle in New York. She who conquered Newport could proceed to dominate New York. Fearsome competition arose on the island for the frenetic weeks of the summer season. Hostesses overstretched themselves as to who could give a better entertainment, could wear lovelier clothes, could capture the most impressive foreign guest, could sport the most amazing jewels. There has never been anything quite so fierce, or funny, as the spectacle of the rich at play in Newport, and we must take ourselves there to see how the strategy for succession crystallized around one lady, on many counts a surprising outsider. Minnie Stevens, the very same whose mother made sure she attended *both* premières on 22 October 1883, watched it all happen and was aghast at the prodigal waste. 'What are you all after anyway?' she asked, with pretended naïvety. She thought the terrific competition was nothing but confusion of mind and fatigue of body. She was right, of course, but then so was Jimmy Cutting, who observed the same activities with approval. 'You do not give parties to enjoy yourselves', he said, 'but to advance yourselves.' What was at stake was social recognition in the most extravagant summer resort the world has ever known, next to which the capitals of Europe were impoverished. Fortunately, most of the women who played the game were not intelligent enough to see how silly it all was, but neither were any of them so hypocritical as to deny the pleasure they derived from being at the summit of world society.

From July 4 until the Saturday of the first week in September the little town of Newport was alive with the great ones of the earth, all translated from New York for a 'holiday' which consumed all their energies and wore them into deep weariness. Every night for seven or eight weeks there would be a dinner, a party, or a ball, taking place in any one of the magnificent houses which the millionaires had caused to be built on this once unpretentious island. The grandest house of all was 'The Breakers', a five-storey palace of paralysing sumptuousness where Alice Vanderbilt, Alice-of-the-Breakers, held court. In open competition with 'The Breakers' were a score of mansions, each in its own grounds and each looking out to the ocean over the cliffs with a verandah offering breath-taking views, with names such as 'Wakehurst', 'Wayside', 'Nethercliff', 'Arleigh', 'Beaulieu'. Mrs Stuyvesant Fish presided at 'Crossways', and the imposing Mrs Belmont at the Marble House, built, as one would only suppose in Newport, entirely of marble. 'A marble palace is the right place for a woman with a marble heart' was the view uncharitably expressed by outsiders. Intruders were ruthlessly excluded from the activities of this élite band, and the local inhabitants of Newport, known as the Footstools, were not even allowed to peer through the gates. No such plebeian establishment as an hotel was permitted to be built, and no trespasser was allowed to stray on to Bailey's Beach, where the owners all had their initials proudly displayed on the bathing huts. It was a risky business appearing in Newport. Some waited four summers before venturing to the sacred reserve, for if you took the plunge and were rejected, your hopes of being invited to the right places in New York were forever dashed. Not until there were at least four houses at which you knew you would be welcome was it advisable to place your future at risk with a visit to Newport, and when you did dare to be seen there, you would have to make sure that you never appeared in diamonds more impressive than those of the reigning hostesses.

The Newport season was carefully planned by a triumvirate of hostesses who arrived a few days before the rest—Mrs Stuyvesant Fish, Mrs Oelrichs, and Mrs Belmont, with Harry Lehr in close attendance as adviser to all three. They would decide upon the events which were to take place and avoid unseemly clashes between two dinners. The inner group of hostesses could not prevent a dinner being planned by one of the fringe group, from Park Avenue, but since they rarely attended a function given by parvenues, a convergence of this sort did not matter. Occasionally a Park Avenue hostess would contrive to trap an illustrious guest, which might oblige the Fifth Avenue ladies to accept an invitation. One such lady who had been thwarted in New York leased an impressive Newport villa, at an exorbitant rent, and determined to break in during the summer. Her social secretary wisely counselled no parties, no invitations, no announcements for the first week or so. Then it became known that a Presidential candidate was coming to Newport and was to stay with the Park Avenue hostess. Consternation erupted. Visiting cards were suddenly delivered to the upstart hostess in dozens, and the delighted lady found herself welcome at all the great receptions. But only during the time that she had her illustrious guest. After he had left, the Park Avenue lady was dropped without ceremony. Her calling card was refused, her attempt to join the Beach Club rejected. She returned, abashed, to New York, and never again took a lease at Newport.

Entertainments given by the sacred few were on a scale of luxury and formality which America had never seen before, and is unlikely ever to see again. Servants wore livery. A receiving line, as for royalty, welcomed each guest on arrival. Girls might wear hundreds of dollars' worth of violets pinned to their dresses, and cascades of fresh roses and jasmine would fall from the chandeliers into guests' laps. A large dinner could cost a quarter of a million dollars to set up in proper fashion, and the opulence displayed would render all but the initiated dumb-struck. Mrs Oelrichs, who never did anything by halves, not only illuminated her grounds, but the very ocean as well, and she once brought to Newport an entire circus from New York to amuse her guests after dinner. (She was also one of the few in the inner circle capable of getting on her hands and knees with a pail of water and scrubbing brush to demonstrate to her staff exactly how well a floor *could* be cleaned.) Grand Duke Boris of Russia, who was well acquainted with the grand style, left Newport after a visit in a state of perplexed amazement. 'I have never even dreamt of such luxury as I have seen in Newport,' he said. 'It is like walking on gold. An enchanted island.' The summer was passed in a veritable pageant of vulgar ostentation and excess. Grand Duke Boris was by no means the only titled European to savour this overwhelming wealth. As the little summer resort grew in reputation, every European nobleman yearned to be sucked into the vortex. A visit to America was a failure unless Newport were included on the itinerary.

The penalty of exclusiveness was boredom. The same people dined together night after night, then spent the afternoon in the absurd ritual of dropping calling cards upon each other. Nobody was at home, of course; everybody was out dropping cards on everyone else. To be caught at home at three in the afternoon would have been a social blunder. This aping of European ways was rendered silly by its own superfluousness; they would all see each other later the same day in any event. The ritual was there, but the purpose which had given it birth was absent.

Should it ever arise that there were too few men for a ball, or even for a bridge session, then conveniently they could be ordered by telephone, by Harry Lehr, from the local Naval Training Station, and bemused officers could find themselves in a cotillion with the richest folk in the world. Their names were of no importance; they had been delivered with the caviare.

A few success stories brightened the predictability of these lavish entertainments. The most unlikely took place at Sherwood, the house of Mr and Mrs Pembroke Jones, in the attic of which languished a freckled and plain relation called Mary Lily Kenan. She was 35, well past the age when she could hope to catch a husband, so she had been hidden away from society to act as unpaid seamstress upstairs. She never attended parties or balls, and was only allowed to eat with the family at informal lunches. An exceedingly rich and lately divorced man, Henry Flagler, was once in the house and needed a button to be sewn on. Mary was called down to help. Henry and Mary fell in love, she duly became Mrs Flagler, and lived, as befits a story of this nature, happily ever after.

Somewhat less attractive is the story of Harry Lehr himself, America's Court Jester, the darling of society, the social leader in succession to Ward McAllister. Adored by women, he was distrusted and avoided by men, who felt uncomfortable with him. Mrs Astor had first taken him up, and 'made' him, after which, with no money but plenty of charm, vitality, and what passed for wit, he established himself by flirting with all the top hostesses. His greatest success was with Mrs Stuyvesant Fish, who called him 'lamb' and scarcely moved without consulting him. He was a professional guest, living off his hostesses and never even paying for his travel, as the hostesses all obtained passes for him on the railroads which their husbands variously controlled.

Eventually, Harry Lehr proposed to wealthy Elizabeth Drexel, married her, then declared that he would behave solicitously in public, but would never sleep with her. She was, he said, repulsive to him, and he only agreed to marry her after making sure that his position in society would not be threatened by the alliance. He consulted Mrs Astor, Mrs Stuyvesant Fish, Mrs Oelrichs and Mrs Vanderbilt, and they all reassured him that his wife would be welcome at their tables. So he was safe. Elizabeth Drexel signed a document giving Harry $25,000 a year pocket money, and agreeing to pay for all their joint expenses in marriage. He admitted to her that he was an adventurer, and a successful one, secure in the knowledge that she would never admit to society that he had made a fool of her. She described their marriage as a 'tragic farce', and after his death in 1929 she married Lord Decies. His diaries revealed that he was homosexual, a fact that could have been gleaned earlier by anyone brought up in a less sheltered world. He delighted in women's clothes, and the society columns in the newspapers mocked him as much as they dared; they knew the truth, but the Fifth Avenue ladies could not discern it beneath the elliptical phrases of the press. His was perhaps the most dazzling social career of that meretricious age. Harry Lehr achieved his ambition in life without earning a penny.

It was a Newport tradition that the last event of the season, on the first Saturday in September and the last day of the Horse Show, was the Farewell Ball given by Mrs Stuyvesant Fish at 'Crossways'. This marked the end of another holiday, and confirmed Mrs Fish's pre-eminent position on the 'Social Strategy Board' of the three consuls. New faces (if there were any) were discussed and evaluated. That Tinplate King, William B. Leeds, though he has always been excluded in the past, will have next season to be brought into the fold, as he and his nice wife have been taken up by Mrs Belmont, who is herself one of the Social Strategy Board. Mrs Leeds is naïve and childish, but very generous and really quite harmless. That dreadful climber, on the other hand, must at all costs be kept distant. She had the effrontery to ask Mrs Fish how big her house was. The nerve of it! Mrs Fish had said she did not know for sure, because it swelled at night, but the stupid woman could not understand she was being snubbed. Whoever brought her here?

After the post-mortem, and the tentative plans for next year, the orchestra played 'Home Sweet Home' and everyone left for their quiet retreats on the Hudson, or Long Island, to rest a little before the torment of the New York season began. Some had even enjoyed their few weeks in Newport. 'Just one more two-step,' pleaded a younger guest. Mrs Fish knew when enough was enough. 'There are just two more steps for you,' she said. 'One upstairs to get your wraps, the other out to your carriage.'

Mr and Mrs Fish would certainly be off to Glenclyffe Farms on the Hudson, a house with no running water, and more importantly for Mr Fish, no chattering guests. Like all the husbands of these ambitious ladies, he did not care for parties at all, tolerating them only for the sake of his wife, whom he adored. An honest and admirable man, he descended directly from a Puritan family among the Mayflower passengers, and had risen to a position of eminence and wealth in very few years, being President of the Illinois Central Railroad while still in his twenties. His social position was due entirely to the wit and perseverance of his unorthodox wife, who had made her reputation as society's *enfant terrible* and gloried in it. The advantages were balanced by the liabilities for a man who enjoyed the quiet life. Mrs Stuyvesant Fish had once offended Mrs Harriman, wife of another railroad king, with a thoughtless remark at tea, and from this tiny cause great dramas had evolved. Mr Harriman did all in his power to embarrass Mr Fish, placing a 'mole' in his Company to sow dissension and almost succeeding in removing Fish from power. It did not do for one hostess to upset another.

Unfortunately, Mrs Stuyvesant Fish was adept at upsetting people. Unlike Mrs Ogden Mills, who was simply starchy and rude, Mrs Fish was witty and rude. She seemed at times even to despise the society of which she was an acknowledged leader, for she was remorseless in pointing out the idiocies which other hostesses had imposed upon the ritual of entertaining. She swept aside the stultifying exclusiveness established by Mrs Astor. Amusing and interesting people found a place at her table more readily than the pompous or boring, however respectable their names. She loosened the tight carapace of ceremonial and formality which made dinner parties in New York so deadly. It was she who decreed that cigarettes could be smoked with the soup, she who got rid of string orchestras playing waltzes to make way for jazz musicians, she who served one wine with the meal instead of the customary five. She went so far as to limit the duration of a meal to fifty minutes, a laudable innovation welcomed by the guest who might otherwise be imprisoned with bores each side for three hours, but it did mean that you had to hold your fork in one hand and keep a grip on your plate with the other, as the servants were instructed to whisk each course away after ten minutes whether or not the diner had finished eating. Her greatest single crime was to belittle the hallowed tradition of a visit to the opera on Mondays. Mamie Fish was nothing if not honest. She could not stand opera ('caterwauling in the street' she called it), and knew full well that most of the other tiara-decked ladies did not like it any more than she. But they would make no such damaging admission, and her forthrightness was an embarrassment in a society swaddled in pretence. Mamie did not feign to enjoy music. 'I'm never quite sure that I've fixed my face right,' she said. 'Sometimes when it is just right for expressing appreciation of a cradle song, I find I'm listening to the cry of the Valkyries, or when I've fixed it for the Two Grenadiers, they sing the duet from Romeo and Juliet.' Ladies of consequence were meant to play at least the piano. A rash man asked Mrs Fish what instrument she played, and received the unadorned answer, 'A comb.' Mamie Fish did not play the game by the rules, and it was no small achievement on her part that she maintained her position in spite of her incurable iconoclasm. She was an original, a woman held aloft by strength of character. Her unpredictability was her protection. She could not abide the banal question or standard remark, and brought freshness and vigour to her dinner-parties. If the rest of society manifested disapproval in whispers and glances, Mamie quite obviously did not care a fig.

For example, no lady would even own to wearing a wig of any sort. Mamie wore a piece, which she openly called her 'seven-dollar curls'. They fell off as she was entering the house of Mrs Gould for a grandiose dinner, and a liveried servant bent down to retrieve them, handing the object to Mrs Fish with a deep bow. She was still pinning them back in place as she entered the drawing-room with the remark, to Mrs Gould, 'Sweet pet, you will have to discharge your man. My secret is known to him.'

Again, she was the only hostess prepared to admit that entertaining could be tiring and tedious. Weary of being hypocritically polite when she least felt like it, she chose instead to tell the truth. 'Oh, how do you do, Mr So-and-so', as she welcomed an unfamiliar guest. 'I had quite forgotten I asked you.' To an assembled crowd Mamie cried, 'Make yourselves perfectly at home, and believe me, there is no one wishes you there more heartily than I do.' To a guest who excused herself for leaving so early, Mamie was heard to say, 'No guest ever left too soon for me.' And which of us who has ever given a dinner party, be it for a mere half dozen, cannot recognize and sympathize with the dejection of Mrs Fish, alone in her dressing-room with fifty people waiting downstairs to eat. 'I wish they'd all go away,' she said to a lady who sought her out. 'Four weeks ago I thought I wanted them to come, but now I have changed my mind.'

The rudeness of Mrs Stuyvesant Fish was for fifteen years a regular talking-point in New York. Some did not care for her cruel repartee, but were obliged perforce to tolerate it if they wished to be included at her table. She normally prefaced a spiky remark with the endearment 'sweet pet', which was recognized as a warning. 'I heard what you said last night,' ventured an injured lady. 'You said I looked like a frog.' 'No, no, sweet pet,' said Mamie. 'Not a frog. A toad, my pet, a toad.' Her breezy manner and vivacity were a delightful shock to the young, a sore test to be endured by the dowagers. Hosting the first dinner of a new season at Newport, Mrs Fish welcomed the ladies with an unpalatable home truth: 'Well, here you all are again, older faces and younger clothes.'

There is one famous remark, often attributed to others, but in fact belonging to Mrs Stuyvesant Fish, who took real pleasure in deflating the pretensions of her rivals. One hostess, who knew no more of history and art than Mamie herself, was rash enough to exclaim in front of Mamie, 'And this is my Louis Quinze salon.' 'Oh?' said Mamie. 'And what makes you think so?'

Insolence of this order was in part justified by Mamie's capacity to stay rooted in good earth. Her own house at Newport, while lavish in its comfort, was stark and plain compared to the others, crammed to the walls with expensive and impressive treasures. But in her declared effort to 'liven things up', she indulged in some ludicrous stunts which finally damaged her cause. She was not satisfied with the stilted routine of entertaining, and could not pretend to be. One of these stunts was the dinner for the Tsar of Russia. Others were adopted into American folklore as 'the monkey dinner' and 'the dog's dinner'.

At the time of the visit to Newport of Grand Duke Boris of Russia already referred to, competition to secure the Grand Duke as dinner guest was intense. The race was won by Mrs Goelet, whose husband, Ogden Goelet, owned more real estate in New York than anyone, and whose daughter would marry the Duke of Roxburghe in 1903 (the present Duke of Roxburghe is May Goelet's grandson). Naturally, everyone in Newport graciously accepted the Goelets' invitation to dine with the distinguished Russian guest. Until, that is, another invitation was delivered, asking everyone to dine with the Tsar of Russia himself, at the table of Mrs Stuyvesant Fish. If ever cat were thrown among pigeons, the animal could hardly cause more disturbance than fell upon Newport with this announcement. Many, after much careful consideration, accepted Mrs Fish's summons and made feeble excuses to Mrs Goelet. The dinner was duly held. The resplendent man seated at Mrs Fish's right as her Guest of Honour, glittering with jewels and decorations, turned out to be Harry Lehr in disguise. What could the assembled guests do but laugh at the joke, while inwardly seething with fury? Mrs Fish's purpose, apart from having a good time at the expense of everyone else, was to demonstrate how gullible and ignorant were the highest echelons of high society, but the ladies could only see that they had passed up a real duke for a bogus king. Lessons were lost on them. It was from that day that Harry Lehr, 'lamb' to Mrs Fish, became 'King Lehr' to the *cognoscenti*.

Even more fuss was generated by the Dog's Dinner which Mamie gave as part of her campaign to find something different to do. Guests were strictly limited to the dogs of ladies in Newport society. No human intruder was allowed. The social columns in the press made a leading story of the feast, telling readers that dogs were seated at a highly-polished and silver-laden dining-table, and waited on by servants as they munched into their *pâté de foie gras*. Unpleasant comparisons were drawn with the starving populace in the Appalachians. In fact, nothing quite so disgraceful took place. The dogs tucked into platefuls of stewed liver and rice, fricassee of bones and shredded dog biscuit, served unceremoniously on the verandah. Mrs Elisha Dyer's dachshund ate so much it fell unconscious by its plate and had to be carried home. But Mrs Fish was never allowed to escape the obloquy of her dog's dinner, which was thought to bring society into disrepute.

Even more damaging was the occasion when Mrs Fish and Joseph Leiter announced that they were bringing a Corsican Prince to dine with Mr and Mrs Lehr, and arrived with a monkey in full evening dress, who sat on Mrs Lehr's right and, according to her, 'behaved beautifully'. This, said the newspapers, was yet a further example of Mrs Fish holding society up to ridicule. They did not say, of course, that were society less ridiculous, Mrs Lehr would have told Mrs Fish to take herself and her Corsican prince straight back home.

It was unquestionably Mrs Fish who kept society on its toes and was constantly surprising the world with original, if slightly daft, ideas. Her sense of humour was adolescent, but as precious as silver in a society where everyone else lacked even the mildest trace of humour. She once persuaded Jimmy Cutting (James de Wolfe Cutting, a far from wealthy bachelor) to give dinner for eight at his modest farmhouse on Rhode Island. Mamie would bring the guests. When they turned up, Cutting was surprised, perhaps relieved, to find that the guests included Mamie Fish, Harry Lehr, a life-size mannequin dressed to look like a young lady whom Jimmy Cutting was known to fancy, two dogs, one parrot, and a framed portrait of a Spanish Infanta. On another occasion, guests for lunch at 'Crossways' found that the footmen had eaten everything, and they had to go home hungry.

For all the embarrassment she caused to the more stuffy of her contemporaries, Mrs Stuyvesant Fish had an influence on society which, in the long term, was salutary. She was more relaxed, more easy-going, less priggish than other hostesses. Her only pretension was to use note-paper so heavily scented that one recipient of her letters had to order her butler to stand in a strong draught while he read them to her. But even that was more probably due to the tastes of Mamie's lap-dog, Harry Lehr.

Nor should it be forgotten that an invitation from Mrs Stuyvesant Fish was a prized possession. Her dinners were spectacular, her cook better than anyone's, her wines more carefully selected than those offered by her rivals. Meals were served in stately splendour by her English butler, Morton, and his copious staff. Morton was as formidable a character as Mrs Fish herself. His face never betrayed any expression, let alone a smile, and his eye for etiquette was faultless. Woe betide the guest who held a fork at the wrong angle; Mrs Fish would not object, but Morton would freeze the offender with his icy stare. Eventually, Morton was fired, for reasons which have been buried. His revenge was perfect. Before leaving, he unscrewed the whole of the gold dinner service into three hundred separate pieces, mixed them up, and left them in a hopeless heap on the dining-room floor. As no one else had any idea how to reassemble them, two men from Tiffany's had to hasten over from New York to Newport to put the lot together again in time for dinner that evening.

'It doesn't make any difference what you decide to do in life', said Mamie Fish, 'but you must do it better than anyone else.' She has earned her place in America's social history, a step behind Mrs Astor, for having broken traditions and established new customs. She is generally recognized as the woman who started what later became known as Café Society. But she did not take herself seriously enough to be accorded the ultimate honour of Mrs Astor's crown. That would require a far more austere nature than Mamie Fish could summon. As the century turned, it became increasingly clear that the hostess best fitted to take on total leadership of New York society, and one who had indeed been consciously planning for just such an eventuality, was young, pretty Mrs Cornelius Vanderbilt.

The Vanderbilt story has been told before, but repetition does not diminish its lustre. The family into which Grace Wilson married was uniquely distinguished by rapid success. As their chronicler has pointed out, they created a fortune in one generation, became the richest family in the world in the second generation, and the first family of America in the third. Their origins were of the simplest. Coming from the little Dutch town of Bilt, near Utrecht, they went to America about 1650 and settled near New Amsterdam (as New York City was then called). They spelt their name van der Bilt, and there is to this day a family bearing the same name in Holland, presumably distantly related to the millionaires. Their fortune grew out of a tiny, unremarked show of initiative in the nineteenth century, when Cornelius Vanderbilt, a small vegetable farmer on Staten Island in New York harbour, ferried his vegetables across to the growing city in a small rowing-boat, and sold them at a decent profit. (At the same time, John Jacob Astor, founder of another fortune, was a baker's errand-boy.) Vanderbilt gave twenty-five per cent of his earnings to his mother, and with the rest opened a small bank account. The turning-point came when he borrowed back from his mother a hundred dollars to buy a larger boat, with sails, which he then used to carry passengers as well as vegetables over to Manhattan. Gradually he bought more and larger boats, until he had a fleet sailing up and down the Hudson river, and ocean-going vessels making the trip to Europe. He built his own ships and the fleet grew to a total of over a hundred. When the American Civil War broke out, he turned over his clippers to the United States government, after which he was always known as the Commodore, which is convenient for the historian as it distinguishes him from all the other Vanderbilts who bore the same name.

Commodore Vanderbilt expanded into the railroad business at the age of 70, and by 73 controlled the New York Central Railroad, building the first Central terminus at 4th Avenue and 42nd Street and becoming the largest employer of labour in the United States, as well as the greatest figure in steam navigation and railroading in the entire country. When he was 81, he said, 'I have made a million dollars for every year of my life, but the best of it is that it has already been worth three times that amount to the people of the United States.' All this from the delivery of potatoes and carrots by a man who could neither read nor write but who would in his lifetime see a university named after him.

The Commodore was married twice, the second time to a woman named Frank Crawford [*sic*] when he was 75. His honesty and industry were widely known, and to the end of his days he maintained the habit of putting away twenty-five per cent of everything he made. It is a nice thought that his Staten Island mother lived to see most of the glorious heights to which her son had risen.

Commodore Vanderbilt left ninety-five million dollars to his son William H. Vanderbilt, who doubled it in less than eight years. It cannot be said, then, that the Vanderbilts idly enjoyed the proceeds of the Commodore's initiative; they inherited his acumen and prospered accordingly. William H. started life also as a farmer, joined his father's enterprises as a clerk, and rose to become the controller of 638 steam-engines. It was he who built the mansion at 640 Fifth Avenue (one of seven Vanderbilt palaces to line the Avenue) which would one day, under Grace Vanderbilt, be the scene of the most glittering dinner-parties New York has ever known. The house, begun in 1881, took eighteen months to complete, employing 600 men and 60 sculptors transported from Europe to make it as much like a genuine royal palace as could be conceived. Unfortunately, as William H. Vanderbilt conceived it, the result was a catastrophic example of vulgar taste which subsequent generations had to remedy. By then, of course, there was so much money falling into the Vanderbilt coffers that they could not possibly spend it fast enough, and renovation on a vast scale absorbed only pin-money.

William H. dropped dead in his grandiose library only nine years after his father the Commodore, leaving sixty-two million dollars to each of his two eldest sons, Cornelius and William K. Vanderbilt. It was Mrs William K. Vanderbilt (*née* Alva Smith from Alabama), a woman whom we have already met, to confuse matters, under her subsequent name of Mrs O. Belmont, who first established the Vanderbilts in society with her famous fancy-dress ball of 1883. This incredible masquerade was modestly intended as a 'house-warming' party to celebrate the completion of her house at 660 Fifth Avenue, which had been built as a copy of the château at Blois. The Astors, already secure at the top of society, still contrived to look down upon the Vanderbilts (much as they, in turn, would look disdainfully upon the Rockefellers), and proposed to ignore the event. But such was the noise generated in anticipation that Mrs Astor could not comfortably pretend the ball was not happening. So she let it be known that her daughter would be pleased to attend and was meanwhile practising her quadrilles. Mrs W.K. was having none of this; she saw her advantage and grabbed it. There was regrettably no question, she said, of inviting Miss Astor to her party, since Mrs Astor had never dropped her calling card. With this, Mrs Astor knew she would have to climb down or be omitted from the biggest event of the year. She called upon Mrs W.K. Vanderbilt, and a kind of amity was forged. The ball of 26 March 1883 turned out to be the most extravagant of its kind ever seen in America, with a guest list totalling 1,200. (Henry Clews compared the event to the entertainments offered by Alexander the Great and Louis XIV.) It was all the more remarkable as never before had any Vanderbilt woman so much as thrown a tea-party; they had been known as repressively shy. Henceforth Mrs W.K. and her sister-in-law, Alice of the Breakers, were twin powers in the organization of the élite.

The seasons of 1895 and 1896 kept the once-shy Vanderbilts at the forefront of public attention with a series of family events virtually seismic in their effect upon future generations. In the first place, Mrs W.K. Vanderbilt divorced her husband, at a time when ladies in society could scarcely spell the word, let alone envisage its realization. What was even more unlikely, she survived the scandal, exchanged one millionaire for another—Mr Belmont—and went on much as before; she became the Mrs Belmont who, along with Mrs Stuyvesant Fish and Mrs Oelrichs, determined the tenor of life at Newport. Secondly, the new Mrs Belmont ruthlessly destroyed the romance of her daughter, Consuelo Vanderbilt, with Winthrop Rutherfurd, by keeping her imprisoned in the house and intercepting her mail, in order that she should forcibly be married to a man she did not know, and did not like when she knew him, the Duke of Marlborough. It was, naturally, the wedding of the decade, and Mrs Belmont was heartily pleased with herself. Hardly had the fuss subsided when the third rumpus occurred, in such a torrent of publicity that it made footnotes of the previous squabbles. Cornelius Vanderbilt and his wife, Alice of the Breakers (that is, the brother and sister-in-law of William K.) were horrified to discover that their eldest son, also called Cornelius but happily known as Neily, was in love with Grace Wilson.

Precisely why Cornelius *père* should have been so horrified has never been satisfactorily explained. It could not have been that Grace was uneducated, ugly, poor, or loose, for she was the opposite on every count. Despite a brief engagement to Cecil Baring, she was utterly unsullied by amorous intrigue. She spoke French and German, was known and liked in all the best European circles, knew how to curtsy, spoke freely and with the correct degree of deference to royalty, had learnt cooking in Paris, was well versed in wines and knew all about precedence. Moreover, she was very pretty.

It could not have been that the Wilsons were not good enough. Richard T. Wilson, Grace's father, had a fortune of fifteen million dollars, small by Vanderbilt standards perhaps, but enough for a Fifth Avenue mansion and a Newport residence, and backed by a success story as impressive as any. Mr Wilson had been born in Gainsville, Georgia, in 1829, the son of a Scottish tanner. Starting as a travelling salesman, he had risen into the banking world and was now so acceptable that he even counted among the twenty names to which Mrs Ogden Mills restricted New York society. His charming southern manners and his overt honesty had made him very popular abroad. His other children had made such illustrious marriages that the Wilsons were famed for their ability to catch the most eligible husbands and wives. Son Orme Wilson married an Astor daughter; the other Wilson daughters married Mr Ogden Goelet, the real estate millionaire, and the Hon. Michael Herbert, British Ambassador and brother to the Earl of Pembroke. Some whispered that Richard T. Wilson would stop at nothing to get his last daughter wed to a Vanderbilt, but since the Wilsons were in some ways more respectable than the Vanderbilts and since Grace could easily have married into the British aristocracy, the argument carried little conviction.

Could it have been that Wilson was a Southerner? The Commodore, it must be remembered, had given his fleet to the United States government and several Vanderbilts had fought for the Yankees while Richard Wilson was selling blankets to the

Confederate army and selling cotton in England to support the
Confederate cause. So identified with the South was he that it
would one day be said the character of Rhett Butler in *Gone With
the Wind* was based upon him. Even that fails to illumine the depth
of Vanderbilt hostility, for after all, Mrs W.K. Vanderbilt (now
Mrs Belmont) had herself been from Alabama.

The reason publicly given for the row was that Grace and Neily
were too young, and that a rich young man should see the world
before choosing a wife. Certainly Cornelius *père* was a puritanical
man, who never said or did anything that he would not have said or
done had his mother been in the room, and puritanism usually finds
itself allied with stubbornness; what Cornelius considered right
must be right. But Richard Wilson was every bit as admirable a
character, declaring that the financier Frick (whose mansion, now
the Frick Museum, is the only one left standing on Fifth Avenue)
was not fit to be in the same house with children. Since Grace was
twenty-five, and Neily twenty-two, it might well have been Wilson
who could object that Vanderbilt was too young for his daughter.

The most likely reason was the one never given. The Vanderbilts
had risen to such heights that, in common with European royalty
and nobility, they had passed the point at which marriages could be
made for love. Neily should wait for his parents to choose a bride for
him, to make a proper dynastic alliance, as Mrs Belmont had so
conspicuously done for Consuelo. The preference of one human
being for another was a paltry basis for the partnership of
millionaires. Neily did not see the matter in this light. He could not
see the matter in any light at all, for he had committed the ultimate
folly of falling in love.

The Vanderbilts did everything in their power to prevent the
liaison from developing, and Cornelius made it quite clear to his son
that he forbade it. Neily was desperately attached and would defy
anyone to be with Grace wherever she went. The Wilsons, who
were not accustomed to being mentioned in newspapers except as
part of a decorous list, were mortified by the huge publicity which
erupted, for the young couple quickly became a symbol of young
love to America, and Grace, in the days before film-stars, was
elevated to the role of national heroine. Grace fled to Europe. Neily

followed her. They returned to announce their engagement on 10 June 1896. The very next day Mr Vanderbilt placed an announcement in the papers to the effect that the proposed marriage was against his express wish. Richard Wilson sent out invitations despite his natural foreboding and the less confident members of New York society escaped the city in droves rather than be obliged to take sides. Then, the day before the wedding was due to take place, Neily fell ill and the nuptials were postponed. Mr Wilson was lumbered with ten thousand red roses which he had then to send to various hospitals. It seemed as if Neily had been broken by the will of his formidable father.

By this time, poor Grace had been so compromised that she was virtually unmarriageable. If Neily abandoned her, she would have to spend the rest of her days a spinster. But Neily had no intention of abandoning her. Father and son quarrelled fiercely every day, to such an extent that the normally discreet servants could not fail to be aware of what was going on. Then Mr Vanderbilt suddenly collapsed with a paralytic stroke, brought on, it was said, by an angry punch from his son. Even if the rumour were a lie, certain it is that the strain told upon the old man. As he lay weakly in bed at his august mansion, a city permit was secured to sprinkle tan-bark on the roads to deaden the noise of traffic, and finally even to divert all traffic from Fifth Avenue. Such was the power of the Vanderbilt name. A week later Mr Vanderbilt was taken to rest at 'The Breakers', his home in Newport, leaving the city clear for Neily and Grace to join in matrimony.

The wedding took place a few days afterwards, quietly, in the drawing-room of the Wilson house. Grace wore a brooch of thirty large diamonds around an immense sapphire, a present from the groom. Apart from Wilsons, there were present Astors, Belmonts and Goelets, but not one person bearing the name Vanderbilt. From 'The Breakers' issued the most pregnant silence.

Old Cornelius Vanderbilt never spoke to his son again after that day.

He survived another three years, and when the Will was produced shortly after his death it was found to carry the date in June 1896 when Neily had first declared his intention of marrying

Grace against his father's wishes; the old man drew it up and had it signed and witnessed that same evening, while his anger was still hot. It was a document of cruel vindictiveness. Neily was ignored as if he no longer existed. The bulk of the huge fortune went to his younger brother Alfred, while he was left with one and a half million dollars, in trust, which his father was unable to divert. Even more humiliating for the eldest was the clause leaving to Alfred the Commodore's gold medal, traditionally passed down to the head of the family. Alfred later made over to Neily an additional seven million dollars, but the brothers never did more than nod to each other for the rest of their lives, and the split within the Vanderbilt clan has never been healed. Mrs Herbert, with alluring hyperbole, called it 'the greatest wickedness of the nineteenth century'. Randolph Hearst said, 'What a fool [he] was to forfeit a fortune for a pretty face.' Ordinary Americans, on the other hand, rejoiced that a millionaire could behave in so human a way as to place happiness before wealth.

For the first years of their marriage the new Vanderbilts lived at 677 Fifth Avenue. A son, Cornelius, and a daughter, Grace, were born, again without any other Vanderbilt moving a finger to acknowledge their existence. The story might have had a miserable ending had Neily been incompetent or stupid, but he was in fact a very clever and resourceful man. He applied for a job, with his earnings studied at Yale, and rose to become a brilliant engineer, whose inventions brought him fame in his own right, and money. It must be admitted that a scholarly husband was not wholly within Grace Vanderbilt's understanding or appreciation, but while she was vivacious and happy in a social atmosphere, and he in an erudite one, as long as they did not conflict, life proceeded pleasantly enough. Grace had money of her own from the Wilson side, so the 'poor' Vanderbilts were able to live in a manner befitting their name. This suited Grace, as she soon set her sights upon the ultimate goal of any socialite, the domination of New York. The wonder of it is that, after such dreadful beginnings, after a scandal which rocked the country and divided a family, after rumours which even suggested she had been pregnant at the time of her marriage (she was not), Grace Vanderbilt overcame all obstacles and succeeded in being crowned Queen of New York.

However 'beautiful and brave and cruelly reviled' she may have been, Grace was as if born to the role of a hostess, and it would take more than a social earthquake to prevent her realizing her destiny. Had she not been groomed well in advance by her very able sisters Mrs Goelet and Mrs Herbert, encouraged by the venerable Mrs Astor herself, educated almost with a throne in view? Grace set her sights upon Mrs Astor's position in 1901 and prepared a solid campaign for the succession. The field was by now wide open, other contenders having disqualified themselves for one reason or another, and the memory of the Vanderbilt feud now five years old. Indeed, the only serious rival left was Alice of the Breakers herself, and she was still in mourning for her husband who had died two years earlier.

With splendid effrontery, the first step Grace took was to buy, from the Astors, a house at Newport practically in the shadow of 'The Breakers' and overlooking the same cliff. Alice, who still did not mention Grace's name, was challenged on her very doorstep. The house was called 'Beaulieu', and Grace saw to it that the style of living there was of such extravagance that one was bound to conclude it was inhabited by a lady who adhered to the principle of primogeniture and the divine right of kings. At 'Beaulieu' she kept 17 vehicles, 30 horses, 15 stableboys, a coachman, a French chef, an English butler and indoor staff of 40, all to demonstrate natural pre-eminence. Yet that was not enough. Mrs Belmont, Mrs Fish, Mrs Oelrichs, Mrs Mills and others all had staff as impressive and homes as ostentatious. Moreover, they enticed the most illustrious guests. Grace was still not unique, and she was terribly young, at 31, to aspire to dominance. She did it, however, with one masterly stroke; she showed that she alone among hostesses was the intimate of genuine royalty.

In 1902, Prince Henry of Prussia, brother of the Kaiser, visited America. With letters to Berlin well in advance and diplomatic gestures from other directions (it helped that her brother-in-law was an Ambassador), Grace organized her ascendancy with machiavellian foresight. The Prince arrived. His obligatory visit to the opera was made remarkable by his joining Grace Vanderbilt in her box. No one but Grace knew this was going to happen, and the effect was as she had hoped—electrifying. What is more, she gave a dinner at which Prince Henry was guest of honour, and it did not pass unnoticed that this was the only private dinner he attended in New York. From that day Grace's position was unassailable. Other Vanderbilts may have inherited the fortune, but Grace was Head of the House of Vanderbilt as far as Society was concerned, and it had all been achieved with a dinner party.

Whenever Grace flashed down Fifth Avenue in a blaze of red, her red carriage upholstered in red velvet, coachmen in maroon livery, plumes, tassels and gold, it was now with a confidently imperious air.

Her '*Fête des Roses*' party in Newport was another demonstration of power. Not only did she have millions of red roses, more than anyone had ever seen in one place, hanging in festoons throughout the garden and falling to be crushed underfoot by astonished guests, but she built a miniature theatre in the grounds of Beaulieu to be used for just this one party. A hundred builders and carpenters worked day and night for a week to complete the edifice, and Grace imported from New York the entire cast, company and scenery of the year's hit show, *Red Rose Inn*. This meant the theatre in New York had to be closed not for one day, but three, and Grace happily settled the bill for a full house three nights in a row.

In 1914, Neily inherited 640 Fifth Avenue from an uncle. This was the house which had been such a monument to the bad taste of an earlier generation, and which the Marquis de Castellane found to be more like a museum than a residence. Grace immediately started to redecorate and refurnish, even to an extent rebuild, the mansion over a period of two years, employing 600 labourers. She installed thirty-three bathrooms and brought in furniture of the finest elegance and authenticity, even including some items which had been in Louis XIV's private apartments at Versailles. When she had finished, the mansion occupying the entire block from 51st to 52nd Street was undeniably one of the most distinguished houses in America. For the next twenty-five years it would receive and host not only the highest East Coast aristocracy, but all degrees of foreign royalty. Grace moved from 677 to 640 Fifth Avenue in 1916 (she had barely noticed the war across the ocean) and almost immediately it became the Buckingham Palace of New York City and she, naturally, assumed the role of New York's reigning monarch.

One wholly pleasant consequence of Grace's elevation to sovereign status was a belated reconciliation with the other Mrs Vanderbilt, Alice of the Breakers. In the twenty years since Grace and Neily married, Alice had consistently refused to receive her, or even to acknowledge her existence. Aloofness of this order was by now beginning to look ridiculous. Besides which, Alice was old, and age sometimes dissolves enmity. In recognition of Grace's quasi-regal status, Alice one day left 'The Breakers' and visited her daughter-in-law at 'Beaulieu'. It was a magnificent gesture, as it might well have been supposed proper that Grace should bestir herself to visit Alice, her senior. Neily was so delighted when he saw his mother in his house that he leapt to his feet with joy. He had in truth been deeply distressed by the feud and entirely remorseful that he had parted from his father, whom he admired, so bitterly.

Alice was among the 125 guests in New York when Grace threw a reception for the Queen of the Belgians in 1919. Once again, the occasion presented an opportunity for a blatant display of power. A red carpet was laid out on the steps up to the entrance. Grace waited at the top of the steps, totally covered, it seemed, in a skin of diamonds, and as the Queen arrived, very simply attired with one row of pearls, Grace walked down to welcome her, so that the two women should meet half-way. Nothing could more vividly emphasize that Grace saw herself as a Queen. Indeed, her friends by now called her simply 'The Queen', and a royal visit to New York was always treated like a State occasion at 640 Fifth Avenue. The address was as familiar to New Yorkers as 10 Downing Street is to Londoners.

Her preoccupation with ceremony bored her husband and alarmed her son. Lessons on behaviour to her children had always been of the nature 'Should the former Governor of New York be seated on the right of the hostess and the former Ambassador of Great Britain on her left, or vice versa?' If the children gave the right answer they were deemed to have been educated in a style befitting their station.

If Mrs Vanderbilt's friends felt justified in calling her 'The

Queen', her detractors saw even more reason for nicknaming her
'The Kingfisher', not only because she had a yacht of that name, nor
simply because she was fascinated by royalty; it was suspected that
she intended her daughter Grace to make a suitable wife for the
Prince of Wales (later Edward VIII).

Unlike Mrs Greville and Mrs Corrigan in London, who both
chased after royalty, Grace did not need to court favours with
kings—she considered it natural and proper that she should be on
terms of intimacy with the crowned heads of Europe. She never
received anyone without a pedigree and ruled New York society
more strictly than Queen Mary regulated the Court of St James.
Her son has claimed that she entertained every British monarch
from Victoria to George VI, as well as the last Tsar and Tsarina of
Russia, but that may stretch a little the meaning of 'entertain'. She
certainly had met them all.

Queen Mary she counted a particular friend, keeping a signed
portrait of her at hand all the time. To her chagrin, English friends
appeared not to take this seriously enough. Cecil Beaton was a
lunch-guest in 1937, by which time Grace was sixty-seven and had
been Queen of New York for thirty-five years. She told Beaton how
upset she had been by the abdication of Edward VIII:

First, she produced a small bag. Then, from inside, she whisked
the wherewithal to make her nose clown-white. Ridiculously, she
began covering her entire face with ugly blobs of powder. The
chin received another heavy patch. During the story-telling, by
dint of gradual smoothing away, a natural face appeared from
under its heavy coating. 'Oh, I can't tell you how I have suffered!
I can't tell you what the family means to me. I was the first person
to be received by the late King after his illness. I was summoned
to tea with Their Majesties and we talked and talked and talked. I
kept waiting to be dismissed. But no, we talked until I began to
get a little faint. My head drooped; I said, "Ma'am, am I not
keeping you? Must I not go?" And the Queen said, "Oh no, if
you *have* to go that is different, but if you can, please stay." And
do you know, I had arrived at the Palace at five o'clock and by the
time I left it was—six o'clock. Oh, they've been so wonderful to
me. I could lay down my life for that family.'

When Osbert Sitwell went to see her some years before, she had asked him to convey her fondest love 'to the dear boys', by which she meant the Prince of Wales and his brothers, a remark which did nothing to impress the arch-snob Sitwell. Her London rival, the royalty-catcher Mrs Greville, professed to hate Mrs Vanderbilt, probably because she was more successful even than Maggie Greville in letting the world know that she was acquainted with kings. She told Mrs Greville once that she had thought of coming to live in England, and received the icy reply, 'No, Grace, we have enough Queens here already.'

The most telling observation Mrs Vanderbilt ever made, with regard to the image she perceived of herself, was apropos 'dear poor Marie Antoinette'. 'I feel so sorry for her,' she said. 'If the revolution ever came to this country, I would be the first to go.'

When George VI came to the throne, she behaved in motherly fashion towards him; she had, after all, known him since he was a baby, and felt quite free to call him 'the little King'. King George called upon Mrs Vanderbilt at Claridge's in London and told her she was 'very naughty' to have smuggled her dog through Customs (he had heard the animal's barks from an adjacent room). 'I could have you locked up for the rest of your life,' he said. 'Why don't you, Your Majesty?' said Grace.

The day before this incident, Grace had had tea with Queen Mary and Mrs Roosevelt, and ingenuously reported that the three of them had decided there would be no world war. She really thought that her influence extended beyond every normal frontier.

Though she had no real influence, the fact remains that Grace Vanderbilt really did count royalty among her friends. She carried on a correspondence with Queen Mary for more than thirty years, the two ageing ladies frequently exchanging recipes (surprisingly, Grace was an accomplished cook), and once wrote a nine-page letter to the Queen telling her that she was unfair towards the Prince of Wales. It says much that the friendship survived this audacity.

She was similarly outspoken with the Soviet Foreign Minister Andrei Gromyko, who came to lunch and had to listen to Mrs Vanderbilt's fond memories of all her Russian friends, by which she meant the Tsar and his family, apparently oblivious of the role Gromyko's party had played in their extinction.

Entertaining on so prodigal a scale cost a frightening amount of money. Grace spent more lavishly than anyone else in New York, for a longer period. In one year, she entertained no less than 37,000 people. Her husband, now General Vanderbilt, watched in dismay as the capital he had tried to protect was frittered away in an endless orgy of dinner parties, an increasingly desperate attempt to maintain social status. Grace need hardly have bothered, as by 1940 she had no rivals within sight, but she seemed not only to identify with Marie Antoinette, but now to behave like her. Grace's spending estranged her from the General, who took to drinking alone in his room rather than watch his wife cling to the past and play hostess to a world which no longer understood the attraction of the role. When she installed a lift at Beaulieu, the General declared that she no doubt hoped it would crash and kill him.

In old age, Grace Vanderbilt retained her beauty, perhaps due to her habit of drinking mineral water with a slice of lemon instead of the smallest amount of alcohol. Her appearance was unmistakable, and she was as immediately recognizable as Queen Mary. She took to wearing a bandeau tight around her head, usually of the same material as her dress, and this bandeau became her trade-mark. She possessed hundreds of them, wearing one even when it meant cramming a tiara between it and her hair. She was never without diamonds, and when fully dressed wore an enormous stomacher of diamonds pouring down her front like a waterfall.

Grace Vanderbilt lived on to become a relic of a former age. The East Coast and New York lost their pre-eminence in the social world with the sprouting of millionaires in California and Texas, all of whom were far more wealthy than Grace. Taxes and over-spending combined to reduce her money to less than two million dollars, and in 1945 she was forced to abandon 640 Fifth Avenue and move into a smaller twenty-eight-room house at 1048 Fifth Avenue, on the corner of 86th Street. The fifty-eight-room mansion was demolished in 1947, and its contents sold off. The walls and trappings of the formal dining-room, scene of the grandest dinner-parties in American history, were bought by Paramount Films for only $975.

Grace Vanderbilt died in 1953, at the age of 83. Like most

hostesses, she had achieved by determination the life she had always wanted for herself and reached a position of power in society more awe-inspiring than that of all other women who made the dining-table the centre of their existence. For more than a quarter of a century, grown men and women would brave illness or earthquake to dine at her table rather than run the risk of being stricken from the most important social register in the world. The Kingfisher was indeed a Queen.

CHAPTER FOUR

Mrs Ronnie Greville

To Mrs Ronnie Greville is attributed perhaps the most snobbish remark made by a twentieth-century hostess. Alluding to her reputation as an intimate friend of half the crowned heads in Europe, and wishing to make that distinction known to anyone who was not yet aware of it, she uttered in a loud voice, and with more than a hint of a sigh, 'One uses up *so* many red carpets in a season!'

This kind of snobbery is attractive if it can be backed up, and in Mrs Greville's case there was no question of fraudulent boasting. When she told an awed guest that three kings had been sitting on the edge of her bed that morning, she was telling the truth. The newspapers of the Twenties bear eloquent testimony to Mrs Greville's royal connections; in 1922 she is entertaining the Prince of Wales. In 1924, she is giving a huge ball at which the crowd was so dense that the King and Queen of Italy had to sit in their car outside while the footmen cleared a way through the assembled guests to the ballroom. In 1927, King Faud of Egypt, on his first visit to England for seventeen years, dined with Mrs Greville as naturally as if she were the crucial aim and purpose of his journey. Ten years later, the Queen of Egypt brought her ill-fated son Farouk to England, and again dined with Mrs Greville. Osbert Sitwell was there, noting that apart from the Queen and 'her clumsy fat-boy son', there were Prince and Princess Chiclitz, and the

Grand Duke and Duchess of Hesse. The Queen of Spain was a particular and genuine friend, to be remembered in Mrs Greville's will. And her unique closeness to the British Royal Family enabled her to deliver the most crushing humiliation to Emerald Cunard, busily embroiled with the Prince of Wales and his 'cutie' Mrs Simpson. 'You mustn't think that I dislike little Lady Cunard,' she said, 'I'm always telling Queen Mary that she isn't half as bad as she is painted.'

Mrs Greville's entrée to the highest royal circles derived from her late husband, the Hon. Ronald Greville, who had been one of Edward VII's favourite people. Greville had also been the closest male friend since childhood of George Keppel, husband of King Edward's delightful mistress (and a significant hostess in her own right) Alice Keppel. Keppel was best man when Ronald Greville married Margaret Helen Anderson in 1891, and the Keppels and Grevilles went so far in mutual devotion as to occupy nearby houses in Charles Street, Mayfair, and demolish a complete house which separated them in order to construct an Italian garden between them and 'pop in' on each other without the formality of an invitation. When Ronald Greville died in 1908, and Edward VII in 1910, Mrs Greville not only maintained the royal connection but built upon it and enlarged it until it became a veritable obsession. Scarcely a day passed without some royal name-dropping. Undoubtedly her finest hour came in 1923, when the Duke of York married Lady Elizabeth Bowes-Lyon and accepted Mrs Greville's offer to spend their honeymoon from April 26 to May 7 at her enchanting country house near Dorking, Polesden Lacey. Thereafter, Mrs Greville was acknowledged by all who were interested in such matters as the intimate friend of the Yorks, later to be King George VI and Queen Elizabeth, though she herself, with that same affectation of mild irritation which caused her to lament the cost of red carpets, professed to be disappointed when her friends came to occupy the throne. 'I was so happy in the days when they used to run in and out of my house as if they were my own children,' she said.

When the Yorks were entertained at Polesden Lacey, which was frequently, other guests had to be chosen with care. One such was

Osbert Sitwell, *persona grata* with the royals as well as one of the very few who did not secretly detest Mrs Greville. He described the occasion, rather ambiguously, as 'like jazz night at the Palladium. All the butlers were drunk—since Maggie was ill—bobbing up every minute during dinner to offer the Duchess of York whisky.'

After their accession to the throne, the King and Queen accorded Mrs Greville more favours than are usually due to a subject, however adept her cook may be. In 1938 she ignored doctor's orders and rose from her sick-bed to attend Ascot. The King and Queen made her life easier by permitting her to use the royal entrance to the racecourse. Most doctors will admit that a boost to the morale does wonders for one's temperature.

To some, Mrs Greville's cultivation of royalty was a harmless hobby, but there were others who seemed to find it offensive. Cecil Beaton was exasperated. She was, he said, 'a galumphing, greedy, snobbish old toad who watered at her chops at the sight of royalty and the Prince of Wales's set, and did nothing for anybody except the rich'. Beaton was wrong, at least as far as her charity was concerned, but he was not alone in his invective. Words still worse were scribbled in diaries after her death.

One must not begrudge Mrs Greville's singular achievement in grabbing many of Europe's kings and queens into her private circle. For the illegitimate daughter of a self-made Scottish brewer this was social climbing without parallel. She managed it, of course, with an inexhaustible supply of money, without which she would have come no further than the railings of Buckingham Palace; royals do not dine at paupers' tables. But she did it also with character. Mrs Greville, 'Maggie' to her friends, had an extremely forceful personality. One could hate her, fawn upon her, be amused by her, but one could not ignore her or feign indifference to her. This marks the one powerful difference between Mrs Greville and Laura Corrigan, with whom otherwise she might appear to have much in common. Both Mrs Greville and Mrs Corrigan collected royals; both had so much money they need not even think about it; both came from obscure, even shameful beginnings; both achieved their ambitions. But while Mrs Corrigan had few brains, Mrs Greville was very clever indeed. Moreover, Laura Corrigan's niceness was nowhere paralleled in Mrs Greville's almost vicious behaviour. Whereas Laura never had an unkind word to say about anyone, Maggie Greville rarely bothered to speak unless impelled by malice. Even a kind word turned to poison on her lips.

They did have this in common: their social appetites were fuelled by business acumen. Mrs Corrigan controlled a multi-million dollar steel company in America. Mrs Greville's pocket-money came from her Scottish breweries. 'I'd rather be a beeress than a peeress' she said, and a very successful beeress she was.

Success, initiative, self-reliance, these were the backbones of Mrs Greville's moral philosophy. She learnt them from a remarkable father. William McEwan, son of John McEwan, a shipowner from Alloa, was born in 1827. From the smallest beginnings, he built up his own brewery business by making shrewd decisions, often against the advice of caution, and by common hard work, until by 1889 the business was worth a million pounds. His sister Janet married a Younger, of another brewing family, and her son William Younger, nephew to McEwan, was eventually Managing Director of McEwan & Co.

McEwan went into politics quite late in life. From 1886 to 1900 he was M.P. for an Edinburgh seat, though the democratic process of persuasion through exchange of ideas was not palatable to him, and he rarely spoke in the House of Commons. McEwan was a plain, blunt man, who gave his outspoken views frankly and did not understand the possibility of dissent. He was severely critical of those who were stupid enough to disagree with him. Surprisingly, he was a staunch Liberal and supporter of Gladstone.

When his first wife died, McEwan was a lonely man. He consoled himself with a woman who has been variously described as his housekeeper, his cook, and the wife of his day-porter; the day-porter was said to have been shifted to night duty so as to facilitate McEwan's attentions to the wife. The issue of this union was Margaret Helen Anderson, and between father and daughter there was a bond of uncommonly deep affection.

Maggie was given the very best education money could buy, but it did not leave her with any taste for metaphysical discussion or the knowledge to be gleaned from books. In later life she would admit,

'My dear, I know I'm not an educated woman.' Nor did it imbue her spirit with much tolerance, but then the McEwan genes were more powerful than any exterior stimuli. Besides, her illegitimacy appalled Edinburgh society, which can be offensively pompous at times, and she and her father were ostracised. This alone would effectively smother any nascent tolerance in Maggie's breast. She never forgave Edinburgh, and any dignitary from that city who visited London when Maggie's star rose high would feel the sharp lash of her tongue.

McEwan and daughter moved south, and Maggie married the awesomely dull Hon. Ronald Greville, son of the second Baron Greville, in 1891. His mother, Lady Violet Greville, only mentions him once in her memoirs, and that is to say that he was fond of steeplechasing and 'rode many races'. His uncle, Reginald Greville, had died in a steeplechase at Sandown Park. Lady Violet manages totally to ignore her daughter-in-law, who does not even figure in a footnote. Perhaps she had in mind the reputation of an earlier Mrs Greville, who had gone to Italy with her husband and another couple, and returned with the husband of the other woman; she, the other woman, returned with Mr Greville, and this early example of wife-swapping had the happiest results, for each woman remained with the husband of the other after the holiday. It is more likely that Lady Violet could not bring herself to acknowledge the stain of a bastard within the family. She was herself a Scot, after all, the daughter of the Duke of Montrose.

Maggie and Ronnie were very happy. It was said that she would have given up her social life, some of it at least, had she had children. As it was, the sparkling kaleidoscope of society held compelling attractions which supplanted the maternal instinct. The Grevilles lived first at Reigate Priory, until Papa McEwan gave them the exquisite property near Dorking, which had once belonged to Richard Brinsley Sheridan, called Polesden Lacey. Here, and at the very large London house in Charles Street, they entertained the most important people in the land.

Ronald Greville fought a very difficult by-election against Keir Hardie and Sir A. Ballson, keeping the seat for the Conservatives with a small majority over the Liberals. His notable contribution to political life was to support Free Trade in opposition to official Conservative policy. Otherwise he made no especial mark on his times. He died at the age of 43, following an operation for cancer of the throat complicated by post-operative pneumonia. George Keppel was at his funeral.

Maggie then went to live with her father a few doors away in Charles Street, where she tended him devotedly as his poor health enfeebled him. In the last years he was so thin that he appeared almost transparent. Still, stubborn as he was, he insisted on taking long walks through the London streets, undeterred by the traffic which more than once had knocked him down. To give up these rambles, or accept a companion, would have been to admit senility and dependence, which a proud self-made man cannot do. Mrs Greville overcame the difficulty with tact and cunning. She employed a private detective whose job it was to shadow Mr McEwan wherever he went and make sure he crossed the roads safely, without ever revealing his presence. This subterfuge went on for a considerable time, and old McEwan never did discover he was being protected.

At the age of 80 he was made a Privy Councillor, and at 85 he died, with Maggie by his bedside in Charles Street. His fortune of £1½ million he left almost entirely to Maggie, with one eccentric and typically vindictive restriction: she was never to invest any money in Australia. Maggie not only accepted the command, but declared she would insert a similar clause in her own will. She did.

Maggie then devoted her energies to entertaining and to business. The directors of McEwan & Co were required to journey down to Polesden Lacey for board meetings, and there was never any danger of their forgetting that she was the boss. Kenneth Clark remembers seeing the gentlemen leave her room after one such meeting, 'in a very chastened frame of mind, some actually trembling'.

As for entertaining, this was pursued with determination and vigour at Polesden Lacey, and the vast London house, 16 Charles Street. Polesden was a perfect venue for a weekend party, peaceful and luxurious. The house looked out over a valley, with glorious gardens and flowing lawns kept to the peak of perfection.

'Everywhere there is the silence, and the spaciousness that comes from long established wealth', wrote Chips Channon. Across these lawns would wander Edwardian and post-Edwardian guests, a lady on one arm, a glass of champagne in the other hand. One can see them now, like ghosts, without very much imaginative effort, for the house and grounds are open to the public.

The interior, save for one room, is no longer as Mrs Greville knew it; furnished and decorated in her style, it was flashy with comfort, but not vulgar. The house, built by Cubitt in 1818, had been refurbished by Maggie to a high degree of excellence after the Great War, when she had turned most of it into a convalescent home for officers and retained for her own use some rooms on the south and east sides. The redecoration was expensive, and fundamental; it included the creation of seven self-contained guest suites each with its own bathroom attached, a rare luxury even among the rich in those days. The reception rooms were dotted with rare pieces of china, collectors' items in furniture, and magnificent paintings. McEwan had given one of his choicest items, a Rembrandt, to the National Gallery, but there were plenty left to decorate the walls of a large country house. Long after Maggie's death, the house continued to exert its hypnotic, relaxing power. 'It is strange how happy I am at Polesden', wrote James Lees-Milne, who never met Mrs Ronnie Greville and only saw the house when arranging its transfer to the National Trust.

Maggie effected a similar transformation at 16 Charles Street, more a palace than a house, even going so far as to install 18-carat gold scroll work in the drawing-room; not since the height of Victorian prosperity had such extravagance been observed. These were indeed sitting rooms in which to receive kings and queens. Osbert Sitwell said that these two houses 'possessed an unobtrusive luxury of life and background that I have never encountered elsewhere'. A hyperbolic remark from some one who had set foot inside most of the grand houses of his time.

Sitwell's testimony conflicts with most other impressions which have survived. 'The potency of her character enabled her to infuse her splendid entertainments with a sense of fun and enjoyment that rendered them more memorable even than did their magnificence, or the beauty of their setting,' he wrote. Kenneth Clark, on the other hand, representing the more general view, thought her dinner parties were the dullest he could remember, 'stuffy members of the government and their mem-sahib wives, ambassadors and royalty'. Perhaps Sitwell's innocent snobbery, normally excited into wrath by the pretensions of some one like Lady Colefax, was quiescent when confronted by regal splendour. He did not care for people stepping out of their class, a sin he ascribed to Lady Colefax but either ignored or forgave in Mrs Greville.

Maggie looked more like a butcher's wife than a *grande dame* of society. She was small, very fat, round like a snowman, and devoid of elegance. Her god-daughter, who was devoted to her, said she resembled 'a small Chinese idol with eyes that blinked', and the same girl once had to be restrained by her mother, in the nick of time, from naming her ugly pet spaniel 'Maggie' in honour of Mrs Greville. Such unattractive dogs surrounded Mrs Greville in lieu of children, and she grew to look like them.

There was no denying what Sitwell called the 'potency' of her character. Having tested power in her youth, she embraced it, enjoyed it, relished it throughout her life, using it with scant regard for the people who trembled before it. She was in many ways a 'power-maniac', and would in different circumstances have made a resolute dictator. As it was, she used her power to exalt the favoured and ridicule the excluded.

Like other contemporary hostesses, she possessed the ability to spot quality in the young and predict their rise to distinction, often helping them along the way. Her 'help' sometimes amounted to interference. Having picked out an unknown and bestowed upon him the benefit of her interest, she expected him to allow her to run his (professional) life ever after. 'Those who were clever enough pretended to let her do so', commented her god-daughter Sonia. All these *protégés* were naturally in the political world, for politics alone interested her outside the private scope of her business and the fantasy of her royals. All three, of course—royalty, business and politics—were different avenues towards the exercise of power, which Maggie revered above all else. Mere pleasure without power was to her useless and base. So little did she know of the intellectual and artistic circles which eddied around Lady Cunard that she once addressed the poet John Drinkwater as Mr Bayswater. 'My name is not Bayswater,' he replied sternly. 'I'm so sorry, Mr Bathwater,' said Maggie. There may well have been intended slight in this mistake.

Another example of her imperious interference arose when Sonia Keppel became engaged to Roland Cubitt, son of Lord Ashcombe, Ashcombe lived only two miles from Polesden Lacey, at Denbies, but he had scarcely dealt with Mrs Greville, whom he contrived with success to avoid. He was Lord Lieutenant of Surrey, a situation which Maggie considered lowly compared to her own. One day Lord Ashcombe's butler announced that Mrs Ronald Greville was outside the front door, in her Rolls-Royce. Would she not come in, asked Ashcombe. 'No, m'lord,' replied the butler, 'Madam prefers to wait in the car.' Lord Ashcombe obediently went out to see. The chauffeur and footman were on the box of the Rolls, Mrs Greville, formally dressed, sat inside. Politely, Ashcombe himself invited her to step in the house. 'No, thank you,' she replied, 'I only called to tell you that I do not consider that your son is good enough for my god-daughter.' Leaving Ashcombe furious with indignation (she enjoyed that), Maggie drove straight back to Polesden.

Mrs Greville knew the ways of the world better than most, which made her advice, usually given in a peremptory, staccato style, sage and sensible. She was acute, shrewd, observant, with a rare gift for appraisal and discernment, and remorselessly cynical. Tact was not among her virtues, and she was as quick to tell a man he was wrong or foolish as she was to guide him along the correct path. In this she was pre-eminently her father's daughter.

Her vanity was boundless. If the Queen of England could give her access to Ascot through the royal entrance, then other European countries should consider it an honour to entertain her. Everywhere she went on the Continent—and she travelled a great deal before illness rendered her a cripple—she expected a private train to be placed at her disposal. If it was not, the resident British Ambassador would be sure to receive a reprimand, or some lesser official would be summarily removed from his post. It is no wonder that European heads of state formed the impression that Mrs Ronnie Greville was an extremely important woman, a fact which was to cause much mischief as the Second World War approached.

If power was the prize to be attained, money was invariably the means to attain it. Mrs Greville equated success with the accumulation of fortune. She did not understand those who would not aspire to wealth, and despised those who did aspire and failed. Kenneth Clark wrote, 'It is rare, and a great source of strength, for anyone to be totally consistent. Mrs Greville was totally material . . . she thought solely in terms of material gain.' Ever on the qui vive for a suitable husband for Sonia Keppel, she did not approve of a nameless young man, whom she nevertheless liked, because he was not rich. Sonia admitted that her godmother might have shown more kindliness if they had waited thirty years, 'by which time T. should have picked up a fortune'. It is a telling remark.

More than any other trait of her personality, it was Mrs Greville's malice and cruelty which excited so much antagonism, for it seemed to many the capricious and irresponsible exercise of power to the detriment of the less successful. She was a true and loyal friend, but a terrible enemy. Some politely called her 'waspish', or even, like Chips Channon, secretly admired her nastiness. 'There is no one on earth quite so skilfully malicious as old Maggie', he wrote. Other normally self-controlled diarists rose to a crescendo of anger when mentioning her name. Harold Nicolson called her 'nothing more than a fat slug filled with venom'. 'How comes it', he wrote, 'that this plump but virulent little bitch should hold such social power?' Lady Leslie said she would sooner have an open sewer in her drawing-room than allow Maggie Greville in it. James Lees-Milne heard that she had a tongue dipped in gall.

Nicolson vividly recalls a *tête-à-tête* with Mrs Greville at a lunch given by Lady Spears (who was Mary Borden, the novelist and author of the satirical story which lampoons Lady Colefax):

Maggie Greville begins by whispering to me how much she dislikes gossip, how much she hopes there will be no gossip at this luncheon and how the one thing she cannot stand in this life is people who say unkind things about other people. Having said this she proceeds to dip her little fountain-pen filler into pots of oily venom and to squirt this mixture at all her friends. Having completed this process she then turns to self-laudation and tells me a long story of how she paid a dentist's bill on behalf of the King of Spain.

Yet, for all that, there were times when Mrs Greville showed kindness, and it is perhaps the fate of the famous that their more colourful faults are recorded more readily than their quiet virtues. Sonia Keppel has always maintained that Mrs Greville was kindness itself to her as a child; her mother would frequently dump Sonia on Mrs Greville when she was ill, and so good a godmother was she that she seriously wanted to adopt Sonia. Mrs Keppel, however, would not let her go. Osbert Sitwell recalled a charming story which, he said, demonstrated Mrs Greville's special understanding of character. His elderly housekeeper, Mrs Powell, had been severely ill after an operation. Maggie wanted to do something for her which would give her genuine pleasure, and she hit upon the idea of asking Mrs Powell to spend the evening in the kitchens of 16 Charles Street, where she could watch the celebrated French chef prepare a gourmet meal for forty covers. Mrs Powell seized the invitation, and enjoyed herself thoroughly. It did her more good, said Sitwell, than a whole month spent by the seaside. There was even the tangential benefit of psychological succour, for Mrs Powell could boast that she, given such a finely equipped kitchen, would have produced a meal superior to that provided by any Frenchman.

It is a pity, after that, to observe that not all the Sitwells found Mrs Greville as enchanting as Osbert apparently did. His brother Sacheverell thought her 'sheer hell and extremely boring'. The answer is that Maggie could not inspire indifference; she was either hated or beloved. Henry 'Bogie' Harris once said, 'One can live without everyone, really; everyone but Maggie; she's like dram drinking.'

Osbert Sitwell's contention that his heroine held fashionable life in contempt looks thin against all the evidence, unless one thinks that entertaining artists and musicians is 'fashionable' while feeding heavy ambassadors is not. More defensible is his plea for an understanding of her charitable work. Like her father, who had given McEwan Hall to the University of Edinburgh at a cost to himself of £115,000, Mrs Greville was generous. She claimed that she understood the people so well because her mother had been in service; honesty was a virtue one could justly attribute to her—she was not at all ashamed of her illegitimacy and scorned the Edinburgh hypocrites who had ostracised her father because of it. Her donations to charities in aid of the poor were unknown to most of her acquaintance, (and her will would demonstrate her assistance to the Edinburgh Working-men's Club and to Guy's Hospital), though they were admittedly much smaller than the sums she bestowed upon 'the deserving rich', the Royal Family, and various animal welfare societies. She had also been particularly kind and helpful to Canadians, as if to insult Australians by pointed contrast.

Her pugnacity remains the dominant feature recalled by posterity. She had courage as well as honesty, and would never dilute her opinions no matter who was present. If she thought someone an imbecile, she would say so. Well aware that she had enemies, she enjoyed the fight and welcomed the battle. 'She was a courageous and accomplished warrior', wrote Sitwell, 'and liked to be able to make use of her technique, acquired through many years . . . if a point had been reached where a bubble had to be pricked, no one could perform the operation with a more delicate skill and, indeed, virtuosity . . . Thus, when she entered an assembly, many a fashionable hostess quailed.' She might question the adjective 'delicate'. The Duke of Portland has said she was poisonous; if she heard a nasty story about some one, she would embellish it and make it even nastier. David Herbert thought her an ugly old beast, and a horrid woman; his mother, the Countess of Pembroke, hated her with passion and would never have her at Wilton.

Occasionally, her malice was actually very amusing. She said of Alice Keppel, 'To hear Alice talk about her escape from France, one would think she had swum the Channel, with her maid between her teeth.' Churchill she did not care for, largely because he was anti-Hitler when she was a shameless Hitler partisan, but also, one suspects, because he was the one man alive who was more belligerent than she and would not be timid in her presence. When his oratory was England's most powerful weapon, Mrs Greville scornfully reflected, 'If only the Prime Minister could have permanent laryngitis we might win the war.' When Lady Chamberlain returned from Rome in 1940, Maggie remarked, 'It is not the first time that Rome has been saved by a goose.'

With utmost cruelty, she kept her funniest and most hurtful story for the man who was devoted to her and might have married her, Sir John Simon. It was said that Simon did not marry Mrs Greville because she might have proved an obstacle to his becoming Prime Minister, by reason of her Nazi sympathies. She often told how he had proposed to her and had bitten and chewed the poker when she refused him.

Naturally, her smartest lashes were reserved for other women who dared to set themselves up as hostesses. Lady Cunard she called 'The Lollipop' (an allusion to Sir Thomas Beecham's collective name for his favourite light classical pieces of music), and pretended, as we have seen, to have told Queen Mary that 'little Lady Cunard' was not as bad as she was painted. She also put about the false story that Emerald had asked her who this Mrs Simpson was, thus making it appear Emerald was a liar (everyone knew she was a good friend of Mrs Simpson's).

She was vicious in her antipathy towards the American hostess, Laura Corrigan, whom she had never met. Asked why she declined all Laura's invitations, she said, 'To be known in the States as an English woman who doesn't go to Mrs Corrigan's parties is to be placed on a pedestal,' adding after a pause, 'I like pedestals.' She also said, in reply to the same question, that she did not go to Laura's receptions because 'I am never hungry enough.'

She similarly detested Mrs Vanderbilt, whom she did at least know. Channon chatted to her for forty minutes, during which time she was vituperative about almost everyone. Osbert Sitwell thought Mrs Greville's acid hostility was reserved for the smug and pretentious, but she was not without pretensions herself. She would wear the most ostentatious though beautiful diamonds from head to toe, which was not very far as she was so noticeably short, and look like a Christmas tree. On one occasion she and Mrs Arthur James, another hostess with airs, went to the same ball, both wearing strings of lovely pearls. When Mrs Greville realized that Mrs James was showing four rows of pearls, when she had visible only three, she dug deep down into her bosom and yanked out another three rows, making six altogether. This was not the conscious action of a woman above the trivial vanities.

Almost as famous as Mrs Greville were her two astonishing butlers, Boles and Bacon—astonishing because they were constantly drunk when serving, constantly reprimanded, and never sacked. The hostess was evidently as devoted to them as they were to her. Sitwell's description of a dinner, with royalty present, as like 'jazz night at the Palladium' could have been applied to countless evenings in Charles Street or at Polesden Lacey. Kenneth Clark has recalled one meal at which Boles, who habitually drank whatever the guests left behind, and moreover claimed to be a communist, surpassed himself. One of the specialities of Mrs Greville's excellent cuisine, usually reserved for when royalty was present, were baby tongues. On this occasion, as the tongues came from the kitchen, Clark saw Bacon eye them 'with insuperable longing'. His bloated red face was transfixed by the view of the delicacy. Finally, unable to contain himself, he began stuffing the baby tongues into his mouth, out of sight of all the guests save Kenneth Clark, who observed that 'the sauce ran down his shirt front, his jaws worked furiously'. Meanwhile, guests sat looking at empty plates, until Mrs Greville called out, 'Boles, what's become of the baby tongues?' Boles tactfully covered the greed of his companion. 'There were none to be had in the market this morning, Madam,' he said, as Bacon hastily put a napkin over his shirt to hide the stains, and brought in the next course.

Even more outrageous behaviour on the part of Bacon (or Boles?) occurred at a dinner when Austen Chamberlain and his daughter Diana were present. Mrs Greville noticed the butler was more than usually drunk, so she quickly scribbled a note on the back of a place card and handed it to him. It said, 'You're drunk. Leave the room at once.' With great presence of mind Bacon put the card on a silver salver, went down the table, and presented it solemnly to

Chamberlain, who looked, looked again, put on his eye-glass to make sure he saw what he thought he saw, and sat in stupified silence for the rest of the meal. The incident caused Mrs Greville much embarrassment, yet the butler kept his post in her household.

Society gleefully recounted these stories in lighter moments, but as the mood of foreboding deepened during the 1930s, it was more likely to be Mrs Greville's pernicious influence to the detriment of the country which dominated as a topic of conversation whenever her name was mentioned. She was no longer merely a rich and forceful personality, but a potentially dangerous one.

No one questioned Mrs Ronnie Greville's patriotism; it was her judgement which caused alarm. Even that would have mattered little had it not been for her determination to influence events, and the apparent willingness of politicians to heed her. Convinced she was right in most things, with a ground of common sense as her ally, she actively sought to insinuate her views into discussions among the powerful. After a glorious meal at Polesden, she would take the most important guests aside, such as Hoare or Simon or an ambassador, and engage in serious talk. Kenneth Clark described the scene thus: 'She sat back in a large chair, like a Phoenician goddess, while the cabinet minister or ambassador leant forward attentively.' He added, 'I have no doubt that she had considerable influence.' To the British Ambassador in Spain she wrote, 'If I were in power I would *clear out* some of the permanent officials at the Foreign Office.' Her wrath was immediate and peremptory.

Since the war, others have doubted whether Mrs Greville, Lady Astor, Lady Londonderry or Lady Cunard really did wield the influence ascribed to them, probably because to admit that they did would be shaming. Yet at the time, it was clear to anyone who cared to observe that Mrs Greville, in particular, had the ear of the mighty. She was not the only hostess with political power, as has been claimed, but she was the most insidious. Osbert Sitwell thought her political antennae were acute, her intelligence sound. Robert Bruce Lockhart, on the other hand, thought she was out of her depth and was fooled by Hitler. Whatever the case, the most significant circumstance was that the Germans took her seriously.

Ribbentrop fawned on Mrs Greville. She was the very first

person he went to see on his visits to London. She was present at the Nazi party rally in Nuremberg, venting her fury on the British Embassy for not sending a representative. After all, she said, the British Ambassador in Moscow attended Communist celebrations in Red Square. Not surprisingly, the Nazis treated her like royalty, offering a curious spectacle. To this dumpy woman who gave splendid dinner parties they showed more evidence of respect than was manifest in their dealings with the British Prime Minister. Doubtless they wanted her pro-Nazi sympathies to be more widely disseminated in Britain, and perhaps they even thought she represented the opinion of the 'ordinary' British citizen. The Italian Ambassador, Count Grandi, sent a letter to 'Darling Maggie' expressing the view that she must never think for a moment that their two countries would go to war.

Harold Nicolson was present at one of her dinners when the pro-German atmosphere almost choked him:

> I sat next to a German woman who tried a little Nazi propaganda. Poor wretch, she did not know that she had a tiger lurking beside her. 'Do you know my country, sir?' she said. 'Yes, I have often visited Germany.' 'Have you been there recently, since our movement?' 'No, except for an hour at Munich, I have not visited Germany since 1930.' 'Oh, but you should come now, you would find it all so changed.' 'Yes, I should find all my old friends either in prison, or exiled, or murdered.' At which she gasped like a fish. Maggie saw that something awful had happened and shouted down the table to find out what it was. In a slow strong voice I repeated my remark. As Ribbentrop's Number Two was there on Maggie's right, it was all to the good.

Ribbentrop's Number Two almost certainly reported back to his master that the mood of the British was tame apart from one or two crypto-Communists like Nicolson; the real people were on Germany's side in the fight against Bolshevism. Some, like Bill Cavendish-Bentinck (later British Ambassador in Poland and now the Duke of Portland), tried to point out that snippets and tittle-tattle picked up from the posh dinner table of Mrs Ronnie Greville were valueless. Cavendish-Bentinck told Ribbentrop that he would do better to visit the German consuls in Manchester or Birmingham if he really wanted to obtain an idea of what the British thought, but Ribbentrop was not impressed. He preferred to rely upon the profoundly Conservative ambience which prevailed at Charles Street.

Harold Nicolson, again, turned to his Diary in anger one day in 1939, a few months before the outbreak of war, to express his contempt for the damage done by Mrs Greville and her like. Speaking of 'the defeatist and pampered group in London' who had long been assuring Mussolini that the capitalists were on his side, he wrote,

> I do not believe that any intelligent man such as Grandi could have left him [Mussolini] under any illusion that the will-power of this country is concentrated in Mrs Ronald Greville. He must know that in the last resort our decision is embodied, not in Mayfair or Cliveden, but in the provinces. The harm which these silly selfish hostesses do is really immense. They convey to foreign envoys the impression that policy is decided in their own drawing-rooms . . . these people have a subversive influence. They dine and wine our younger politicians and they create an atmosphere of authority and responsibility and grandeur, whereas the whole thing is a mere flatulence of the spirit. That is always what happens with us. The silly people are regarded as representative of British opinion and the informed people are dismissed as 'intellectuals'.

Habits change little. Even now the Conservative distrust of intelligent people would offer a wide avenue to any ambitious hostess, with conviction rather than power of analysis, to have her views heard, applauded, and admired. Mrs Greville merely took advantage of the deeply ingrained anti-intellectualism of the British upper class, and found an audience of powerful men ready to agree with her.

The French, far more mature in matters of the *salon* tradition than the English, kept well away from Mrs Greville, whom they thought faintly ridiculous. A woman such as that would surely never be taken seriously in France. The French painter and author Paul Maze once flew into a rage of astonishment, at lunch with Lady Colefax, as he contemplated the absurd degree of importance attached to Mrs Greville's views. He had heard her praising Hitler. Was it possible that such a stupid woman could have any influence on British policy? When French women interfered in politics they were at least intelligent; they read books and they slept with diplomats. 'And, believe me,' he said, 'to sleep with M. Briand one has to have a high degree of intelligence.'

The coming of war was almost like a personal blow to Mrs Greville, the denial of everything she had advised and counselled her friends, the pulling up of a drawbridge thus preventing access to a whole world of 'society' beyond. War, she thought, was a criminal mistake, the prelude to a Bolshevik invasion. She continued to think the Nazis were our friends. Finding herself suddenly holding a minority and unpopular view, she sank into torpor and submitted to illness. Her debilitating disease had by now almost rendered her immobile, and she willingly yielded to the necessity of spending the rest of her life in a wheelchair. There seemed no longer much point in resisting—the world had become a hostile, vulgar place.

Like Emerald Cunard, and (monthly) Sibyl Colefax, Maggie Greville took a suite at the Dorchester Hotel, now the last refuge of the hostesses and arguably the centre of High Society resistance to Hitler's irritating bombs; life went on at the Dorchester as if Hitler had never existed. Mrs Greville gave a lunch party on 30 April 1942, to which she invited the Mountbattens, the Duke and Duchess of Kent, the Duchess of Buccleuch, Prince Philip of Greece (later husband of Queen Elizabeth II), and the most successful social climber of twentieth-century London—Chips Channon. It was to be her last grand occasion. Confined to her chair and obviously in pain, she nevertheless got out all the famous jewellery and wore it—too much of it—proudly. The diamonds and emeralds were world-famous, probably one of the finest private collections of jewels in London. As the last great Edwardian hostess slipped gradually away, people openly wondered what would happen to these magnificent gems.

Four months after her last 'royal' lunch party, Mrs Greville died at the Dorchester Hotel, at the age of seventy-five. She was buried in the rose-garden at Polesden Lacey, next to the dog cemetery, on 18 September 1942, in the presence of the Belgian Ambassador, Sonia Keppel, Chips Channon, Osbert Sitwell, Mrs Ralph Younger, Lord Ilchester and Lady Crewe. The staff also stood by the graveside—Boles the faithful butler, Mrs Stroud the secretary, and Captain Thorpe the agent. Apart from the dogs who lay near by, and upon whom Mrs Greville had bestowed the more affectionate side of her nature, she was interred in a quiet space, alone.

Five days later, the memorial service at St Mark's, North Audley Street, was one of the most packed that had been seen there in wartime. There were six ambassadors, the Lord President of the Council Sir John Anderson, archdukes of Austria, Youngers, McEwans and it seemed half the nobility of England. Even Margot Asquith, who knew Maggie Greville for what she was and did not hesitate to say so, was there. In the minds of all present was one persistent and fascinating question: what would become of the houses, the wealth, the jewels? When would the Will be published?

The furniture at Charles Street was stacked up, labelled, and packed ready for auction. Boles was there to help, wandering from room to room, sobbing into his handkerchief. For him the death of Mrs Greville was virtually the slamming shut of his own life. He had been in service with her for forty-two years, and knew no other existence. The sale at Christie's, including not only furniture but 1,000 bottles of claret and six rare bottles of Grande Champagne 1810 brandy, realized £6,000.

Professor Richardson was commissioned to prepare a tombstone which, when it was in place, looked like 'the top of an old-fashioned servants' trunk, half buried in the grass', according to James Lees-Milne. It can be seen to the west of the house today.

Rumours about the will circulated before details were published, which caused some embarrassment to the Queen, as it was widely thought that she would have Mrs Greville's jewels, yet she was not supposed to know anything about it and had to feign surprise whenever it was mentioned.

Dame Margaret Greville, D.B.E., left £1½ million, with specific bequests of all her jewellery 'with my loving thoughts' to the Queen, £20,000 to Princess Margaret, £12,500 to the Queen of Spain 'with deep affection and in memory of the great kindness and affection which Her Majesty has shown me', £10,000 to Sir Osbert Sitwell, £10,000 to the National Anti-Vivisection Society, with smaller amounts to the R.S.P.C.A. and the Canine Defence League. Boles received a legacy, as did the Edinburgh Workingmen's Club, though significantly less than the handsome bequest to Princess Margaret. As for the jewels, now the world knew that Mrs Greville had kept her promise and given them where they would be best worn. To this day, Queen Elizabeth the Queen Mother may on occasion be seen wearing some of the Greville jewels, including the magnificent diamond necklace which had once belonged to Marie-Antoinette. She wore them during the celebrations for her eightieth birthday in 1980.

Mrs Ronnie Greville is not often remembered with kindly thoughts. As a hostess she possessed some of the essential benefits, but lacked others just as crucial. She gave superb dinners, probably with better food than any of her contemporary rivals, in magnificent settings. She knew the powerful. She could tell a good story. And she was rich. Yet she was a businesswoman before she was a hostess, and the canny judgement which enabled her to prosper in business was antipathetic to the finest human qualities. She was thought by many to be a shrewd judge of men and women, sagacious and sensible, yet her judgement rarely ventured further than an appraisal of who would be successful and who would not, and why. Success and making money were the forces she respected, leaving no room for those artistic motions of the mind which make a man interesting. In this way she was far less brilliant a hostess than Emerald Cunard. You cannot build a *salon* uniquely around statesmen, diplomats and members of royal families. That magic spark of improvisation and unpredictability was missing.

Moreover, it is no accident that so many people called her vicious and poisonous. She enjoyed mocking and lacked that sensitivity which would permit her to see that by constantly speaking ill of people she rendered herself gross. Her malice was unrelieved by a twinkle in the eye; on the contrary, she meant what she said. Courage and bold speaking are all very well for a businesswoman, but they do not sit well in the lap of a hostess. Mrs Corrigan and Lady Colefax were wholly kind, Lady Cunard mischievous but good, Mrs Greville quite simply malevolent.

There was finally something sinister in her allegiance to the Nazi leaders. Her correspondence might well have proved especially interesting to scholars, if only because she had been on the edge of political power for so long. Scholars were not to be afforded the chance to pry. She instructed Boles to destroy all her private papers after her death, and he faithfully burnt the entire collection.

The Visitors' Books, however, survived, and there can be seen the lists of guests meticulously kept for every occasion, in strict order of precedence. Weekends at Polesden Lacey generally catered for about fourteen, and dinners at 16 Charles Street were attended by anything from ten to sixty people. There is an evening when, of sixty-one names mentioned, over fifty are titled, and many others when the guest of honour was a King, and of the thirteen other guests, ten were themselves royals. Queen Mary is there on 6 July 1937, interestingly with no Germans present—that would be too indiscreet. The Queen of Spain's name occurs dozens of times, and less frequently there can be found the Kings of Egypt and Greece. George VI and his Queen occur constantly, both as sovereigns and as Duke and Duchess of York before 1936; in fact, one of their last dinners out before the abdication of Edward VIII was with Mrs Greville. On 29 June 1937 (one week before Queen Mary!), the King and Queen dined with three dukes, four duchesses, marquesses, earls, Sonia Cubitt and Osbert Sitwell, a total of thirty-six, and their last visit before the outbreak of war was in February, 1939.

Alongside the Visitors' Books there is a Bridge Book, and lists of all the menus served. A large Christmas party mentions seven courses, all in French, including Plum Pudding de Noël, and a mysterious dish concocted in honour of the hostess's most esteemed guest—Oeufs Duc d'York.

Other relics of the Greville era are Maggie's little round spectacles, still lying in their case on her desk, various photograph albums, all the Christmas cards she received from Buckingham

Palace, and the red carpets which were put to such frequent royal use. They are still in use today, although Mrs Greville would perhaps not approve their function; they now line the route around the house and bear the tread of the ordinary public.

CHAPTER FIVE

Emerald Cunard

At a Cabinet meeting shortly after the First World War, the Prime Minister, Lloyd George, asked an unusual question. 'Does anyone know a Lady Cunard?' he said. 'She is a most dangerous woman.' Among those present in the Cabinet were some of Lady Cunard's most frequent guests at luncheon and dinner parties—Winston Churchill, Arthur Balfour, Alfred Milner, Lord Curzon—but not one of them spoke up to acknowledge acquaintance with her.

Their reticence seems now surprising in the light of the avalanche of admiration which descended upon Lady Cunard after her death. Dozens of those who knew her have joined in a chorus of praise for her unique combination of qualities and have assured her place as London's pre-eminent hostess of the twentieth century. Far from wishing to deny her, writers of memoirs have made her the glittering centre-piece of their reminiscences and given us to understand that their lives would have been truly impoverished without her beneficent, invigorating influence. Yet Lloyd George's question, and its reception, did touch upon a truth which lay at the heart of Lady Cunard's success. At her table, politicians were rarely allowed to behave like politicians. Gravity, earnestness, solemnity were forbidden; boredom was banished. A politician used to uttering banal circumlocutions relating to economic forecasts would, at Lady Cunard's, find himself reciting French poetry and rediscovering a joy which he had almost forgotten. An awe-inspiring general would be questioned about his collection of butterflies. Emerald Cunard could detect gold in a slag-heap, she had an almost infallible instinct for the nugget of interest concealed by the most intractable exterior, with the result that politicians would find their guard spirited away by her uncanny charm, and would unbend to an amazing degree. 'She made heavy politicians and financiers aware of another world beyond their ken', wrote Harold Acton, 'and in a subtle way she influenced and educated them.' This is no doubt what Lloyd George meant in calling her 'dangerous', that she threatened to reveal to ponderous men with important decisions to make, that they were human, gay, light-hearted, that conversation and literature held more charm than matters of state. In 1918 echoes of Victorian formality still persisted, and old-fashioned men were not ready to admit gaiety as a life-enhancing force with its own dignity in the scale of human values. Emerald Cunard swept all that aside like a swift, cleansing winter breeze from the Atlantic. She was, indeed, American, but the marvel is that she was more than this—she was Californian, the only woman from that sunshine state ever to have dominated the social life of a cosmopolitan city.

Charm is a gossamer thing, virtually impossible to describe. One can feel the transfusing vigour of its rays, and be unable to account for it retrospectively in words. Emerald had charm. She has been called bewitching, entrancing, beguiling, scintillating, and it has been said that her presence could banish gloom. 'You charm even the morose,' said George Moore. Harold Acton said that when the cloud of melancholy threatened to envelop him, he would visit Lady Cunard. 'More than any man or woman I knew she could dissipate it in a few sparkling sentences.' Roderick Cameron wrote, 'The moment she entered a room one was conscious of her presence. The diamond-like glitter of her wit was a tangible thing and she wore it like a jewel; it glowed round her like an aura round the moon, pale and phosphorescent, as exhilarating as the cold air of a frosty night.' Cameron also said she had the gift of inspiring enthusiasm, a gift which caught by surprise many a first-time guest, who expected to talk at length on a subject about which he knew too much, and found instead that he was expatiating on a matter in which he thought he had no interest at all. To this end, she never invited like with like; there was no question of dividing her friends into social categories, with ambassadors on one evening and musicians on another. They would all be thrown in together, famous and unknown, old and young, the extrovert and the reflective, no matter what their calling or position in life. Peter Quennell has said this made her evenings 'stimulating, however exhausting and bewildering'. She even paid scant attention to numbers, or the careful balancing of the sexes, proclaiming that she invited people for conversation, not for mating.

George Moore, who was in love with Lady Cunard to the end of his days, told her that her life was a work of art, adding that 'perhaps you would not be so wonderful if you were self-conscious'. She was completely a stranger to that premeditation which makes an apparently chance remark the product of much troublesome thought. Her chance remarks were never anything else but spontaneous, in fact everything she said was impromptu, always astonishing, and often hilarious, so that it would have been quite impossible for her to be self-conscious without shrinking with alarm at the contemplation of her own effervescent character. Others contemplated it with delight. To revert once more to Sir Harold Acton, who spoke of the electric crackle in the air when Emerald was around, eloquent metaphor comes to service when he captures the especial charm of the woman. She was 'like a spiritual dowser in a desert. As she walked along with her willow, springs bubbled from the sand . . . her sweet presence was a passing benediction whose influence did not pass: she offered one the chalice of her own eternal youth . . . lights glimmered at her house which flickered out elsewhere.' 'You come into a room filling the air with unpremeditated music', wrote George Moore.

She knew when to encourage indiscretion, if the sparks would harmlessly kindle a flagging conversation, and she could be mischievous without malice. Her wit was not damaging. Yet she had a challenging way of talking, very direct, and she would not accept a mild amorphous banality for a reply. She was said to have 'a whim of steel'. It was, as is already clear, Lady Cunard's

conversation which rendered her unique. She used language in a
way which was entirely her own, so that it is even now possible to
make a remark in the style of Emerald Cunard, as it is to mimic Noël
Coward. She was aggressively comic and personal; to Lady Cynthia
Asquith, priceless, startling. You never knew, when she began a
sentence, where it would end, as the normal sequence of controlled
thought would not be the one that would occur to her, yet her
sweeping inconsequential absurdities could, more often than not,
reveal a subtle significance that would set one's reflection along new
and rewarding lines. Osbert Sitwell said that her wit consisted in a
particular and individual use of syllogism, 'so that it was impossible
beforehand ever to tell to what conclusion any given premise might
bring you'. Surprise was the essence of her style, a comic view of the
obsessions of mankind its inspiration. George Moore was right:
Lady Cunard was an artist. Though she left no book of maxims, no
collection of letters, she was as much a social observer as La
Rochefoucauld, or Madame de Sévigné, both of whom she
admired. Her art lay in her conversation, that most evanescent
form, and there was no Boswell to record it. Later in this chapter an
attempt must be made to recapture some of that conversation. For
the moment, let it suffice to point out that she had no rivals among
the hostesses of the twentieth century. Laura Corrigan could not
talk about anything, and Sibyl Colefax had the intelligence, but not
the spark necessary to give it vivid verbal expression. Lady
Cunard's conversation could probe delicately, 'like the act of
sunshine on a garden', or it could provoke teasingly, like a matador
goading a bull. Whichever the case, it was hers and hers alone, and it
made her the supreme exemplar of the social talents in her time.

Emerald Cunard having spent virtually all her adult life in England,
one was apt to forget that she had once been Maud Burke, from San
Francisco, California. She was quite happy to forget it herself, as
she tended to bemoan the lack of culture among Americans and to
regret their want of humour. If she continued to see the cultureless
and humourless Laura Corrigan, it was because Laura was a
marvellously innocent butt for her gentle teasing. Not that she was
to any degree a 'European' snob. She once chastized 'Chips'

Channon who was rash enough to belittle the Kenneth Clarks in her presence, saying they were bourgeois and not in society: 'You are as much an upstart as Kenneth Clark, and so am I,' retorted Emerald. 'We are both from across the Atlantic.' Nevertheless, this was a rare admission. On the whole, she never made reference to her origins, and was irritated when they were brought to her notice inadvertently. When she rented a friend's house while her own was being redecorated, she loudly proclaimed that there were no faucets near the basin. 'Faucets, Emerald? What *are* faucets?' asked someone. '*Faucets*,' she shouted, 'Everybody knows what a faucet is.' Of course, nobody did, until it was pointed out by some well-travelled friend that faucet was American for tap. Emerald was visibly displeased.

Maud Burke had been born in San Francisco on 3 August 1872. Her father was related to the Irish patriot, Robert Emmet, her mother was half-French. They were well off, but not rich. All the records relating to her origins and childhood were destroyed in the San Francisco earthquake of 1906, so the only information available was derived from Lady Cunard's own very sparse references to the past. Thus people learnt that she had had an older brother, who died in infancy, and that she grew up surrounded by Chinese servants. Precious little else was ever divulged. Living entirely for the present, she simply could not be bothered to revert to her childhood, and if the subject did unexpectedly occur, perhaps once in five years, it was not dwelt upon. 'Unexpected confidences alternated with mysterious reticences', wrote Peter Quennell. 'Many episodes she preferred to leave obscure.'

One of the most obscure was the part played in her life by Horace Carpentier. A former general in the American Civil War, kind and very well-read, Carpentier had become a millionaire from dealings in real estate. His hobby was to educate and advise pretty adolescent girls, whom he called his 'nieces', the favourite among whom was the obviously intelligent Maud Burke. Mr Burke had recently died, and Mrs Burke, still young, was pursued by rich admirers. One of these was Carpentier, who in this way made the acquaintance of little Maud and took her under his wing. She was extremely lucky to have such a protector, for it was under his influence that the two great passions of her life, literature and opera, were first formed. In his splendid library, a bibliophile's treasure-house, Maud discovered Balzac, Richardson, and Shakespeare. From that moment until the end of her life, she devoured Balzac and Shakespeare until she knew them practically by heart, and Richardson's *Pamela* remained her favourite English novel. All of French literature, Greek and Latin poetry, taste and discernment, came from hours spent in Carpentier's library in San Francisco. He took her to her first opera at the Metropolitan in New York, which likewise marked her for life, and would one day bring her acute suffering.

When Maud was eighteen, her mother married a stockbroker called Frederick Tichenor, leaving Maud to set up house with her 'guardian'. Mother and daughter remained close, however, visiting Europe frequently on trips financed by Carpentier, who was anxious that Maud's cultural experience should accumulate. She was a pretty girl, with ash-blonde hair and penetrating, intelligent eyes, likely to attract attention. But her finest asset was her ebullient impetuosity. She was carefree, bright, impulsive, liable to say and do the most unpredictable things. This characteristic was to enslave George Moore to her for the rest of his life.

On a visit with her mother to London in 1894, when she was 22, Maud discovered that Moore was to be a fellow-guest at a large luncheon party in the Savoy Hotel. She greatly admired Moore's writing. Slipping surreptitiously into the restaurant before anyone else, she changed the place-cards to ensure that she would be sitting next to the great man. Moore lavished fulsome praise upon Emile Zola during the meal, at which Miss Maud Burke, who also cherished Zola, placed her hand on his arm and exclaimed, 'George Moore, you have a soul of fire!' From that moment, Moore tells us, he was in love.

He also tells us that it was Maud, a few weeks later, after being constantly in his company day after day, who turned to him and said, 'You can make love to me now, if you like.'

Eventually, Maud had to go back to America with her mother. It seems Moore's adoration touched her only lightly, whereas he was metamorphosed by the encounter. The beautiful letters he addressed her leave no doubt that she was the most important woman in his life. 'You are at once the poet and the poem', he wrote, 'and you create yourself not with silks and pearls, though these things are beautiful upon you, but by your intense desire of beauty and life . . . In you Nature has succeeded in expressing herself and completely . . . surely the most fortunate man in the world is he who meets a woman who enchants him as a work of art enchants . . . You are at once the vase and the wine in the vase. You are the music and the instrument which produces the music, and you are a prodigious virtuoso, and while thinking of you one thinks of all that one loves most intimately . . . very few men have seen their ideal as close to them and as clearly as I have seen mine. Very few have possessed all they were capable of desiring of beauty and grace; I have possessed more, for the reality has exceeded the desire.'

Meanwhile, Maud had met in New York a member of the Polish royal family, Prince Andre Poniatowski, and this time her impetuous nature did her a disservice. She and the Prince were fond companions, but she allowed the rumour to be put about that she was engaged to him. Poniatowski demanded a public denial, which Maud granted in a newspaper announcement, claiming that it was her guardian, Carpentier, who objected to the match. She was ever after to entertain a very pessimistic view of the married state, and it was with only moderate enthusiasm that she welcomed the courtship of Sir Bache Cunard, grandson of the founder of the Cunard Line, and the current baronet. 'I like Sir Bache better than any man I know,' she said. But she did not say that she loved him. They were married in New York on 17 April 1895, and shortly afterwards Maud left America with her husband to take up her new life in the English countryside.

There was scarcely even a remote possibility that Sir Bache Cunard and Maud Burke could learn to enjoy a compatible life together. She was original and sparkling, 23 years old, already an intellectual steeped in the love of books, and devoted to metropolitan life. He was 43, dull, serious, philistine, and equally devoted to the country life of hunting and fishing. In spite of their similar ancestry (Bache was three-quarters American, his mother American and his grandfather born in Philadelphia), Sir Bache Cunard was the quintessential English country gentleman, educated at Rugby, with a commanding presence dominated by a walrus moustache.

Maud's new home was a vast mansion in Leicestershire called Nevill Holt, full of gloomy panelled rooms, swords, stuffed animal heads, and forty servants. For four centuries it had been the seat of the Nevill family, until it was bought by the Cunards in 1876. Though he was now head of the family, Sir Bache took no interest whatever in the shipping business. When he was not riding to hounds, he spent his time making decorative ironwork in a remote room in the tower. He also supervised the gardens, instructing his men to feed the yew hedges with buckets of bull's blood.

All this was daunting in the extreme to Lady Cunard. She positively despised the country and made but little effort to accustom herself to her husband's pleasures. She did ride to hounds a few times (and astonished her later friends by her unexpected knowledge of hunting), but the only welcome aspect of her pregnancy later in the year was the release it afforded her from this uncongenial obligation. She offended her husband by her rejection of stuffy formality, by her habit, for example, of giving orders to the footmen herself, instead of transmitting them through the butler. She entertained ideas of decoration which were thoroughly at odds with those of her husband. Once, on discovering that she had engaged workmen to paint a room white in his absence, Sir Bache sent his carriage to the village to bring the men back and scrape it all off again. Nor does she appear to have endeared herself to the locals, though the hysterical reaction of Lord Mexborough upon seeing her for the first time must surely be ascribed to his eccentricity. In a wheelchair, his white beard reaching down to his knees, Mexborough screamed, 'Take her away! Take her away!'

At least at the beginning, Sir Bache was as much in love with his bride as could be expected, but as the months went by, he wondered why he had not been able to catch one of the demure and well-behaved East Coast beauties, many of whom married into the English aristocracy, instead of this self-willed and unpredictable Californian. Working for hours at his forge, he built an ornamental gate for his wife, with the words 'Come into the garden, Maud' picked out in small horse-shoes. Maud's reception of this gift was said to be chilly. Bache told her she was beautiful, like Queen Victoria; 'that plain woman', said Maud. Gradually, two separate lives were lived at Nevill Holt, husband and wife rarely being found in residence together. The villagers noticed and commented upon the fact that Lady Cunard was there whenever the baronet was away, and as soon as he returned, her ladyship was off to the theatre in London or the couturiers in Paris. Soon there were three separate lives. Nancy Cunard, destined to be as famous as her mother and even more original, was born on 10 March 1896, and immediately accorded her own set of nurses and servants. Her mother had little to do with her. She had no maternal instinct and did nothing to conceal her distaste.

Nevill Holt is now a boys' boarding school, but it still shows on the wall of the servants' quarters the bells of the last century: 'Sir Bache's room', 'Lady Cunard's room', 'Miss Nancy', 'Schoolroom', 'Governess'. For fifteen years this remote palace was Emerald Cunard's home. However unlikely a place for a high-spirited young woman, it has this significance in her story, that it enabled her to discover the talent for entertaining which was to make her an historical figure. At first the only guests were her husband's hunting friends and local squires, none of whom could respond to Maud's effervescent personality. When Sir Bache was away, she would bring in friends of hers from London, musicians, men of letters, men of intellect, and the atmosphere of the house would change within hours. On one occasion, guests sang Wagnerian arias, each from a different bedroom in the dead of night, until the whole huge house was bursting with song. Sir Bache was away; he did not care for amusement of this sort. When he returned the following day he detected a light-hearted ambience in the air. His wife told Cecil Beaton, years later, that he noticed an atmosphere of *love*. 'I don't understand what is going on in this house,' he said, 'but I don't like it.'

In the end, it was Maud who won. Her circle of friends grew, she was noticed with approval by the Prince of Wales, and society opened its doors. Having at first been rather cold towards the immigrant wife, the mentors of English society were finally captivated by her brilliance, her indefinable knack of making

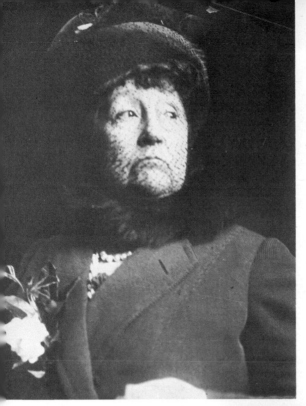

Mrs Stuyvesant Fish, *enfant terrible* of New York society at the turn of the century

Mrs Cornelius Vanderbilt (*née* Grace Wilson), the Queen of New York

The Vanderbilt mansion on Fifth Avenue

'The Breakers', summer cottage of the Vanderbilts
at Newport, Rhode Island

everyone near her feel exhilarated. Maurice Baring announced that he felt no longer any need to belong to 'The Society for the Prevention of Cruelty to Lady Cunard'. She could look after herself, and that is precisely what, increasingly, she did. Nevill Holt saw the beginnings of her career as a hostess and the neglect of her role as wife and mother. London would be the beneficiary.

But this is to anticipate. There were still a number of tedious years at Nevill Holt, brightened by the ever longer list of weekend guests. Maud's marriage did nothing to dilute the ardour of George Moore, called simply G.M. by everyone who knew him. For a year after the birth of Nancy, Maud did not invite him, feeling with reason that his attentions could become embarrassing. Though she enjoyed the romance, it is probable that she discouraged its expression. Nevertheless, the suspicion that they had been lovers endured among their acquaintance. G.M. himself had said that they must 'stint their desires to blessed adultery', and it was often suggested that Nancy had really been G.M.'s child. This is unlikely, but the fact that the story was spread at least indicates that it was thought a serious possibility. As Nancy grew older she became very close to the old man, and once asked him outright if he was her father. His reply was ambiguous. 'You must ask your mother,' he said.

He continued to write beautiful letters to Lady Cunard, which usually went unanswered, as Maud did not care for writing letters. In later years, he refused to use the telephone, so contact between them was unnecessarily difficult. One year after Nancy's birth, Maud encountered G.M. unexpectedly in a London street, and they resumed their friendship. Thereafter, G.M. was a frequent visitor at Nevill Holt, sometimes for long stays, when Maud's withdrawal hurt him. 'She turned her head aside, that she might not see my tears', he wrote. 'Every night she locked her door, and the sound is and will ever be in my ears.' Maud's affection for G.M. occupied every layer of love and esteem except that which leads to passion. He was one of the giants of European culture, a man not only respected for his own work, but the friend of painters and writers at the summit of achievement. It is not easy now, when Moore is little read, to appreciate just how revered he was at the time. A supreme stylist and a prolific worker, his books were admired above most others. He was the perfect 'man of letters', the guardian of English literary tradition. He was also, for Maud, a wonderfully entertaining guest, for he was completely free from inhibition, iconoclastic, and acutely perceptive.

Harold Acton and Max Beerbohm have both given vivid impressions of the old man with 'baby-pink complexion and aquamarine eyes which gazed as if he were seeing the world for the first time, white-haired and mustachio'd Adam in the garden of Eden, surprised by what he saw'. Acton spoke further of his 'pure simplicity, mischievous humour, and the frank innocence of his comments', which could be awkward. He would tell of his troubles with an enlarged prostate, making no allowance for the susceptibilities of his listeners. Max Beerbohm wrote, 'Whatever was in his mind, no matter where he was or what his audience, he said. And when he had nothing to say, he said nothing. Which of these courses in an average drawing-room needs the greater courage—to say simply anything, or to sit saying simply nothing? I think I used to rate Moore's silences his finer triumph. They were so unutterably blank. And yet, in some remote way, they so dominated the current chatter.' Some one might raise the matter of Roman Catholicism. G.M. would intervene briefly: 'You can't change God into a *biscuit!*'

Lady Cunard relished G.M.'s imperturbability, and his quixotic remarks, in some ways very much like her own. She could steer the conversation in unforeseeable directions, and he would willingly follow. Harold Nicolson thought him 'a silly old man' (this is thirty years later, when he really was old) and declared that he talked rubbish, but then Nicolson's perceptions were more mundane. It is hardly surprising that he found the fanciful conceits of a George Moore or a Lady Cunard offensive. He preferred the more predictable cosy qualities of a Lady Colefax.

G.M. would have preferred to have Maud all to himself, but the days on which they could talk alone became less and less frequent as Lady Cunard's social life increased. He went to see her surrounded by people because he could not see her alone, but he did not care for what he saw, and told her so. 'I wished to fly from your world, which is not my world', he wrote. 'You continue to imagine that these people interest me, but you are the only one in Society who interests me.' 'Society is a snare, and he who gets entangled will never come to fruition.' The garrulous crowd which encircled his beloved, barring his access, was to him as 'squeaking dolls: excellent folk, no doubt, but I have lost my taste for them, that is all'.

G.M.'s devotion to Maud could not be countered by any rebuff or show of indifference. 'You are a hard woman in many ways' he told her, 'but if you were less hard I don't think you would have held me captive such a long time;' [this is in 1906] 'I do not complain of my captivity—good heavens no; it is the only allegiance I acknowledge and man without allegiance is like a ball of thistledown.' 'Very often I fall on my knees and thank God for his great mercy in having made you known to me.' Few women are fortunate enough to receive such glorious declarations, or to see proof of a man's fidelity. G.M. cherished the first gift Maud had ever made to him, a tortoiseshell comb; long after it had broken in two, he kept the pieces before him on his writing-desk.

Lady Cunard was soon to change her life drastically, and lose her heart to another man, who understood less how to value it than did Moore. In 1911 she finally left Nevill Holt and her husband for ever, choosing to settle in London with her daughter Nancy, now an elegant young woman of sixteen. For almost forty years London would be the décor of her social and emotional existence, the scene of her emergence as a hostess *sans pareille* and of her descent into ultimate loneliness. 1911 was also the year that she met Thomas Beecham.

Maud was 38 and Beecham 32 when they were introduced by another hostess of the day, Mrs Charles Hunter. (This lady had more in common with Lady Colefax than Lady Cunard, being an acknowledged chaser of celebrities. From the very beginning, Lady Cunard was never tempted to cultivate people simply because they were grand or well-known.) According to local gossip, Beecham was discovered in bed with Maud by workmen repairing the clock-tower and peering through the window, on a subsequent visit to Nevill Holt. Whether or not this is true, certainly it was shortly afterwards that Maud made her decision to move to London. Her

involvement with Beecham grew ever more intense, and through
him, her dedication to the opera was established. In the days before
government subsidy, it needed warriors with perseverance and
spunk to keep opera going and to make it fashionable. Beecham and
Lady Cunard were a formidable pair. Beecham sank his fortune,
derived from the famous liver pills launched by his grandfather,
into his Imperial Opera League. Maud's contribution, in addition
to providing a great deal of her own money, was to galvanize
London society into giving its support. She was by now in a fine
position to bully and cajole a vast number of people into making
financial contributions and attending performances at Covent
Garden. As Osbert Sitwell has pointed out, Maud grasped the fact
that it was 'necessary to rely on regular attendance by numskulls,
nitwits and morons addicted to the mode' in order to fill the house.
She tolerated the foolish and the illiterate, for the first time, if they
could be made to donate a large sum to the cause. She flattered their
snobbery, their hopes of being 'in the swim' and likely to find
themselves in the same theatre as royalty, if dear Thomas's beloved
opera could be helped thereby. Nor was her own interest either
dilettante or solely rooted in love for the man. Maud genuinely
appreciated opera, knew arias from Verdi, Puccini, Wagner and a
vast repertoire by heart, regularly attended rehearsals. While it is
now common knowledge that the respect which opera enjoys in
England is owed in large part to the pioneering influence of
Beecham, it is not always acknowledged that Lady Cunard herself
played an indispensable part. Whole seasons at Covent Garden
depended upon her efforts. Osbert Sitwell, again, says that all who
enjoy opera are in her debt; 'there was no limit to the number of
boxes she could fill. Her will-power was sufficient, her passion for
music fervent enough, to make opera almost compulsory for those
who wished to be fashionable.' With malice, Evelyn Waugh called
her 'the Duchess of Covent Garden', but at least he recognized
where her allegiance lay. In war-time London, in 1917, she would
be at the opera come what might, to set an example to the public.
Her friend Diana Cooper reflected that 'she really, I expect, wanted
to die with Thomas Beecham if Covent Garden was to be hit'.
Hence the malice of men like Waugh. The affair of Lady Cunard

and Thomas Beecham was no secret.

Mischievously, she appeared to enjoy the very openness of the liaison. She once received by anonymous registered post a caricature of Beecham, disguised as a dull organ man with a monkey on his shoulder. Others might have torn it up and thrown it away, but Lady Cunard revealed it to her guests, saying that she was intrigued as to whether it came from a man or a woman, who hated him or her.

If Maud had stumbled upon the right man to fire her intellect and marshal her energies, she had made an unhappy mistake where the heart was concerned. Beecham was a notorious womaniser who found it irksome to be faithful. He had already been involved in one divorce scandal, and had broken the dreams of a number of women who had hoped for more than lust. Lady Cunard was to endure in his affections longer than most, but their relationship went forward upon his terms, which were visibly selfish. Maud was careful never to call him anything but 'Mr Beecham' or 'Sir Thomas' (after his knighthood in 1916), and she never lived with him, but she admitted to Cecil Beaton years later that Beecham resented people who loved him. 'He's very grudging', she said. She knew, therefore, that he resented her love, but who can determine *not* to love by design?

The Beecham liaison also soured Maud's already difficult relationship with her daughter. It had never been good, as the two women had been virtual strangers and Maud had been a lamentably neglectful mother, though perhaps no more so than many others in her position. Nancy's biographer allows that Lady Cunard was not dramatically worse than other mothers, and that Nancy was not ill-treated. She was not, however, given much time. Now that she was on the threshold of womanhood, with a mind very vigorous for a girl her age, she watched her mother cavort with a famous conductor. She told Diana Cooper (then Lady Diana Manners) that her mother was a hypocrite, and that if this affair with Beecham were to continue then she, Nancy, could do as she liked. There was even an occasion when Nancy participated in a parlour game in which players were required to tell who they would most like to see come into the room. It was an innocent and silly game, much loved by adolescents, but Nancy's choice was far from innocent. 'Lady Cunard *dead*', she announced.

Nancy was, of course, deeply attached to old G.M., and she witnessed his suffering when he realized that his 'ideal' woman had forsaken him. It is small wonder she was angry. Moore never allowed himself bitterness, but he did let slip some gently sarcastic remarks in his letters which concealed a gnawing sense of loss. 'Of course life is intolerable if it be not always at concert pitch', he told her (was the pun intended?), and he confessed he found Beecham's taste questionable. Why did he dilute *Tristan* and the *Siegfried Idyll* with Delius rather than leave the original versions as they stood? 'It never occurred to me that these works required to be rewritten.' None of this had the smallest effect on Maud, whose adoration was carried to the summit of excitement.

Lady Cunard's reputation as a hostess was now growing apace, despite the fears expressed by such as Lloyd George. In keeping with her new status on the London scene, she decided to adopt a new name. 'Maud' was undeniably prosaic and dreary, virtually the most unsuitable name a woman of spirit could possibly have. Emeralds were her favourite jewels—she wore them all the time— so why not 'Emerald Cunard'? Some had already nicknamed her 'Emerald' before she made the decision, so the transition from one name to another was easy. One friend wickedly suggested that 'Emerald' was hardly appropriate, since there was nothing green about Lady Cunard. The one person who had no idea, and had not been informed, was G.M. At the end of a charming letter to him, she signed 'Maud Emerald', adding in brackets that this was her new name. G.M. was disconcerted, to say the least. What could 'Maud Emerald' mean? Only one thing, surely: she had married again, and the lucky man was Mr Emerald. G.M. took out the telephone directory and searched frenetically for the name of his rival. No Mr Emerald. Was it a mere whimsy, this new name? He could not bear the uncertainty. What if it were true? G.M. sat down and wrote a plaintive letter to Maud Emerald begging elucidation. 'A yes or a no will be enough', he said. 'You cannot fail to understand that it is unfair to leave a man who has loved you dearly for more than thirty years in doubt.'

The following day G.M. could contain himself no longer. The letter would take days to arrive, the reply even longer. He must know. He sent forthwith a telegram: WHO IS EMERALD ARE YOU MARRIED? G.M. Before he could receive a reply to this anxious message G.M. encountered Sir Joseph Duveen, who found him incredibly distraught, pacing up and down like a caged animal. He looked ill. G.M. explained the cause of his worry, compounded by the knowledge that there was, after all, a Mr Emerald; he had found him in another directory, and he was a manufacturer of paint! Duveen gently explained that Lady Cunard had frequently been called Queen of the Emeralds, and that there was no question of a mysterious man, let alone a marriage. The relief was so great that G.M. began to cry. To Edmund Gosse he wrote that day, 'Rossetti says in a little poem that the greatest happiness is the passing of pain, and yesterday I felt he was right.'

When Lady Cunard had first moved to London, she had taken the Asquiths' house at 20 Cavendish Square while they occupied 10 Downing Street. At last she could decorate according to her own taste after years of 'making do' with the grim oppressiveness of Nevill Holt, its Great Hall and its flagstone floors. She bought furniture and paintings as easily as she would buy flowers or hats, for she was still rich, the Beecham ambitions not having yet swallowed her fortune. She really came to prominence, however, when she took the lease on a large house in Grosvenor Square which became, in the twenties and thirties, her *salon* and where she presided over a style of entertaining which was to make her the twentieth-century equivalent of Lady Holland in an earlier time. One of her closest friends, the American-born Member of Parliament and arch-snob Chips Channon, described the Grosvenor Square attraction in his diary:

It was in her house in Grosvenor Square that the great met the gay, that statesmen consorted with society, and writers with the rich—and where, for over a year the drama of Edward VIII was enacted. It had a rococo atmosphere—the conversation in the candlelight, the elegance, the bibelots and the books: more, it was a rallying point for most of London society: only those that were too stupid to amuse the hostess, and so were not invited, were disdainful. The Court always frowned on so brilliant a salon: indeed Emerald's only failures were the two Queens and Lady Astor and Lady Derby. Everyone else flocked, if they had the chance. To some it was the most consummate bliss even to cross her threshold. She is as kind as she is witty, and her curious mind, and the lilt of wonder in her voice when she says something calculatedly absurd, are quite unique.

Another entry in Channon's diary conveys some of the excitement she aroused. 'Emerald was gay, exquisite, full of life and fun and we sat enthralled for three hours. She is an amazing dazzling creature . . . her spritely gaiety is infectious.' Osbert Sitwell likened her to a tortoiseshell wind that rustles through a room, billowing the curtains, quickening the inanimate as it passes, and Roderick Cameron, quoting this, agrees that to his own recollection she was exactly like that. 'She stood in the door or came into a room, and immediately there was tension in the air, a nervous crackling; people, one knew, were on their mettle.' George Moore, too, noticed this amazing life-giving quality which bristled around her, and though he would still rather she had bestowed her sun upon him in intimate *tête-à-tête*, he could not withhold his admiration. 'I was glad to see you brightening as usual the lives of dull people', he said. Sir Thomas Beecham was never so gracious.

Emerald's power to bewitch was so tangible that there was always the danger she would overwhelm everybody present. James Lees-Milne said her personality was so strong that she monopolized. But if she did so, it was never by intent. She was neither selfish nor complacent, her aim being to stimulate conversation, not appropriate or usurp it. She would subtly mould the conversation and point it in the most interesting direction; if that appeared too dominant a role, it could only be because others were not sharp enough to follow. Moore chastized her for being addicted to an audience. Not so; she wanted to prod the audience and watch them addict each other. She seemed to be showing off when she was in fact searching. Her mind was incisive, as brilliant as diamond and as keen, 'as nimble and quick as an aria from *Figaro*', wrote Roderick Cameron: 'she was Elizabethan in her robustness of spirit'. Robust, but fine and subtle too, with a subtlety which was quite lost on cruder hostesses such as Laura Corrigan. Sacheverell Sitwell remembered her 'wit, subtlety and nuance'; only the most alert minds could discern such qualities behind an appearance of frivolity.

Not surprisingly, the fresh vigour of her mind led many to depict Emerald as an eternally Spring-like figure, enemy to the staid and the hackneyed. Her mother had called her 'Primavera', a name which G.M. had found especially fitting. Virtually everybody, however, when called upon to describe her, was drawn to use a bird simile, for her physical appearance, as much as her alertness and swiftness, inevitably suggested a bird. 'Her appearance was exquisite in an original way,' wrote Harold Acton, 'like a brilliant humming-bird.' She was 'Lady Amherst's pheasant' (Kenneth Clark); 'a twittering, bejewelled bird' (Chips Channon); 'a canary flitting from perch to perch and scattering feathers and shrill cries' (James Lees-Milne); 'a jewelled bird uncaged' (Diana Cooper); 'a yellow canary' (Mrs Greville); 'an inebriate canary' (Cynthia Asquith); 'instinctive and courageous as a sparrow-hawk' (George Moore, who also noted that she had the bright eyes of a bird). Some, less kindly, turned the bird simile against her, like Virginia Woolf, who described her as 'a ridiculous little parakeet-faced woman', and another close friend, who hit upon 'a canary of prey'—a nice turn of phrase but with little justification in fact.

Emerald's face, too, seemed to excite near-unanimity of approbation. She gave an impression of perky prettiness, which was quite charming in its effect, even in her sixties. Chips Channon said she had a 'pretty, wrinkled, Watteau face', and that she appeared 'aged, wrinkled, vivacious and glittering in the candle-light'. To James Lees-Milne upon first encounter she was 'small and incredibly vivacious and about seventy'. [She was then seventy-one.] 'She has a white powdered, twisted little face and deeply mascaraed eyes. She frolicked in like a gusty breeze, talking volubly, and quite unconscious of the impression she was making.' A week later, Lees-Milne returned to his description in more detail. 'She waltzed in on her small, beautiful little legs (the Sergeant* says I must notice her feet, the most beautiful in the world), looking frail and ill as the old do who are made up to the eyes. Hers had mysterious drops exuding from the corners.' Cecil Beaton's famous photograph, taken about the time Lees-Milne was writing, is a perfect visual compliment to this description. John Lehmann thought her eyes more like semi-precious stones than human eyes, '*trouvailles* applied to the face in whose glaze none of the transitory emotions of the soul could be seen to stir, an effect no doubt produced by the severe face-lifting she had undergone'. Peter Quennell noted the innumerable tiny wrinkles on her skin, which had none the less kept the fineness and softness which customarily vanish during middle-age. There was, he said, a dark line encircling the inner margin of her eyelids, her hair was still ash-blonde, and she had a slightly receding chin. She wore youthful colours, pale blues and pinks. The whole gave 'a beguiling air of spontaneity'. One of the varieties of make-up she used had the unfortunate property of attracting wasps in swarms around her; it must, thought Diana Cooper, be made of wasps' vomit. Emerald changed to another brand which attracted a wasp of another breed; Harold Nicolson said she looked like a third-dynasty mummy painted pink by amateurs. Roderick Cameron, a committed devotee, spoke of her 'fragile' appearance:

> The door into her sitting-room would open and in would prance Emerald, a figure painted by Fragonard and Greuze and Marie Laurencin, a composition in which all three had had a hand. When I write 'prance' I mean it literally; Emerald had an extraordinary walk, like a temperamental race-horse being led to the paddock. She had tiny ankles and feet, and her feet came right up off the ground, stamping, almost it might be called, like a doe. I once saw her from the window of a car, walking down Piccadilly by herself, and it is a picture of her I have never forgotten.

She was also, said Cameron, one of the best-dressed women he had ever met. 'Her toilet had about it a great sense of luxury, as sumptuous almost as a Tiepolo fresco, rich but never vulgar.' She

* Stuart Preston

had a quantity of hats, feathered, that 'sat lightly on her small head, as lightly as her tiny satin feet trod the floor'.

Habitually, she wore three strings of pearls, but would take them off when the lights went down at the opera and stuff them, clattering, into her bag. Or, in her box (known as the omnibus box because there were always such a crowd of friends and paying patrons with her), she would thrust them into someone's hand, Baron Radowitz's for example, with the request, 'Hold on to those for me, dear, they're far too heavy for me to wear.'

Even Lady Cunard's speech, the manner of it as much as the matter, was unique, calling forth spirited attempts from writers to capture it. She would call one 'dear' in the most surprised tone, pausing before and after the word, before making some outrageously iconoclastic remark, as if she lived in a state of perpetual astonishment at the follies and comedy of the world. Her voice fluctuated, undulated, with 'trilling cadences' (according to Peter Quennell), 'like the springtime song of a delighted canary'. To herald an irony or a paradox, she would say 'You know' in a tone of utter disbelief, the first word high-pitched, the second emphatic and in a lower key. It could hardly fail to win attention for what followed. There was a curious, unparalleled gaiety in the way she used voice and inflection. Peter Quennell said that her high spirits 'appeared to arise from regions far below the surface, irradiating her whole demeanour, lending an electric quality to her smallest gestures, giving her flow of talk, however inconsequent, a curious prismatic sparkle'. James Lees-Milne captured the delight of listening to Emerald Cunard in a few lines:

> All sorts of nonsense sparkled off her like miniature fireworks. Emerald gets gay on one sip of cherry brandy and pours forth stories helter-skelter, wholly unpremeditated, in an abandoned, halting, enquiring manner that appears to be ingenuous, and is deliberate. Her charm can be devastating.

Since her wit was fanciful, always unexpected, always amusing, always startling, it was appropriate that she should be endowed naturally with a voice of wonder, and the art to use it as an instrument and not merely a vessel of communication.

So totally urban a character did Lady Cunard become that she positively dreaded an excursion into the country, and when called upon to make one, she would not compromise her chic with head scarves or wellington boots. It required a tremendous imaginative jolt even to remember that she had known country life intimately in the first years of her marriage. Emerald in a field was, in Roderick Cameron's words, 'like putting a Sèvres vase in a hen-coop'. The incongruity of it was simply funny. 'All those views make me dizzy,' she said, and when indoors she would pull down the blinds, saying, 'I hate the sun. I hate the elements. We must get away from nature, or we shall get nowhere.' She was the very antithesis of Rousseauesque. Nor did she care for the traditional country pastimes of a lady. She loathed parlour games, and never so much as owned a knitting-needle. Indeed, it is no exaggeration to say that Lady Cunard lived for music, literature, conversation and romantic attachments, probably in that order. Rural pleasures which formed a natural part of Lady Desborough's life were quite unknown to Lady Cunard.

Gamely, she tried not to appear *de trop*. On a visit to Diana Cooper at her farm near Bognor, she insisted on carrying the milk in a pail after Diana had milked the cow. She wore high-heeled shoes, pearls, and a leopard-skin coat. The cow dimly realized that leopard-skin was not human, and butted her to the ground.

Emerald was abstemious. She rarely drank more than a mild glass of hock, and ate the tiniest portions, in keeping with the little bird she was said to resemble. At the first sign of a cold, she would fast relentlessly for several days, while her guests ate as much as they wanted. (On one occasion Princess Bibesco passed out during dinner. 'Her Highness has fainted,' said Emerald to the butler. 'Give Her Highness a little brandy.' The butler replied, not quietly enough, 'Her Highness has had seven brandies since dinner.')

She could sing, play the piano (Beethoven and Chopin sonatas especially), and above all she would read, endlessly and comprehensively. When the last guest had gone, Emerald's reading would begin. She suffered from insomnia to such an extent that she would spend half the night reading, and with blithe disregard for other people's habits, telephone a friend at two or three in the morning to read out a passage she particularly liked, or discuss a character in Balzac or Suetonius. These literary telephone chats in the dead of night might easily go on for over an hour and, despite their having been woken up, her victims usually found such calls invigorating. They happened to Patrick Leigh-Fermor, to Harold Acton, to Roderick Cameron, to James Lees-Milne, to Peter Coats, and dozens of others. None was tempted to consider her behaviour selfish. She had herself given such pleasure during the day, why should she not be indulged when sleeplessness beset her? Many of them intuited that Emerald was far more lonely than her gregarious life would seem to indicate, but it was a loneliness without the sour tinge of sadness. She simply dreaded being left alone with the night. Besides, she well knew that her friends enjoyed these late-night calls. From anyone else, they would not even have been tolerated.

Frequent tribute has been paid to Lady Cunard's kindness and warmth of heart. She was, wrote Acton, capable of profound affection, and her affections were, moreover, enduring and genuine. She knew how to make friendship precious. Again, there were dozens of people whom she helped. She possessed, as we have said, an extraordinary ability to detect the qualities and talents of people who might have passed unnoticed by others (at least two of her friends have independently compared her to a water-diviner with his twig) and she liked nothing better than to help promote these talents and bring them out. She was justifiably proud of her successes. If there was a young author whom she wished to encourage, she would not only praise his work in the right places, but buy twenty or more copies of his latest book and distribute them. This was rare and true patronage. Her judgement was almost unfailingly sound. She had wisdom, and the tact to withhold advice when she sensed it would not be welcome. Advice to herself she never bothered to give. Emerald was a woman entirely foreign to the sterile habit of introspection.

She was not, however, a saint. Surprising shortcomings freckled her character. Though she adored giving, she hated receiving gifts and lacked even the grace to feign a pleasure. A guest would arrive with a parcel, perhaps carefully chosen, and Emerald would place it aside unopened, uninspected. There was, too, an old-fashioned conventional side to her which married ill with her mock-heroic wit. Certain topics were declared '*on*pleasant' and discussion about them forbidden. *Gros mots* never passed her lips. She stuck rigidly to certain precepts and cared not if others regarded them with amusement. 'A gentleman does not blow his nose in public', she said, and 'a lady does not show her garters'. She sat with a perfectly straight back, demanding similar attention from her guests; she only lounged in private. A sharp edge was thereby kept to the conversation; floppy bodies hide floppy minds. Emerald's conventional traits were soon to be cruelly tried by the behaviour of her daughter Nancy.

She was, moreover, unsufferably rude to waiters, telephonists and chefs, berating them for the smallest offence and calling them Nazis and Bolsheviks. When annoyed, she rarely managed to keep her temper or dissemble serenity, and many of her friends were deeply shocked by this unexpected splash of vulgarity.

There were certainly a few, notably the inhabitants of Bloomsbury, who could not stand Emerald at all, for various reasons. Lady Astor thought her a disintegrating influence, if only because she was a Californian with a vague pedigree instead of an accomplished daughter of one of the best Virginian families. Perhaps not jealousy, but certainly irritation at Emerald's popularity fed Lady Astor's animosity. Evelyn Waugh said she was 'an old trout . . . gibbering down the telephone' who always gave him the shivers. That view, also, need not be taken too seriously; to be insulted by Waugh was often a proof of excellence. The wicked wit and Member of Parliament Malcolm Bullock boasted that he had refused sixty-eight invitations from Lady Cunard in one year, whereas he was precisely the kind of intelligent talker and amusing raconteur one would expect to enjoy Emerald's society. Perhaps he was a bad listener; he chose instead to accept Lady Colefax's invitations, knowing that he could talk at Argyll House for as long as he liked without fear of the hostess making a remark which bettered his own. Nor was Max Beerbohm especially fond of the lady. When Lord Berners told him that Emerald was in absolutely wonderful form, that she never changed, Beerbohm murmured, 'I am sorry to hear that.' Noël Coward and Emerald squabbled in public. Virginia Woolf said Emerald did not know one picture from another and had a drawing-room filled with the riff-raff of London, which was demonstrably silly. Lytton Strachey was even more damning. 'Lady Cunard is rather a sport', he wrote to Mary Hutchinson, 'with her frankly lower-class bounce; she makes the rest of 'em look like the withered leaves of Autumn, poor things. But she herself I fancy is really pathetic too. So lost — so utterly lost!' How strangely wrong can so many bright people be! Without prejudice, it is now perfectly clear that Strachey's assessment was hasty and immature. Lady Cunard was the last person to evoke pathos, and if lower-class bounce is the kind of quality possessed by Charlie Chester or Tommy Handley (and what else could it be?), then it found no echo in Emerald's behaviour.

The obvious answer to critics, which may contain at least some of the truth, is that Lady Cunard was just a trifle too successful, too popular, inspired too much affection. While other hostesses were busy gathering celebrities, as Lady Colefax did, Emerald, by 1930, had become a celebrity herself.

An evening with Lady Cunard usually began with some anxiety, owing to her compulsive unpunctuality. The young Robert Boothby thought that it was part of her act always to appear late, an indulgence of her sense of the dramatic which she derived, probably, from Beecham. If so, then Beecham was not especially pleased with this manifestation of his influence. There was an occasion when Sir Thomas was giving a concert at the Sheldonian in Oxford, and kept the audience waiting until Emerald had arrived, on the arm of Kenneth Clark. Clark recalled, 'when I led this painted Jezebel, chattering like a parakeet, to her place in the middle of the auditorium, Sir Thomas turned round and said "You're late. Sit down."' Even for lectures she would turn up well after the lecturer had begun, and if slides were being shown, the audience would know Lady Cunard had arrived by the shadow of her osprey feathers bobbing up and down on the screen as she made her way to her seat. It is doubtful whether this really was a theatrical gesture; unpunctuality was as much an addiction for her as gambling is for other people. When the King (Edward VIII) was guest of honour at a dinner given by Chips Channon, and Emerald had been accorded the place next to His Majesty, everyone had to sit down without her because she was so late, causing Chips no end of worry. This was, after all, little less than treason! Emerald bounced in, apologized, and all was well. King Edward rather enjoyed that kind of informality—it made him feel human. Had his mother, Queen Mary, been sitting in his place, Emerald's lateness would have had catastrophic social consequences.

The only man known to have reprimanded her for this habit was Lord d'Abernon. Emerald was three-quarters of an hour late for a luncheon party he was giving. 'My dear,' she said, 'I was held up. I went to buy a chandelier.' Lord d'Abernon fixed her firmly with his eye and told her, 'I once had a friend who bought a chandelier *after* lunch.'

Most curious of all, Lady Cunard was late even for her own parties. Guests would arrive for dinner at the house in Grosvenor Square and find everyone there except the hostess. If they already knew each other, there was no great problem, but a stray ambassador or a young author invited for the first time would find that he had to fend for himself for perhaps half an hour and might look as if he had come to the wrong house. Then, last of all, in would come Emerald. She was, said Harold Acton, 'always worth waiting for, a scented breeze of welcome'. Elsewhere he writes, 'The arrival of the hostess was like a burst of melody.'

Rather belatedly, she then introduced various people in a few, brief, incongruous phrases with a touch of fantasy all her own. If they had nicknames, bestowed upon them by herself, they were introduced by these, without reference to true identity, sometimes to total strangers: 'The Idealist', 'The Great Lover', 'Lord Paramour', 'Charming Prince Florimund'. Many thus designated shrank with embarrassment, but there was nothing they could do to stem Emerald's flow of whimsy. Others had slightly more elaborate but no less capricious descriptions:

'This is our great poet from the Foreign Office.'

'This is Gerald Berners—he's a musician, and a saucy fellow.'
'This is Dr Stewart, a worldly prelate, the final authority on Pascal and a professional beauty.'
'This is Mr Evan Morgan, who looks like the poet Shelley and whose mother makes birds' nests.'
'This is Lord Alington, dear. He drives in a taxi at dawn from Paris to Rome, wearing evening dress and a gardenia, without any *luggage*.'
'This is Lady Kelmsley, whose husband owns all the newspapers.'
'This is Mr Peter Hesketh, who owns a whole town.'

James Lees-Milne, then in charge of the National Trust, was introduced as the man 'who looks after all the public houses', and an unfortunate lady as the person whose mother was killed on the Underground. One guest at least took exception to being exposed in a nutshell. Prince Youssoupoff, described as 'the man who murdered Rasputin', turned on his heels and left. The phrases spun out of Emerald's mind without preparation, often placing her in the ridiculous situation of introducing people to others whom they had known intimately for years. Unperturbed, she sailed on to the next one. There is a busy host in New York now, Milton Goldman the theatrical agent, who uses much the same encapsulatory technique, and was once seen introducing Sheridan Morley to his father Robert Morley.

At the dining-table Lady Cunard's vitality utterly dominated the proceedings. It 'flowed like champagne into the conversation' (Acton); 'Emerald's prattle, sometimes very funny nonsense, flowed like a river' (Lees-Milne). She liked to suggest a topic, unfailingly the most unexpected and introduced in the most nonchalant manner, and then see what happened. One such opening was, 'Tiberius must have been charming. Why are so many historians against him?' If that did not produce some entertaining talk, she would abruptly change to another subject, equally inconsequential, so that she gave the false, but intended, impression of being quite scatter-brained. Her mind leapt from one reflection to another, which might be unrelated in any obvious way, sometimes in mid-sentence, and it was up to the guests, however eminent they might be, to keep up with her. She had a gift for paring her narrative of all extraneous detail, making it glide and prance like a gazelle, and could hold the attention of her listeners better than any other hostess. Many there were who preferred to listen to Lady Cunard than make a contribution, which was likely to be ponderous by comparison. She was also blessed with a prodigious memory, which often made her conversation enlightening as well as fascinating.

Should the talk threaten to subside, she would throw in a ball and scatter fresh ripples around the table, conducting her guests with the same deft control that her idol Beecham used on the Covent Garden orchestra. She welcomed some harmless friction which might put someone on the spot, and would mischievously encourage dispute, though not if it involved the tearing apart of someone else's character; she did not approve of malicious gossip, in contrast with Mrs Greville, who thrived upon it. Nor did she approve of coarse language, frowning upon Mrs Cory when the latter had the temerity to mention the word 'brothel'. Emerald had very strong ideas upon what were, and were not, permitted subjects for ladies and gentlemen to discourse upon. All the more mortifying, then, that her own daughter used the word 'fuck' as if it were the most necessary ingredient in daily conversation; nobody knows if she ever spoke in this way in her mother's presence. As they saw less and less of each other, she quite probably did not.

Emerald would make exception for G.M., who liked to dwell upon the most gory details of his operations, especially if they involved the bowels, but would gingerly steer others away from the subject at the first opportunity. To her discredit, she did not much care for two of her guests sinking into a conversation together, but would interrupt them and prise the conversation on to the table. This gave the impression that she wanted all subjects to start and finish with herself, much as it does by etiquette with a royal personage, but the truth was she thought it bad manners to indulge in tête-à-têtes when others were present. Dinner conversation must be general.

Emerald's detractors observed only the surface of her technique.

Lytton Strachey told Mary Hutchinson, 'That blasted woman wouldn't let Max [Beerbohm] open his mouth once—a ceaseless stream of pointless babble, really too maddening! In a few asides edged in between her blitherings, he seemed charming.' Harold Nicolson attended 'a ghastly dinner supposed to be literary' at which, he said, gloom hung over the table.

A little of Emerald's dinner-table manner has come down to us through the assiduous efforts of diarists. There was an occasion when conversation turned to the animal world and its relation to the human. Archie Clark Kerr, sometime British Ambassador in Moscow, later to take the same post in Washington, said that everyone had an *alter ego* among the animals, and they then had to decide which animal concealed the identity of each person present. Clark Kerr opined that Emerald was to be found in the fruit-eating bat, at which, according to Peter Quennell, she assumed an expression of half-horrified, half-enchanted surprise. 'Dear me, what is the Ambassador *saying*?' Kenneth Clark, also present, thought she looked rather put out for the first time in her life. To prove his point, Clark Kerr went on to say that the wives of Scottish fishermen, when their husbands were away, made love to the seals. 'Archie, you must please stop,' exclaimed Emerald. 'To what do you suppose he is referring? Can it be something—something they call *bestiality*?'

Cecil Beaton recalled another typically whimsical remark. 'Really, we can't watch people trying to lift up a Scot's kilt to see what's underneath. We all know what's underneath: it can't be anything new! It isn't as if it were a sea anemone or a salamander!' The choice of over-emphatic words turns a trite observation, not necessarily very funny, into a hysterical fantasy.

The slow-witted and self-important might find themselves mercilessly teased. Kenneth Clark said that whenever Emerald was faced with a pompous public man 'she would whizz round him like a humming bird till he became completely dizzy and began to doubt his own identity'. Clark was present when the victim was a heavy rich American called Myron Taylor. Emerald deflated her guest at one stroke.

'Now, Mr Taylor, what do you think about incest?'

'Well, er, ah, well, there seems to be no doubt at all that biologically the results are deleterious. In some of our small prairie towns statistics show . . .'

'But, Mr Taylor, what about Siegmund and Sieglinde?' And Lady Cunard proceeded to sing the end of Act I of *The Valkyrie*. Mr Taylor went on as if no interruption had occurred.

'. . . and it is proved conclusively in some Near Eastern countries . . .'

'Kenneth, what do you think about incest?'

'I'm in favour of it, Emerald.'

'Oh Kenneth, what a wicked thing to say! Think of the Greeks.' She then recited a passage from the *Oresteia* while Mr Taylor looked bemused and nervous. 'But all the same it was just a silly old taboo, like Pythagoras saying it was wicked to eat beans. Mr Taylor, do you think it wicked to eat beans?' Clark noticed that by this time the poor Mr Taylor was sweating profusely.

Emerald's habit of teasing her guests did not stop short of the great and influential. One day in 1935 she entertained to lunch two cabinet ministers, Walter Elliot and Anthony Eden, along with various foreign notables from whom it was important cabinet discussions should be kept secret. Emerald's question to Eden was impossibly indiscreet in the circumstances. 'You are all wrong about Italy,' she said. 'Why should she not have Abyssinia? You must tell me that.' Eden responded flippantly, so Harold Nicolson tells us. In similar vein, she provoked the Italian Ambassador, Count Dino Grandi, accusing him of having led Mussolini's march on Rome, then provoked Foreign Office friends by pretending that she was violently in favour of Mussolini. She hoped thereby to tease out some important admission. It was all fun to her. Osbert Sitwell once wrote that one should not tell the truth to the Emeralds of this life.

Lady Cunard would have understood Sitwell's warning. She herself maintained that one should never be sincere. 'The whole structure of society falls if you start to be sincere,' she said, 'and you can hardly ever afford to tell the truth.'

When she was not teasing, the epigrams, aphorisms, *bons mots*, 'some mild, some penetrating, darted like flashes from a crystal girandole'. Chips Channon, who paid this tribute, recorded some of her remarks in his diary. On Wavell: 'The trouble about Wavell is that he is riddled with idealism.' On Margot Asquith: 'black and wicked and with only a nodding acquaintance with truth.' On Tacitus, who did not think well of her beloved Tiberius: 'he was the creature of Germanicus, and a gross libeller and pamphleteer. As for Capri! It was only the Chequers of the time.'

Her views on the arts, other than opera, have filtered through the years. John Masefield she dismissed as belonging to the 'police gazette' school of poetry, while John Donne was 'a most lecherous poet'. Somerset Maugham, whom she respected, was not above teasing. He once attempted to excuse himself early from one of her soirées, resisting her entreaties on the grounds that he had to go to bed early, a point of view which the insomniac Emerald could not possibly understand. 'I have to keep my youth,' he said. 'Then why don't you bring him with you?' was Lady Cunard's arch reply.

Mrs Greville's uncommonly large quails were obviously blown up with a bicycle pump. James Lees-Milne remembers this absurd remark: 'Robert Byron's father used to poke his daughters with a sadistic fork.'

There were moments of splendidly unorthodox wisdom, not especially profound, but memorable if only because they were so original. 'You forget that most people do have tongues because you never see them, but a tongue is a charming addition if you like a person . . . teeth should never be a reality, only an indication.' 'A witty woman can never keep a man. She can't afford to laugh at the wrong moment.' 'Only a brilliant man knows how to be ridiculous.' 'Supreme self-confidence is the essential quality if one is to achieve anything; and one must be an expert on at least one subject.'

Emerald's direct, challenging approach could be unnerving, even frightening, to a young man. There were few with the confidence of Noël Coward to cope with her sudden sallies. He upset her by calling her 'Darling' when, in her view, he did not know her well enough. She called him 'common', but there is no evidence that Coward was downhearted for a second. At the dinner-table, one never knew whom she would turn to next, and the young might perspire with apprehension lest they be placed in the centre of the spotlight by a prickly question from the hostess. On a first visit you might hope to escape attention, but such hope was usually vain. When Nigel Nicolson was 19, Emerald shouted at him, down the length of the table, 'Are you in love with anyone at the moment?' Laura, Duchess of Marlborough, was only 18 when Emerald bade everyone keep quiet with the terrifying remark, 'I think it is time we heard something from little Laura Charteris.' Lord Ivor Churchill, aged 19, might well have wished for less attention from Lady Cunard, who kept seizing his 'dear little sympathetic hand'.

The young inevitably benefited from their hostess's slightly intimidating manner, for once the finger was pointed, they were obliged to acquit themselves with some sort of honour. It was education through alarm and through comedy. Emerald made a point of mixing the young and inexperienced with the old and accomplished, the 'lions' with the 'gazelles'. The old would feel young and careless, as Sacheverell Sitwell pointed out, and probably flattered too, while the young would feel they were at the centre of the nation's affairs listening to ambassadors and cabinet ministers. Of course, both were victims of their own vanity, but it was harmless enough. And what better lesson than to watch Emerald turn her probing, fresh and very personal mind upon the latent pomposities of public persons. She had, said Harold Acton, a delicate sense of comedy: 'she could enjoy a Malvolio and lead him on without cruelty.' Not for a second did one suspect her of real malice in her conversational pirouettes.

There was, too, calculated drama in her seemingly impulsive acts, as when she threw her copy of *Beaton's Book of Beauty*, in which she figured, into the fire, energetically poking the burning covers. 'He calls me a hostess,' she said, 'that shows he's a low fellow.' And what more theatrical than to call up the Postmaster-General to complain that her telephone was out of order?

Frequently, a dinner party at Grosvenor Square would terminate with a play-reading or recital, all the more memorable for being impromptu, and with a surprising cast-list. A soldier such as Wavell might recite Browning, and Lord Queensberry would follow with Shakespeare's sonnets, declaimed thunderously. Delius would sit at the piano and play one of his compositions. On one occasion at least,

Richard Strauss himself played selections from *Der Rosenkavalier*. Such were perfect endings to brilliant evenings, 'evenings when nothing in the world mattered but the purest art, whose essence was all around us like the fragrance of cassia.' This is Harold Acton's memory. Life at Grosvenor Square, he said, was thoroughly spent, not economized.

Lady Cunard's lightness of touch made her appear frivolous to the undiscerning, and the odd remarks which have been preserved, in stark print do little to dispel that notion. In truth, she was deeply civilized, even scholarly. Her patronage of the Old Vic and the Phoenix Society, the encouragement she gave to writers and playwrights who on occasion gave the first performances of their works in her drawing-room when less adventurous theatrical managements looked askance, are of course no real indication, for one needs only money to be a patron. But when the last guest had gone home and Emerald began her nightly struggle with insomnia, her real interests would be paramount. She would read for hours, and telephone friends up to three or four in the morning to discuss a poem of Horace, or a character in Saint-Simon, or Madame de Lieven, the works of Thomas Mann, Theocritus, Goethe, Santayana, Webster, Balzac. Balzac she read again and again, and Webster she knew by heart long before the revival of *The Duchess of Malfi* brought his work to wider notice. She would never accept at face value a new book, loudly acclaimed, as would, for example, Lady Colefax, for whom the fame mattered more than the worth. She deplored the lack of culture among many Americans and the English middle classes, for whom a fascinating excursion into the etymology of 'euphemism' in the middle of the night would have held little charm. Lady Cunard was certainly far more than a social figure.

Living for art, Lady Cunard never aspired to political influence. She told how Curzon used to come straight from a Cabinet meeting and divulge the details of important discussions, but she attached no great significance to the antics of politicians, which she regarded with amusement. Those politicians whom she liked were welcomed for their extra-curricular interest in painting, opera or poetry. Like other hostesses, she was courted by the Nazi and Fascist

Ambassadors, Herr Ribbentrop and Count Grandi, who were quite possibly foolish enough to believe that Emerald Cunard represented the common view in England. She tended towards a reactionary stance, finding most manifestations of modern life irksome and unattractive, and for a while saw Hitler as the saviour of traditional values. For all that, her sole determined effort to sway men of power was her (unsuccessful) advocacy of the Order of Merit for George Moore.

There was, however, one person in the land with whom Lady Cunard's influence appeared to outsiders to be pervasive and potentially dangerous, because he, in turn, appeared to seek her counsel in preference to that of Ministers of State. This was no less than the heir to the throne, the Prince of Wales.

Emerald had known the Prince for many years before the crisis of 1936. He is on record as having dined with her as early as December, 1922. At that stage it was important for Emerald to secure the highest possible support for her crusade in favour of Thomas Beecham's beloved opera, and she even aspired to bringing the King and Queen on her side. This was Emerald's one lapse of taste, her one error of judgement. She was heard to say, 'Who do the King and Queen *see*? Who is in the King's *set*?' Even if the reigning monarch had a 'set', it would not have included Lady Cunard, of whom it was no secret that Queen Mary strongly disapproved. The Prince had very different ideas about whom he should mix with.

When Mrs Simpson came upon the scene, Emerald's association with the heir to the throne intensified. She liked the elegant American woman. 'Little Mrs Simpson is a woman of character and reads Balzac,' she said. This endeared the Prince to her, for a while. He would sometimes turn up unexpectedly, at first with both Mr and Mrs Simpson in tow. At a dinner Emerald gave for Diana Cooper at the beginning of 1935, the doorbell rang at 11.30 p.m., and there were the three of them. The whole crowd went on for another meal (supper!) at the Embassy Club. 'You are not David, Sir, but Daniel,' Emerald told the Prince.

As the relationship of Prince and *divorcée* grew more obvious, London society divided into two factions, those who saw danger ahead, and those rallying around Lady Cunard who were in favour of the fresh, vital, young spirit which lay in wait to galvanize the throne. The Prince and Mrs Simpson wanted very much to see a play called *A Storm in a Teacup* in which was depicted a relationship very like their own, but considered that their presence at such a performance might be *mal vu*. So Emerald arranged for the most important scene to be performed for them privately after supper at her house.

There were times when Emerald's pre-eminence among the Prince's friends was questioned, apparently to her fury. She took the Royal Box and the Bedford box next to it at the Opera House, for a performance of *Ariadne auf Naxos*. Too many people turned up, and there was an unseemly scrum to be with Mrs Simpson, now the acknowledged favourite and in the view of many, probably a future Queen. Emerald was separated from her, even her friends noticing that she scowled. On another occasion, she was put out to discover that not only was she a guest of Mrs Simpson at the Bryanston Square apartment, but so were Lady Colefax and Lady Astor. All three were seething with petulance at finding the other two there. Emerald tried shouting 'Your Majesty' (the Prince had by now acceded as Edward VIII) but she was ignored. One glorious snub she received was from Noël Coward, whom she asked to join her in a quiet supper for the King. 'I am sick to *death* of having quiet suppers with the King, *and* Mrs Simpson,' screamed Coward. 'Tell her I can't.'

Nancy Astor was particularly vehement in her anger at Lady Cunard's infiltration. She thought none but the best Virginian families should be allowed close to the throne, and announced that Emerald was 'a disintegrating influence'. This, in fact, was unfair, for Emerald's learning and musical sophistication could have been an influence for the good; it was far better that the King should rub shoulders with her than with the many empty socialites who worshipped the dust in his turn-ups. In personality and style as well as learning, Emerald was considerably superior to the Prince of Wales, and Mrs Simpson, knowing this, brought him more and more into her circle, for his own benefit, to educate him. That Emerald's influence upon the Prince was not immediately discernible was entirely to his discredit.

Far more insidious was the suggestion that Lady Cunard was responsible for the King's pro-Nazi sympathies. When still Prince of Wales, he had made a notorious speech at the Annual Conference of the British Legion recommending that its members should 'stretch forth the hand of friendship' to Germany. This had caused no small rumpus, and in an effort to find a scapegoat it was put about by some that Lady Cunard had brought the Prince into the wrong company, notably that of Herr Ribbentrop. This, too, was unfair. Emerald was pleasant to Ribbentrop, but teased him as much as she teased other self-important men. She once told him that the French Ambassador thought highly of him, an idea which stunned him into silence. Emerald had simply invented it to test his reaction.

Peter Quennell tells the remarkable story of Wyndham Lewis lunching with Emerald and the Prince of Wales, Lewis pensive and taciturn, then nonchalantly placing a small pearl-handed revolver next to his wine glass. There was consternation among all present, yet no one dared utter a word. Emerald was the only person to have the presence of mind to rescue the situation. While everyone else pretended the pistol was not there, she picked it up, said what a pretty little pistol it was, admired its artistry, and dropped it into her hand-bag while continuing the conversation.

The Prince became King, and Emerald was seen to encourage the royal romance. She entertained the delightful idea that she would be appointed as Mistress of the Robes to Queen Wallis and would preside over a renaissance of artistic endeavour at the English Court. The King himself would be the enlightened patron of poets, painters, musicians. She took to referring to Edward VIII as 'our King' in a subtly proprietorial manner.

But there were signs that Emerald's glorious ambitions would come to little. She received an anonymous letter, beginning, 'You old bitch, trying to make up to Mrs Simpson, in order to curry favour with the King', and she was once hissed at a private dinner party. Her own star reached its lowest point when it was rumoured the King was growing tired of her, that he had always hated her, and would hate her again.

When the Abdication Crisis was brewing, Emerald was among

the first to receive news of what was afoot, though her information, as it happened, was incorrect. She plied Hore-Belisha with drink and was told that Baldwin had presented the King with an ultimatum: either he gave up Mrs Simpson, or the Government would resign. Hore-Belisha said the King was defiant, that he intended to marry Mrs Simpson in the chapel at Windsor, and that a new government would be in office within weeks. Emerald was very excited. The prospect of dreams coming true opened before her. Alas, it was not to be. Days later, Edward VIII was plain Duke of Windsor and an exile. Emerald told Sir Robert Bruce Lockhart, in bitter tones, that she blamed Mrs Simpson for the abdication.

Emerald was no more *persona grata* with the Court of George VI than she had been with that of George V. Her brief glimpse of Versailles was abruptly shut off. Gossips said that she took it very hard. The Duke and Duchess of Sutherland gave a ball to celebrate the coronation. George VI suggested that Lady Cunard might be invited after supper, by which time he and Queen Elizabeth would have left. So Emerald waited in Grosvenor Square for a telephone call to alert her to the departure of the sovereign, at which point her own presence would be welcome. It was a sad fall.

Queen Mary went so far as to forbid her family ever to have anything to do with Emerald. The order, of course, had to come through the reigning sovereign, now George VI, and the chief offenders, who must be kept in line, were the Duke and Duchess of Kent. Queen Mary wrote, (as recently quoted by Alistair Forbes),

the other day in my presence Bertie [George VI] told George [Duke of Kent] he wished him and Marina never to see Lady Cunard again and George said he would not do so. I fear she has done David [Edward VIII] a great deal of harm as there is no doubt she was great friends with Mrs S at one time and gave parties for her. Under the circumstances I feel none of us, in fact people in society, should meet her . . . I feel very strongly on the matter but several people have mentioned to me what harm she has done.

If this could be described as a social setback, it was as nothing

compared to the tragic consequences of Emerald's soured relationship with her daughter Nancy. This, too, she largely brought upon
herself. She had never made any secret of the fact that she
considered motherhood 'a low thing' and had wantonly neglected
her only child. Harold Acton, the only person to remain a friend of
them both, put it charitably when he wrote, 'Perhaps the daughters
of prominent hostesses are apt to feel like unwanted guests at home.
Left to the care of governesses, they nurse grudges along with their
dolls.' Nancy Cunard's grudge developed into the most implacable,
intolerant hatred.

She began by marrying a man she knew her mother would not
like, a Guards officer with little to recommend him. Still, Lady
Cunard gave her a house as a wedding present. The marriage was
doomed from the beginning, and soon fizzled out. Nancy then
became a rebellious young woman, fashioning her dress, language,
behaviour and friendships with a view to shocking as many people
as possible, paramount among whom must be her mother. She was
blatantly promiscuous, and, as if in recognition of her mother's
maternal failings, had her womb removed. She began to embrace
causes which her mother would find least attractive—
homosexuality, Communism, modern art, and most of all, negro
emancipation. Above all, she loathed the social life which her
mother led, despised its emptiness and what she considered its
hypocrisy. From the 1920s until the end of her life, she always
referred to her mother as 'Her Ladyship'.

The irony was, Nancy and Emerald had much in common.
Where Emerald was bird-like, Nancy, in Diana Mosley's apt
comparison, was snake-like. She was supremely intelligent, wrote a
very good book on George Moore, and for a while published some
esoteric volumes under the imprint of the Hours Press (books
which are now extremely rare and pursued by collectors). She had
the same kind of squeaky voice as her mother, with a fine choice of
vocabulary and precise enunciation. Some thought her poetry very
fine. Kenneth Clark, comparing mother and daughter, invented a
neat antithesis. Nancy, he wrote, 'liked black people and squalor,
whereas her mother liked pink people and luxury'.

As Nancy Cunard's style of life evolved, it grew more and more
bizarre and self-damaging. She drank hugely all day long, but could

be persuaded to eat little more than a very thin slice of smoked salmon. 'Fucking food, darling,' she said, 'if only one didn't have to eat!' Norman Douglas said she had the appetite of a dyspeptic butterfly. Much of her was of heroic size. She encouraged non-European art, and would therefore wear not one, but thirty ivory bangles on her wrists. Her opinions were sound, as she was at heart a woman who cared genuinely about injustice and humbug, but she pushed them to volcanic excess. Whatever excited her disapproval was '*pestilential*, darling'. Her drinking was also carried to the most violent extremes. She would become 'incandescent with alcohol', uncontrollable, murderous. It has even been suggested that she might have tried to murder a policeman or two. It was Harold Acton, again, who declared that Nancy had 'the hard puritanical core of an extremist'.

Her finest expression of extremism was her love affair with the black musician Henry Crowder. Nancy had had many other affairs before, often with black people, but this was a defiant act against all the established *mores* of England at a time when there was no significant black population and prejudice and fear were both deeply ingrained in the national psyche.

Nancy had lived openly with Crowder, in Paris and London, for two years without anyone daring to mention the subject to Emerald, who could thereby comfortably pretend not to know. Nancy gave a party in the basement of a London hotel to raise money for seven negroes imprisoned in America; black and white people danced together, possibly for the first time in London, at this gathering. Augustus John was present. Mother and daughter had long since ceased to have any contact. Nancy's allowance had been stopped, though Emerald occasionally sent her clothes, which Nancy promptly gave to female black friends. Meanwhile, Emerald continued with her social life as if the most outrageous and controversial figure in London, inimical to everything she stood for, were not her own daughter. The contrast, and the irony, were overwhelmingly stark.

The open breach came when Margot Asquith (Lady Oxford) shouted on arrival for lunch one day, 'Well, Maud, what's Nancy up to now? Is it dope, drink, or niggers?' (Margot insisted on calling her Maud long after she had adopted her new name.)

The effect was catastrophic. Emerald managed to control herself in public, but she was deeply shocked, and very unhappy. She cried. Nancy had never cared for her, she said. Her daughter's behaviour, her contempt for the conventions, were beyond Emerald's comprehension. She had her daughter and her black lover followed by detectives, which only served the more to outrage Nancy, who shortly afterwards published a vitriolic pamphlet, entitled *Black Man and White Ladyship*, which was so nasty that it did more harm to the author than to its intended victim. In spite of the army of friends, said Nancy, Her Ladyship was in reality 'so alone . . . one touch of ridicule goes straight to her heart'. She was a snob and a hypocrite, with so little knowledge of art that she was habitually swindled by dealers. There was prurient *double-entendre* in the reference to how much blacks were in fact 'received' in society, however much Her Ladyship might deplore it.

Thomas Beecham tried to intercede, but the two women were by now so far apart that reconciliation was not even a possibility. Emerald, sickened by the thought of her daughter having sexual relations with a black man, threatened to have Crowder deported. This only made Nancy more intransigent.

Thereafter, Nancy was not mentioned in Emerald's presence. Mother and daughter never met again. Emerald even told Baron Radowitz that she had never had a child, and when on one unhappy occasion Peter Rodd touched upon the forbidden subject, Emerald quietly said, 'Mr Rodd, Nancy does not like me. It is a painful subject.' To intimates she would sometimes admit that she admired her daughter's talents, and that one could always forgive someone who was ill. For her part, Nancy was incapable of forgiveness. Her heart was big for everyone else, but closed to her mother. She told Diana Cooper that she viewed Her Ladyship with total objectivity. 'She was at all times very far from me.'

Emerald only saw Nancy once more, by accident. Driving down a London street one day after the war, her car had to swerve in order to avoid an obviously distraught skeletal figure who lurched in front. It was Nancy. No one in the car admitted to having recognized her. Emerald was unusually quiet for a long time afterward.

Though Nancy survived her mother by fifteen years, she became a gothic, unreal creature, hallucinatory, sordid, virtually inhuman. She continued to drink and to avoid food, with the result that at the end only bones remained. She had burned away the rest, as if the flesh had eaten itself. She died in the bleakest circumstances in Paris.

Nancy's promiscuity had caused distress and bewilderment to Emerald, who had always cherished quite different ideas about love. Physical passion was something she professed not to understand, claiming (absurdly) that she had never been alone with a man, and had never wanted to be. Stories that soldiers were fond of having girls against walls in the dark wartime streets of London horrified her. 'I am told they do these things,' she said. 'Whatever for?' Sex, in her view, had nothing whatever to do with love; she could not understand the need for it, and loudly asked why people did it. If one loved a person, one did not even think of sex. Still less did one think of marriage, the severest enemy of love and not a subject fit for sensitive people. '*Il n'y a pas d'hommes impuissants; il n'y a que des femmes maladroites*', was another of her pronouncements.

'Of course I know by this time that it is no part of your pleasure to see me hanging on to your words', George Moore had written. 'Your instinct was to love not to inspire love; to be loved bored you, and when the inevitable happened you passed on to another chapel to enter a new set of devotions.' Moore was the one man who had loved Emerald selflessly for a lifetime, gently irritating her with his uncommon loyalty. (This was yet another factor in Nancy's contempt for her mother; she knew and valued Moore deeply, and saw the unhappiness his devotion caused him. He once asked to see her bare back, some say it was actually her 'bum', and she obliged.) Emerald in her turn had loved Thomas Beecham for thirty-four years and had been treated shabbily by him. 'I pray that one day I may be sent to prison so that I may spend some weeks undisturbed', he had told her, scarcely bothering to conceal that he meant undisturbed by her. The most awful blow of her life came when, after lavishing most of her fortune to encourage Beecham's ambitions, after giving him her admiration and her heart for more than three decades, she heard, quite by accident, that he had married Betty Humby. The news, and the manner of it, crushed her spirit. She had previously questioned him about the rumours of his love affair, and he had told her that Betty Humby was 'impossible', descended from a long line of dentists. To then discover, in casual gossip at a formal dinner, that her beloved Thomas had deserted her, without even the courtesy of informing her, was as a sharp pain between the ribs. Yet she never spoke ill of him. Wistfully, she would ask acquaintances how he was, and her eyes would betray an enduring sadness. 'She will never know him as well as I do,' she said.

Yet she hardly ever ceased talking about love, and was not averse to some wild semi-public flirtations.* She was heard to declare that her life had been a whirlwind of passionate love affairs, a remark only fully sensible when one remembers that for Emerald 'passion' did not occur beneath bed-sheets. Whether one should kiss on the mouth or on the cheek was a subject she frequently raised, and some of her listeners afterwards thought that her ingenuous remarks were a pose. Pose or not, she permitted herself in old age some powerful flirtations with young men in every way the opposite of the rotund sarcastic man who had disappointed her. They were tall, elegant, cultured men, protégés whose careers she sought to advance, and whose artistic sensibilities she wished to nurture. The most important of these romantic attachments had as its object a brilliant young man at the Foreign Office, Nicholas Lawford.

Lawford was a poetic, attentive suitor in the best traditions of chivalry. He would pick early morning flowers every day and quietly hang them on her bedroom door before going off to Whitehall. She would write him the most effusive endearing letters, flickering with almost adolescent notions of romance. 'How happy I was with you, oh so happy', she wrote after an evening in Lawford's company. 'It was strange but I would not have had it otherwise. I have never been happy with anyone before.' Emerald, sitting up

* Sir Ronald Storrs recorded this snippet of Emerald's conversation: 'A young man called Glyn—I think he was the son of a bishop—asked me if ever I had been the mistress of a cabinet minister. I said, "You must let me think a little." He said, "What about George Wyndham?" I said, 'Well, I suppose I was kissing him a good deal in 1907 and 1908.'''

Mrs Ronnie Greville on the steps of her home, Polesden Lacey, with King Feisal and the Brazilian Ambassador

[Mr]s Ronnie Greville with [Lo]rd Cochrane, later Earl of [Du]ndonald (*left*) and H.R.H. [th]e Duke of York, later [Kin]g George VI (*right*)

Polesden Lacey, home of Mrs Ronnie Greville near Dorking, Surrey

late at night, would talk of poetry and of music in her letters, of love
and devotion, of her desire to give her admirer one moment of
happiness. 'Darling, in all the world there is no one like you', she
said, 'and I again reiterate, I am entirely yours. If you leave England
I must die, I can't go on. Everything I do in your absence is only to
fill in the time, for I long to be with you and only see life through the
magic of your lovely eyes.'

Many of her friends thought Emerald was simply playing with
Lawford's undoubtedly genuine affection. He wrote to her, just as
often, between appointments, and would have his letters delivered
by hand, constantly surprising her with an unplanned *billet-doux*.
She begged him to write her a poem. Her rhapsodic letters
demonstrate that her latent idealism, the purity of her spiritual
quest for an undemanding reciprocal adoration, was indeed
touched by the young man's attention. There was no play-acting in
the thoughts which were evidently consumed with his vision the
day long. She pictured the walls of his flat at Albany 'permeated
with love and suffering', declared that they could not dine there for
it was too unbearably romantic a place, and promised that she was
moved to the depths of her being for the first time in her life. 'You
are the world, your heart cannot be crushed like Atlas, nor your soul
dissolved . . .'

The most powerful impression is of a woman surrounded by
scores of friends, celebrated in cosmopolitan and intelligent society,
yet at heart so painfully alone that she did not scruple to declare
herself to a man forty years her junior, a man for whom she would
remain a '*flocon de neige*', admiring, if necessary, from a distance.
The great hostess wished nothing more than to be the subordinate
worshipper. She would see him in a crowd at the ball given by
Michael Duff for Princess Elizabeth, the heir to the throne, but she
would not interfere or attempt to monopolize him. 'I must not love
a star and try to touch it in its progress.'

Always it is the poetic expression which comes easily to her, not
the torrid or banal. The brittle, airy wit of her public life stood in
bold contrast to this deep flow of idealism which had never, in the
past, been satisfied. She told Lawford, 'I see you pale with
lassitude, stretched upon a bed which I have never seen. But music

brings you to me, and deep conversations . . . You have lit the only candle in my heart and its flame will burn throughout eternity.'

Eternity, for Lady Cunard, did not last long. A friend pointed out to Nicholas Lawford that this absurd *amitié amoureuse* was making him look a fool. Emerald's late discovery of her own personal Dante dribbled to its forlorn and realistic close. Had she not lived so much in literature she might have expected it.

Emerald's financial affairs had for long been lurching into a wretched state. Once a rich woman, she had neglected to look after her capital which had been progressively plundered by her own extravagance and her reckless support of Beecham-inspired schemes. She did not bother to investigate her bank balance and had no desire to learn how money worked. Most of her holdings had been in the United States, which meant that the Wall Street crash had suddenly made her relatively poor. Then she had silver mines in Mexico which turned out to be worthless by the time the Second World War was looming, almost all the ore having been worked out years before. 'If you do not apply yourself to understanding your affairs I am afraid that your money will melt away', G.M. had warned her. Emerald took little heed, and her money did melt away. Her jewellery was sold and replaced with paste copies. Still the entertaining did not cease.

The outbreak of war caught Lady Cunard in America (Margot Oxford later accused her of doing a bunk to the States to avoid the bombing, which was malicious and untrue.) In her absence, No. 7 Grosvenor Square was hit by a bomb, but this did not deter her from returning to London as soon as she could, coming back 'home' to the city where she felt she belonged. She rescued what she could of the contents of the house, and arranged with the management of the Dorchester Hotel in Park Lane to take a small suite of rooms on the seventh floor, Suite 707 on a corner overlooking the park. No doubt she realized that the days of great house entertaining were over, and that she would spend her remaining years as an hotel guest. Yet there was no sense of resignation in her move. She took some of her finest furniture to the Dorchester and transformed the three rooms, plus one for her maid Gordon, into an exquisite little palace. There was not too much room for acrobatics, and stacks of paintings were stored under the bed, but the Cunard suite at the Dorchester soon became the *salon* of wartime London, into which statesmen and soldiers, British and American, would drop in daily for a drink. Emerald gave dinner parties virtually every day, in unspoken competition with the less glamorous 'Ordinaries' given once a month by Sibyl Colefax in the same hotel. The style of Grosvenor Square was naturally missing, Emerald having to rely upon Italian hotel waiters clumsily spilling wine or serving her guests with no respect to the proper order. Nevertheless, Emerald's spirit soared above every inconvenience, and in spite of her frequent complaints and her confession that she was too tired to cope with life, people flocked to her rooms as to a health-giving spa, where they would find her 'gently relaxed among her outspread plumage' (Peter Quennell), and often in bed. Many a chat with a Cabinet Minister took place on the side of Lady Cunard's bed.

Emerald detested the war ('so vulgar', she said) and contrived to pretend that it was not happening. Entirely fearless of the bombs which came in 1944, she refused to use the air-raid shelter in the Dorchester or to have her movements clogged by doodlebugs; they might as well have been bluebottles. If an air-raid trapped her guests in the hotel for a few hours, she was delighted, for Hitler was thus affording the assembled friends a longer period for literary and musical discussion sitting in darkened rooms packed with buhl furniture. Should a bomb come perilously near, Emerald would sit under the table with Shakespeare or Proust.

A fashionable wedding reception soon after the war was the scene of Lady Cunard's most celebrated remark. Chips Channon told her how remarkable it was that London had resumed normal life so quickly. He surveyed the crowded room with a proud air, and indicating the bejewelled guests with a sweep of the hand, said, '*This* is what we have been fighting for!' 'Why, dear,' said Emerald, 'are they all *Poles*?'

As Emerald's health deteriorated her age and fragility began to show. She suffered from a racking cough caused by acute bronchitis and visitors gradually grew aware that the great hostess was slipping away in the Dorchester Hotel. By 1948 she was very weak, though she managed some outings. She attended the memorial service for that other, more meretricious hostess Laura Corrigan in January and went to a party which Sacheverell Sitwell gave for Mae West, about to open in *Diamond Lil*, in February. By the end of the spring it was clear that there was little life left to her. Chips Channon eloquently voiced the desperate feeling of loss: 'our beloved, dazzling, bright, fantastic Emerald dying. I cannot believe it.'

Diana Cooper, probably Emerald's closest female friend, came from Paris to be with her. She sat up for hours listening to Emerald's wandering thoughts, interrupted by long periods of quiet. Her last words were recorded by Cecil Beaton, as told to him by the maid Gordon. Gordon had stayed at the bedside for eight weeks, with scarcely a couple of hours' sleep at a stretch. On the last day, she, the doctor, and the nurse assembled around the bed while Emerald struggled to say something. Her weak lips whispered the same word over and over. It seemed like 'pain'. The doctor asked where the pain was. No, Emerald shook her head. 'Pain', she repeated. Gordon gave her a book and a pen, and on the fly-leaf Emerald just managed to scrawl the word 'champagne'. This was odd, thought Gordon, as Lady Cunard scarcely drank more than an occasional glass of German wine. Still, she produced a tea-spoon and placed a little on Emerald's lips. No, that was not right. Emerald shook her head, lifted her hand with difficulty and pointed to the bottle, then nodded gently to the doctor, to the nurse, and to Gordon in turn. At last they understood. Glasses were brought out, and the three drank to Lady Cunard, who managed a feeble smile.

Diana Cooper went on from one death-bed to that of another friend. Nancy Mitford commiserated with her. 'Oh, let's be frank,' said Diana. 'I mind terribly that Venetia should suffer but I shan't miss her so very much. I do miss Emerald.' Nancy Mitford herself had to admit to an unworthy thought. 'Well, you don't get two Emeralds in one life-time', she wrote to her sister. 'Why couldn't it have been Sibyl instead? (awful of me).'

Emerald had said she wanted to be cremated with as little fuss as possible. Her ashes were scattered in Grosvenor Square.

CHAPTER SIX

Sibyl Colefax

All are agreed she was a hunter of lions, indeed the most persistent and successful lion-hunter that London has ever known. Every eminent person, every famous name, everyone whose achievements had attracted attention or whose position inspired awe, sooner or later was inveigled to her oval dining-table. Resistance was futile. Sibyl Colefax was not abashed by the refusal of one of her invitations. She simply issued another, and another, she would mount up scores of them if necessary, until the prey eventually succumbed, like a fox pursued by hounds, through sheer weariness. Thus by attrition did the collection of famous guests grow to unrivalled dimensions, and when Fielding the parlourmaid announced 'Mr Winston Churchill, Mr Max Beerbohm, Mr Yehudi Menuhin', she was not making fun at the expense of her employer, as many a new recruit might be tempted to suspect. In walked all three gentlemen.

It was no doubt mischievous and unkind of Osbert Sitwell to call her house 'Lions' Corner House', but it was not merely a *bon mot*; the accuracy of the observation was recognized by everyone who knew Sibyl Colefax. Since her death, some of the hundreds of people who were entertained by her have looked back with a denigratory glance. 'The need to collect celebrities was for her an addiction as strong as alcohol or drugs', wrote Kenneth Clark. She was 'a professional dealer in what she considered to be human masterpieces', in Peter Quennell's view. Her social mission, said John Lehmann, was a heroic, scarcely credible phenomenon. Private letters written during her lifetime and only recently published confirm the impression that it was commonplace to speak ill of Lady Colefax behind her back. Virginia Woolf said that she collected 'all the intellects about her, as a parrot picks up beads', and in the same vein she spoke of 'Colefax persistently pecking like a parrot with corns on her toes. No, no, no, I say: it only makes the pecking frantic.' Mrs Woolf learnt that a collector of people cannot rest if one of her specimens threatens to slip out of her grasp. She 'can't believe that it's not a personal insult that I won't roast myself and fry myself talking to her and Noël Coward. Lord—what dusty souls these women get.' Of course, it *was* an insult, for Lady Colefax's self-esteem rose in proportion to the number of celebrated persons she assembled around her, and diminished by reason of their defection. The Germans have a word for it— *Geltungsbedürfnis*, or the craving to acquire value by association. This was the root of Lady Colefax's obsession, and its strength made her the very centre of London social life, on the intimate scale, for several decades. There was far more to her than this, and far more that is admirable and endearing, but since the memoirs in which she still lives naturally dwell upon her manic gathering of the great, we shall consider this first, and then bring to the fore the kindly, inoffensive and guileless woman lurking in her shadow.

A 'colefaxismus' in the thirties was a remark made with a view to impressing the listener with one's privileged knowledge of people and events. If you launched into conversation with a boast which indicated you were privy to Charlie Chaplin's movements, you were guilty of a 'colefaxismus'. Theatrical agents do it even now. In Lady Colefax's case, it was almost certainly true. Charlie Chaplin *was* a friend, and she *did* know where he was and what he was doing, but that did not excuse the tactlessness. She appeared proud to be in possession of the latest off-the-record news. 'I don't care who people know,' said Margot Asquith in one of her spiky moods. 'It is so tiresome that Sibyl is always on the spot. One can't talk about the birth of Christ without that Astrakhan ass saying she was there in the manger.'

Ronald Storrs referred to this habit as 'capping everything with a more celebrated but less well-fitting cap', and described a 'tiresome' meal during which Sibyl was determined to supply appropriate and inevitable anecdotes, clinching and improving every situation. 'If H tried to describe the recent Papal ceremonies, she must needs tell us what Pacelli said to Harold Nicolson when they were both in Berlin.'

That this was not a perverse view of Lady Colefax's extravagance is attested by a short story which Mary Borden wrote, and which is based on Sibyl. Entitled 'To meet J.C.', it tells of a hostess who invites a number of people to the greatest of all her dinner-parties, at which the guest of honour is to be a surprise, revealed only by those initials. When Jesus fails to turn up, the hostess, now obviously mad, is quite undaunted and prattles on in conversation with an empty chair, asking questions about the climate in Palestine and so on. The embarrassed guests conclude that lion-hunting leads ultimately to insanity. By way of a tease, Osbert Sitwell once borrowed a loudspeaker and bellowed out in the garden, for the neighbours to hear, a long list of preposterously grand guests, mostly dead, who were supposed to be coming through Sibyl's front door. She did not think it funny. 'You know how huffy dogs look if you laugh at them,' said Virginia Woolf. 'So do women of the world.'

In her desperation to expand her collection, Lady Colefax more than once made herself appear foolish, which in essence she was not; it was only her hobby which was foolish. Having captured Mrs Woolf, with much laboursome petition, she turned to the other Bloomsbury luminaries and implored her to bring them into her ken. She proposed that they should give joint weekly parties, thus bringing Bloomsbury to Chelsea and Chelsea to Bloomsbury. 'There's Sibyl Colefax pining for one real Bloomsbury party', wrote Mrs Woolf to Ethel Sands. 'She thinks we eat off the floor and spit into large pots of common bedroom china. Well, I can't get a single friend of mine to meet her; no painter at any rate.' Lytton Strachey was enticed, and begged not to be dragged to Colefax again. The great conductor Wilhelm Fürtwangler, an intensely private man, was also enticed, and whispered to a fellow-guest that he was bored to tears. He did not know Lady Colefax, and she did not know him.

Not knowing someone, especially someone who ought to be known, was Lady Colefax's deepest fear. Jealousy attacked her if a person of renown was seen in the company of one of her friends, and was not on her list. Kenneth Clark recalls that he encountered Lady Colefax when he was lunching with the actress Vivien Leigh, and failed to introduce her. She was, he says, 'hysterical with fury', and telephoned him immediately with the plea 'Who was that? Who was that?' Before long, Vivien Leigh and Laurence Olivier were intimates at Argyll House, the Colefax home. She was worse at the theatre, where it was essential she should be seen to greet and exchange words with absolutely everyone she had ever met. Robert Bruce Lockhart found this habit 'tiresome', and commented, 'The scrum was stupendous.' Alfred Lunt was less patient. He took her to the theatre and was irritated by her standing up, looking around with the eyes of a hunter to see who was there and with whom. 'Sibyl,' he said, 'you have been taken to the first night of a very interesting play by one of the greatest living actors. You will sit down, talk to me and listen to the play, or I shall leave.' This brutal instruction, apparently, she obeyed.

If you were not especially well-known, Lady Colefax's attention might the more easily be diverted elsewhere. Many are those who remember her eyes wandering around the room as they were talking to her, looking over shoulders, glancing sideways with a questing energy, in case there might be a more interesting conversation in progress in another corner with someone it was important to impress. One could see her thinking, 'I hope they remember to get out the best cigars for the Ambassador, and keep the ordinary Jamaican ones for everybody else' while she appeared to be listening. The art of pleasing was characteristic of Edwardian society; it belonged effortlessly to such as Lady Desborough and Mrs Keppel, and consisted in giving the impression that you were concentrating on what was being said to you. Your whole attention was focused, for the moment, on your guest. You took an interest in his opinion or experience. This was by no means false; it was a combination of good manners, which arose naturally, and a desire to stimulate people. One could only stimulate by taking an interest in people, not merely as public personages, but as human beings. This was one of the essential qualities of a good hostess which Lady Colefax lacked. She regarded people as prize objects, assessed according to value. Those who had not yet been publicly acclaimed were caught in a less warm embrace than those who were, and the transition from Mr So-and-so to a dear personal friend addressed by his first name fell upon one immediately after one's name had become public property. Sibyl Colefax was a follower, not a leader. Careful calculation played too large a part in her enthusiasms.

She was frequently told as much, and denied the imputation hotly. Why, it was pure accident that all her friends were famous! She was simply interested in people for their own sake and wanted her home to be a place where interesting people could meet and enjoy each other's company. Was it her fault if they happened to be famous? She did not pay attention to such trifles.

It was true, as we shall see, that Sibyl Colefax did love company and was nice to people. It was also true that she was rather more helpful to the young and unconnected than most of her denigrators have allowed. But this was largely after her reputation had been established and when an important ingredient of that reputation consisted in Sibyl's being able to introduce anyone to anyone. That she should fail to recognize the deep springs of her own motives was only to be expected. *Geltungsbedürfnis* is wholly unconscious.

One may watch the process of pursuit and capture with the history of Sibyl's relationship with Virginia Woolf, which began with the publication of Mrs Woolf's second novel, *Night and Day*, in 1919. By this time Mrs Colefax (her husband had not yet been knighted) was already the established centre of a large circle which included Austen Chamberlain, Lilian Braithwaite the actress, Olga Lynn the singer, Garvin the journalist, Owen Seaman the editor of *Punch*, E.F. Benson, Osbert Sitwell, Lady Randolph Churchill, Hugh Walpole, Ruth Draper, J.M. Barrie, Ivor Novello, Bernard Berenson, Hilaire Belloc and Logan Pearsall Smith, but Virginia Woolf was not yet the great literary personage she was soon to become. She had, however, caused a sufficient stir with *The Voyage Out* and *Night and Day* to excite Sibyl's interest. On 2 November

1919, Mrs Woolf wrote to Roger Fry, 'Mrs Colefax—this is the first fruits of *Night and Day*—has intimated through Logan [Pearsall Smith] her willingness to receive me; to which I have replied that I have no clothes. It is now her part to provide them; but so far she continues to think the matter over.' Sibyl was nothing if not tenacious. She repeated the invitation, several times, and when Mrs Woolf made it perfectly clear that she did not wish to have to buy white gloves and a new hat and shoes in order to come to tea, describing herself as 'dirty, dowdy and disreputable', Sibyl reassured her. Virginia Woolf visited. She was now on the list.

Once on the list, there was no simple avenue by which one could get off. Sibyl took to inviting Virginia Woolf to dinner rather than tea, promising that she would meet other (famous) writers, not pausing to consider that writers met each other anyway without her help. It was no lure to Virginia Woolf to have the names of her own acquaintances thrown to her as bait, especially as she preferred to encounter them in less contrived surroundings. 'We shall have to dress up, Vita [Sackville-West] and I, and behave like ladies, in the King's Road, instead of toasting buns over my gas fire.' After *Orlando* was published, it received a vicious review in the *Evening Standard* over the signature of Arnold Bennett. Sibyl invited Virginia Woolf to dinner 'to meet Arnold Bennett'. She went. The two writers were pushed towards each other to lock in combat. In fact, they behaved decently and got on very well together, but the hostess, according to Virginia Woolf, 'was gloating', for here was a scene which she knew would redound to her credit; famous novelist and famous reviewer were face to face in *her* house.

Nevertheless, Mrs Woolf became a regular guest. In the first place, she was fascinated by a world in which behaviour followed rules very different from those of Bloomsbury; she had a lively curiosity and ventured into society as a geologist pores over metamorphic rocks. 'They all seem like people enchanted', she wrote, 'and chained to a particular patch of the carpet, which they can't cross for fear of death.' But more importantly, she grew to like Sibyl. From thinking her 'silly', and 'hard, shiny and bright', she eventually recognized that the hostess was 'a nice, good, discerning woman' whose kindness she appreciated and whose company, when alone, she enjoyed. To Vita Sackville-West she confessed, 'Lord, how one does treat that woman, and seen privately alone at tea here, she's so nice: only glittering as a cheap cherry in her own house.' The fact that Vita was one of Sibyl's closest friends did not weigh in Virginia Woolf's judgement, which was always scrupulously honest. Independently of Vita, she wrote seventy-one letters to Lady Colefax over a period, which was seventy more than she would have written to a woman she only despised for her collecting habits. Sibyl won through because she was inoffensive and good, and the observant Virginia Woolf could see that her desire to please was as strong as her desire to impress, and far more conscious.

The scene of all these conquests, from 1921 to 1936, was Argyll House in King's Road, Chelsea, London, a beautifully proportioned house set back from the road behind railings, with a handsome garden behind. It can still be seen, dark and grubby now, but with its elegance undimmed. Here for fifteen years Sibyl Colefax gave lunch and dinner parties for the select and distinguished virtually every day, with the help of only her faithful maid, Fielding, Briance the chauffeur and Mrs Gray the cook. The food was always excellent, but there were no pretensions to grandeur. The setting was fundamentally intimate and domestic. It was a family home, where Sibyl lived with her husband, Sir Arthur Colefax, and their two sons, Peter and Michael, so that guests were invited to join the family for a meal in their small, comfortable house, rather than to attend a great party. Thus was Sibyl's entertaining distinguished from the opulent country-house gatherings of Lady Desborough and Mrs Greville, the lavish, wasteful, night-club parties of Mrs Corrigan, and the sparkling extravagancies of Lady Cunard. Sibyl Colefax was modest, even humble, compared with the others, for she had not the advantages of a Whig aristocratic upbringing or inherited fortune, nor any American wealth based on trade. She was English, middle-class, and relatively poor.

Sibyl was the granddaughter of James Wilson, from a Scottish family of woollen manufacturers in Hawick, Roxburghshire. Having set up business in London as a hat-maker, Wilson, a self-educated man, eventually became a Member of Parliament and founded the *Economist* which, in its early days, he not only edited but wrote almost single-handed. He was then only 38. When he was 54 he was appointed Paymaster-General in Palmerston's government, and created a Privy Councillor, shortly afterwards to be sent to India as the finance member of the Council of India, set up to restore the chaotic economy of that country after the mutiny. Wilson's last, most glorious year was spent in India, where he took his wife and five daughters, and where he died in 1860. He is buried in Calcutta. One of his daughters married Walter Bagehot, while the youngest, Sophia, married Wilson's private secretary who was a member of the Indian Civil Service, James Halsey. Their youngest daughter, Sibyl, was born in London in 1874, and taken to India at the age of nine months. Thus Walter Bagehot was Sibyl's uncle, though since she was barely three when he died, he cannot be said to have had any influence upon her.

Something even more mysterious hovered in the background of earlier generations. There was much talk of Sibyl's having 'a touch of the tarbrush' and being descended, in one line, from some exotic ancestress. Certainly her dark eyes and complexion were not essentially English.

Sibyl's childhood was nomadic and lonely. She lived sometimes with an aunt, sometimes with other relations in England when her mother had to be in India, sometimes at school. She was largely self-educated, with patches of schooling in Putney whenever circumstances allowed. She learnt perforce to be self-sufficient and to read avidly everything she could lay her hands on. She also grew accustomed to the society of eminent men, her father moving in the lower reaches of Indian political life. One of the first people she knew was Lockwood Kipling, Rudyard's father. At the age of 20 she first went to Florence, where she always maintained her life really began. She fell in with Bernard Berenson, who was to be a life-long friend, and his multifarious relations. Berenson's wife, Mary, was sister-in-law to Bertrand Russell and sister of Logan Pearsall Smith, the man later entrusted with the commission to catch Virginia Woolf.

At 23, Sibyl Halsey met Arthur Colefax, an up-and-coming patent lawyer from Bradford, the son of another woollen merchant.

Colefax had been educated at Bradford Grammar School, Strasbourg, and Merton College, Oxford, and despite his father's wish that he stay in the woollen trade, he had turned down the first job that was offered him and chose instead to study for the Bar, whither he was called in 1894. He and Sibyl fell in love and determined to marry, but decided to wait until his career was established. They did not have to wait long, for Colefax's Yorkshire shrewdness and assiduity led him to specialize in the unspectacular but vitally important branch of the law dealing with patents. He was soon one of the country's leading experts in the field.

The Colefaxes were married in 1901 and spent the first thirteen years of their life together as rolling stones, tumbling all over Europe and gathering friends wherever they went. With a London house in Onslow Square and a country residence at Old Buckhurst, they gradually accumulated a vast number of acquaintances whose names were filling the Visitors' Book, by 1914, at the rate of two pages a week. They were, in the early stages, mostly literary and theatrical, but when Arthur was a Member of Parliament for ten months, political contacts arrived to swell the numbers. Colefax was a Bencher of Lincoln's Inn by 1916 and Solicitor-General for the County Palatine of Durham in 1918. He was now firmly recognized as the leader of a small group of specialists at the Bar who dealt with the law of patents and trade marks (another was his colleague, Stafford Cripps), an eminence acknowledged in 1920 with his knighthood. Social life had reached such proportions, and Sir Arthur's work was so securely London-based, that he and Lady Colefax decided to sell both Old Buckhurst and the Onslow Square house, and bought Argyll House in 1921. Now it would be easier for everyone to meet in more regular fashion.

Easier, too, to organize the receptions for special occasions, some of which have passed into history and earned for Sibyl Colefax a place in the annals of English life which would have surprised her. There had already been, in December 1917, the historic poetry reading when all three Sitwells, Edith, Osbert and Sacheverell, read their works to an assembly which included T.S. Eliot, Aldous Huxley and Edmund Gosse. Of course, it was not 'historic' at the time, but in retrospect one may see that it was the first occasion on which the ambitious trio (Huxley called them the 'Shufflebottoms') made their mark on London society. Some of those present found the scene distasteful and artificial, but that is by the by. The fact was that the Sitwells' growing reputation was enhanced by the impact of this reading, and Sibyl's standing as hostess to the intelligentsia was advanced. There were to be many more such occasions. It was *chez* Colefax that Fred and Adèle Astaire were entertained to a reception after their first performance in London. Paul Valéry was presented to London at Argyll House. Gertie Lawrence and Olga Lynn sang, Artur Rubinstein played. The culmination was to come with the accession of Edward VIII, but that was still many years ahead.

She was at pains to make an 'occasion' of her evenings, which frequently involved bullying a guest to perform. Rubinstein played for her often, but other artists were reluctant to be coaxed. At a party given by Georgia and Sacheverell Sitwell for the American actress Mae West in 1948, Sibyl declared that their mistake had been in trying to induce Mae to perform. This was too much for Ronald Storrs. He wrote, 'Don't I remember having a dinner in Argyll House ruined by being put next to Ruth Draper, with instructions to nag her into one or two turns, she resisting at first firmly and later sternly: a hateful Assignment.'

As Sibyl's hold on London entertainment grew, so did her popularity as a figure of fun. People openly referred to her as 'old Coalbox' and derided her lion-hunting technique. She was well aware of this, and professed not to mind, yet she was hurt if her sincerity was questioned and steadfastly refused to admit that the single quality possessed by all her *invités* was fame. Her 'rivals' during the 1920s (if so they can be called) were Laura Corrigan and Emerald Cunard. Mrs Corrigan never crossed her path and would never have invited the same people. They might have been operating in different cities. Corrigan guests were titled and flighty, Colefax people were intellectual and of some consequence. It is doubtful if Laura Corrigan ever read a book, so she would have been well out of her depth with people who wrote them. She rather endearingly looked down upon Lady Colefax because she could not capture the kings, queens, princesses and dukes who regularly attended a Corrigan feast. In fact, Sibyl was not remotely a snob in this sense, and never chased after royal highnesses simply because they were royal. The only characteristic she shared with Mrs Corrigan was a kindly nature. Neither of them was malicious or offensive, in contrast with Mrs Greville, who was malice personified, and Lady Cunard, who was at least mischievous. Sibyl detested malice and intrigue.

There was rather more contact and grounds for comparison between Sibyl and Emerald Cunard. In the first place, many of the *habitués* of the one were invited by the other, making it inevitable that their relative qualities should be a frequent subject of conversation, or rather gossip. They knew that they were considered 'rivals' and kept each other at a polite distance, referring to each other invariably as 'Lady Cunard' and 'Lady Colefax' with a palpable hint of scorn. They went so far as to invite each other; in 1935, for instance, Lady Cunard is several times among the guests at Argyll House. But the atmosphere generated by their presence in the same room was never warm. As personalities they were so discordant they might have been constructed from different clay. While Emerald was indiscreet as a matter of policy and mischief, Sibyl was totally reliable and discreet; she could be entrusted with a secret. While Emerald contributed to conversation, even invented it as she went along, Sibyl launched it and then lost control. Emerald was a brilliant impresario who challenged her guests and drew a performance from them, whereas Sibyl, having assembled them, did not know quite what to do with them. Undeniably, however, Sibyl was much the more caring person, a decent honourable soul who wanted only to do good. This was the very last sentiment that would occur to Lady Cunard. Lord Berners said that Sibyl Colefax's evenings were a party of lunatics presided over by an efficient, trained hospital nurse, while Emerald Cunard's were a party of lunatics presided over by a lunatic.

Their rivalry occasionally gave rise to open competition, with marks scored by the onlookers. Lady Cunard saying, 'Oh dear, I simply must stop. I'm becoming a bore, like Lady Colefax.' Or Sibyl very appropriately capping Emerald's attempt at a colefaxismus, when she declared, at a moment of extremely strained relations between Italy and England, that she had received a very nice letter from Count Grandi (the Italian Ambassador). 'Have you also heard from him, Lady Colefax?' 'Only by telegram,' responded Sibyl.

That the rivalry also engendered simmering jealousy in Sibyl is attested by an account given by Virginia Woolf of an afternoon in Bloomsbury, when the two women were having tea alone. The telephone rang, and Lady Cunard's butler was pressing Mrs Woolf to dine. Sibyl was furious. 'I've never heard of such insolence,' she said, exclaiming that it was impertinent beyond endurance to ask a person to dine when one did not know her (this was, of course, precisely what Sibyl had always done). Lady Cunard was nothing but a snob. Mrs Woolf said that Sibyl's face was 'contorted with a look that reminded me of the look on a tigress's face when some one snatches a bone from its paws'.

The question whether or not Lady Colefax was a snob is a vexed one, dependent for its answer on an impossible clarity of definition. 'Snobbish' is a word which conveys different meanings to different people. Certainly, there were those who told stories about her alleged snobbery. At a dinner in Londonderry House, when the Prime Minister was present, Sibyl in her eagerness to get close bumped into Lady Ilchester. Immediately an imaginary headline for the morning papers was concocted: 'Social Upstart Knocks Down Elderly Countess'. Another story held that during the black-out in the war, the only sound that could be heard was of Lady Colefax climbing the social ladder. The arch-tease Lord Berners once played a splendid trick on her by inviting her to a meal 'to meet the P of W'. She naturally accepted, chucking whatever else was in the diary, and found herself sitting next to the Provost of Worcester. Berners enjoyed himself hugely and fingered the wound with glee. 'But Sibyl,' he said, 'I didn't think you were a social snob. I assumed you would be delighted to meet an estimable clergyman.'

A similar mistake occurred when she told her maid to invite Mr B. Shaw. The gathering was highly intellectual. Fielding for some reason thought she meant Bobbie Shaw, the very unsatisfactory drunken homosexual son of Lady Astor by a previous marriage. 'Can't think why they asked *me*,' said Shaw when he discovered himself entirely out of place.

Sibyl's friends, however, point out that she was only an intellectual snob, which is somehow less offensive; she was impressed by achievement, not by titles. Even better, she was an élitist, which is even less of a bad thing. There is a sense in which every professional hostess must be an élitist, for if she only invited the milkman and the newsvendor, however interesting they might be, no one would ever hear of it. There may well be scores of such humble hostesses entertaining in Stockwell every week, but their evenings necessarily lack the one crucial ingredient which every real hostess nurtures—that they be the subject of comment in as wide a field as possible. The essence of snobbery is to arrange your life in such a way that you must be considered a person of importance if you know so many important people; that you know such people must be an observable fact, or it is wasted.

It also follows that if you have an engagement with one important person, and an alternative meeting with a *more* important person is proposed, then you must needs cancel the first. There are some who recall having been 'chucked' by Sibyl in this way.

The fearsomely acute Virginia Woolf observed another more recondite manifestation of snobbery in Lady Colefax. Inviting her to tea in Bloomsbury, she tidied up the room and bought iced cakes. Sibyl was a trifle disappointed. She wanted a burnt bun and a room as untidy as possible, 'and if my fingers were covered with ink stains it was all to the good'. The point was that Lady Colefax should be on such terms of intimacy with the great writer that no attempt be made to organize anything 'special'. Snobbery demanded that Virginia Woolf be discovered in all her relaxed squalor; she would tart herself up only for less privileged folk.

Having said that, it must in fairness be averred that Lady Colefax took as much trouble with her less elevated guests as she did with her pride of lions. She was painstaking and energetic on behalf of mere cubs, the young and the promising. She took trouble to learn about people, what they had done and what they hoped to do, and never forgot a detail. She was in every way a 'caring' person. A research assistant on the track of some obscure literary or historical figure would be introduced to exactly the right person, or persons, who could help point him in the right direction, and Sibyl would not rest until she had found the way in which she could help most efficiently. When Henry McIlhenny, the Philadelphia art collector, came to London, Sibyl assembled together for him the directors of the National Gallery, the Wallace Collection and the Tate Gallery, all precisely the people he most wanted to meet, a gesture which took time to organize and which could not contribute to her own aggrandizement. It was simply to give McIlhenny pleasure. Lady Colefax has, indeed, the distinction of being the first hostess to make museum directors 'smart', to bring them into London social life. Lady Cunard would not have bothered, Mrs Corrigan would not have known how to, and Mrs Greville would have looked down her nose.

Another circumstance which made Lady Colefax unique among hostesses was that she was happily married to a man on whom she doted. Family life was so central to her existence that entertaining was a complement, not a compensation. Lady Cunard's husband was satisfactorily dead, Mrs Corrigan's helpfully absent most of the time. Sir Arthur was a sweet and good man, thoroughly reliable, amiable, of equable temperament and kindly disposition, like his wife devoid of malice and an enemy to violent or disruptive emotion. All splendid attributes, no doubt, but hardly likely to inject lively banter at the dinner-table. Though the best possible husband, Sir Arthur was the worst possible husband to a hostess. He was, in company, a liability, and as he was deaf, he was never to realise that his wife's guests considered him a bore.

It is little short of awe-inspiring that there should be such universal consent on Sir Arthur Colefax's conversational style. 'Chips' Channon was the most laconic; he was, he wrote, 'deaf, and unfortunately the very reverse of dumb . . . boring beyond belief'. David Herbert thought him 'the most boring man that's ever been born', and Sonia Keppel 'the biggest bore ever'. Once he had started on a topic, it was virtually impossible to stop him. Her sister, Violet Trefusis, once fell asleep as Sir Arthur was in mid-stream, waking up twenty minutes later to hear him say, 'And then we got to Bergamo and it began to rain . . .' Nor was she the only one. Lady Hambleden nodded off during a monologue about patents. The acid Lytton Strachey described him as 'a dreadful pompous lawyer and politician with a very dull large face pétri with insincerity', which was a trifle strong. Virginia Woolf was rather more tolerant. 'Sir Arthur was very kind,' she said, 'he did his best to entertain me; but why he thought that I was primarily interested in the Dye-stuffs Bill I have never found out . . . At one time I was the second leading authority in England on that measure.' He was usually at work all day and not present at a lunch party, but dinner invariably found him at the head of the table. Mrs Woolf thought of him as an old piece of furniture that had always been there.

Guests would often consult with each other and pray God that they were not placed next to him. He was usually flanked by two docile guests, or old friends who knew how to interrupt him. Kenneth Clark said that he was 'not an asset' and was only thought to be the biggest bore in England by those who had not visited the provinces. Lord Berners wickedly suggested that the Government had offered him £30,000 a year to bore the Channel Tunnel.

Sibyl was aware of her husband's reputation even if he was not. She told Jimmy Smith (the Hon. James Smith, of the bookshop family) not to mention umbrellas, for that was the only subject on which Sir Arthur was *really* a bore, and when she saw him with Max Beerbohm in the garden, she exclaimed in wonderment, 'Oh *do* look! Max is *laughing!*'

There were the exceptional few who enjoyed Sir Arthur, in addition to the many who liked him. Max Beerbohm was indeed one of them, as he lived so much out of England and never read the newspapers, so he looked to Colefax for information. This he received in plenty. Sir Robert Bruce Lockhart was another who sought his company, to talk about fishing. The most surprising of his conquests was Mrs Simpson, the King's friend, who engaged him in animated conversation when no one else would address a word to him. No wonder Mrs Simpson was socially so successful; she possessed to the finest degree that quality which was second nature to the Edwardians but which had been neglected by most Englishmen since—good manners. Those who talked loudly of the tedium of Sir Arthur's company certainly lacked his grace. Virginia Woolf's was the most controlled and accurate observation, in a letter to Vanessa Bell. His conversation, she said, 'though full of substance, lacks atmosphere'.

As for Sibyl, the same people who chastized Sir Arthur were

quick to enumerate her shortcomings. Chips Channon thought her garrulous, gracious and absurd, Roger Fry dismissed her as an old nuisance. The Sitwells, having been helped by her, turned viciously against her and seldom missed a chance to belittle or denigrate. Osbert Sitwell in particular saw in Sibyl all the smug complacency of the middle classes which he most despised. In fact, he was seriously off target; Lady Colefax was made more firmly than that. What he, who admired the loathsome Mrs Greville, most objected to was that Sibyl was not a large, impressive personality. Osbert liked to be overwhelmed by women.

It is difficult to capture Lady Colefax's appearance, for she had a horror of being photographed, and only sat for one portrait, which will be reproduced in Michael Bloch's biography. She was not beautiful in any exciting way. Small and short, tending to plumpness, with large black eyes which rolled, she seemed more mousy than carnivorous. In a throng, she would be completely lost beneath the shoulders of everyone else. James Lees-Milne thought she must have been pretty once, but that now, in middle age, she had a face like an intelligent pug's or a dolphin's. A number of people emphasized the bright hardness of her features. She was 'shiny and metallic' according to Chips Channon, reminding him of obsidian or onyx. To Edith Sitwell she was like a wrought-iron railing. Peter Quennell described her 'terrible eye—dark and narrow and penetrating', while Kenneth Clark though she could give a black look unlike anyone else. Virginia Woolf likened her to a bunch of red cherries on a hard black straw hat, and her husband Leonard, reverting again to the metallic appearance, said she was armour-plated and enamelled.

All of which suggests that her appearance was especially noticeable. It was not. Whereas Lady Cunard's exotic looks would make heads turn, and Mrs Corrigan or Mrs Greville dazzled with their jewellery, Lady Colefax was unremarkable in aspect. Had she not been a celebrated hostess, few would have bothered to describe her at all. She was essentially simple and unpretentious. James Lees-Milne says that she never played the great lady, and could not have done so had she wished, for she was quite the poorest of the London hostesses. In her youth she had bicycled and read books, both inexpensive hobbies, and never since had she been rich enough to indulge herself. She spent money only on entertaining, and even that was not done on any exorbitant scale. In the years to come she would be even poorer.

Her conversation, too, was unremarkable. She would talk ceaselessly, hardly drawing breath, but would have nothing memorable to say. Virginia Woolf said she went on talking, talking, in consecutive sentences like the shavings that came from planes, artificial, but unbroken. Harold Acton thought she practised Wilde's dictum that conversation should touch on everything but should concentrate on nothing. (Cynthia Gladwyn, on the other hand, remembers Sibyl like Madame Récamier, hardly talking at all.) Chips Channon referred to her 'jabbering' and Ronald Storrs to her 'talking far too much and insistently'. Harold Nicolson, a real champion, gave an example of the sort of sentence with which she hoped to generate conversation at her table. 'Who is the dullest celebrity you have ever known?' she asked everyone. Not only was it an uninspiring subject, but since most of those present would have volunteered 'Lady Colefax', it was also embarrassing. She was not a *raconteuse*, and ought to have avoided telling stories, as they inevitably fell flat. She was quite likely to make a *faux pas* and ask a question to which all present already knew the answer, or to make a perfectly just comment at the wrong time. There was an occasion when she asked a youngish writer to escort her to the Belgian Embassy ball, but she wanted first to go to the Curzon Cinema in Curzon Street, to see the Movietone News. There was bound to be some item on her friends the Mountbattens, who had just returned from India. In the cinema, Sibyl whispered to her companion, 'Of course, what they won't show is Edwina kissing Nehru at the airport, which undid all the good they had done in India for the past years.' At which a lady in the row in front turned round and said, 'Hello Sibyl, I thought I recognized your voice.' It was Edwina Mountbatten. To make matters worse, they all four arrived at the Belgian Embassy together. Sibyl was mortified, but managed to rise above the awkward moment. She was very resilient.

She rarely allowed the conversation of her guests to proceed unchecked without jumping in with a remark which she hoped

would help divert attention to another speaker. Her contribution
was light talk. It was not usually the apposite moment, and her
butting in caused irritation more often than not. Just as you were
entering into an interesting conversation, she would take your arm
and whisk you off to someone else. Too flustered and anxious about
how the party was going, she had not the gift of relaxation, and even
at the table would be busy fussing with knives and forks or putting
the salt cellars in the correct position. Her tenseness was an
encumbrance to a party. Lady Cunard did not suffer from this; she
made conversations, and Sibyl collapsed them. 'She makes
everyone stony', said Mrs Woolf, 'and breaks up talk with a
hammer—good, deserving, industrious, kind-hearted woman as
she is.' One had the impression she was already thinking about the
next party.

Those who spent time alone with Lady Colefax found a very
different person, at ease and *décontractée*. Her charm won over
Virginia Woolf, with whom she spent many chatty afternoons, and
David Herbert remembers an afternoon walking through his
garden in the country when he could not have wished for more
agreeable, relaxed company. She told him the most important thing
in a garden was to look after your nose. In the end, however, even
her self-revelations were guarded and circumspect. David Cecil
spent a weekend with her and did not know her any better
afterwards than before.

Among Sibyl's closest friends were Harold Nicolson and Vita
Sackville-West, living at the exquisite Sissinghurst Castle in Kent.
Vita stayed most of the time in the country, but Harold was in
London all week, and would lunch or dine at Argyll House several
times a month. He once promised he would never take a drastic step
in his career or in Parliament without first consulting Sibyl, while
both he and Vita grew genuinely to love her. Even they, however,
devoted and loyal as they were, found themselves obliged to
dissemble in order to avoid too-frequent visits from Lady Colefax.
They arranged that their sons, Ben and Nigel, should share a
bedroom. Had they been allocated separate rooms, and one been
away for any reason, Sibyl would have proposed herself and
suggested she use the vacant bedroom. If they shared it, the room

was likely to be occupied most of the time by one or the other, and Sibyl could be politely refused with good reason.

Lady Colefax was intelligent and read widely. She contrived to get hold of all the latest books and, since she woke early, managed at least to dip into each of them. Mudie's, the lending library, had to remind her that she had thirty of their books on loan at one time. The latest books were piled into a basket of the kind normally reserved for logs, and placed at the top of the stairs. Her knowledge of art was immense, far greater than any of her bemused guests would have suspected, and moreover she had the sensitivity not to press this knowledge upon people. For years she corresponded regularly with Bernard Berenson, who had first brought art into her life in Florence. She also wrote once a week to Thornton Wilder, one among many who respected her intelligence. Her knowledge of ancient history and archaeology was surprising. Lytton Strachey, who called her 'thoroughly stupid', did not look further than his prejudices. Harold Nicolson praised her as a clever old bean who ought to have concentrated on intellectual, not social guests. (She did.) Virginia Woolf discerned her intelligence, but saw also that it lacked depth and tenacity. 'Her mind flickers like an arc lamp,' she said. And yet she was able to act as interpreter between Sir James Frazer and l'Abbé Breuil.

On one occasion, Mrs Woolf celebrated Sibyl's unsuspected percipience, revealing what she called 'astonishing sensibility'. Sibyl had left her umbrella behind in Bloomsbury, and Virginia mischievously described it as glowing and gleaming among her old gamps. Sibyl blushed. 'Mrs Woolf,' she said, 'I know what you think of my umbrella—a cheap, stubby, vulgar umbrella, you think my umbrella; and you think I have a bag like it—a cheap flashy bag covered with embroidery.' As this was precisely what Mrs Woolf did think, she had to accord full marks to Sibyl for perception. 'Must there not be depths in Lady Colefax?'

Uncommon energy being a prerequisite of the successful hostess, Lady Colefax was especially well endowed in this respect. Dynamic and indefatigable, she had reserves of vigour to keep her going all day long, with never an unoccupied moment. She was awake every morning at 6.30, and at her avocations by 8.45. The interim period was spent at her most pressing duty, writing cards of invitation for forthcoming lunches and dinners. When staying with friends in the country, the interval would stretch until perhaps noon, by which time she might well have written between thirty and fifty invitations. She never flagged. By the time she left the house, there might be some cards still unwritten. So she took them into her old Rolls-Royce, and continued scribbling on her knee. The car would swerve round a corner, Sibyl and invitations would clatter to the floor, but her pen never stopped; she picked herself and cards up and carried on the long list. Jimmy Smith accompanied her once on a train journey to Wales, where they were both invited for the weekend. She hardly uttered a word, but spent the entire journey writing out invitations to this and that until the heavy collection spewed off her lap on to the floor of the carriage, to be left untended by the writer until the end of the ride. The following week the most popular guest might receive three of four of these cards by the same post, each for a different occasion. Lord Berners had a Victorian blackamoor statue which he adapted so that, when a hidden button was pushed, its mouth opened and out poured a stream of Colefax invitation cards.

The cards would not be so acutely recalled by all their recipients were it not for one startling circumstance: they were virtually illegible. Lady Colefax's handwriting has been likened to an intoxicated hoop and a bicycle race. It was quite obviously fashioned in a frenzy, with sometimes the date and the time indecipherable, making a telephone call necessary for elucidation. Other guests were mentioned by initials—H.G. [Wells] and R.A. B[utler]. One usually placed the card on a mantelpiece and glanced at it from time to time, hoping that its secrets would suddenly be revealed; or threw it on the floor in the hope that the odd angle would make all clear. Mr Cox, the legendary character who worked all his life at the London Library, was deluged with cards asking for certain books. He pinned the cards on the shelf behind him and would study them several times a day until, usually in consultation with his colleagues, the titles hidden in the scrawl would be prised out. Karel Radowitz remembers that people would carry Sibyl's cards with them, and pass them on to others, on the grounds that a concerted effort to interpret them might be successful. On one occasion a letter of hers (not a card) was passed round the table at lunch, everyone making an attempt at it; they never proceeded further than the opening sentence, 'The once a day steamer has just passed . . .'

None of this bothered Lady Colefax in the smallest degree. She well knew that her script was bizarre, and did not mind being teased about it. Virginia Woolf was frequently inclined to be gently satirical. 'My dear Sibyl, I have actually made out every word of your letter, an author's vanity, I suppose', she wrote, and again, 'The joy of it is that one of your letters can be read twelve times before grasping the full beauty.' The joke was carried even to the offices of the Hogarth Press, whence Lady Colefax received a formal letter presenting their compliments but regretting that they were unable to accede to her request owing to their inability, notwithstanding several hours spent at the task, to interpret it.

Sibyl, however, was never confused by her erratic handwriting. Having scribbled fifty invitations, she would remember the substance of all of them, the combinations and linkings. She never once made a mistake and guests rarely showed up for the wrong assignation. That alone, in the circumstances, was a triumph. (Ronald Storrs once arrived a week early, having misread 'Sibyl's cuneiform'.)

In 1926 Lady Colefax added another, vitally important dimension to her activities. She paid her first visit to the United States of America, and returned with the continent in her pocket, or at least with its Most Famous People on her list. Some she knew already— Condé Nast, Frank Crowninshield, Douglas Fairbanks and Mary Pickford, Charlie Chaplin—but the scope of her American acquaintance was to widen significantly. Americans have vast energy, yet even they wilted a little after a series of dinner parties with Lady Colefax. Fairbanks and Pickford were reduced to the verge of the tomb, according to Aldous Huxley. Sibyl met scores of people, nibbled at some, devoured others. The theatre critic Alexander Woollcott became one of her devoted transatlantic friends, Thornton Wilder another. Virginia Woolf thought this accumulation of people and distance travelled unwholesome. 'Does it matter what Sibyl does? A coal mine, heaven, it's all the same. She pants a little harder—that is all.'

From that moment on, Lady Colefax's American connections were as important to her as her English friends. More to the point, her work in bringing together English and American personalities was crucial in improving Anglo-American relations on an informal, social level. Before Sibyl's efforts, Americans tended, with exceptions of course, to regard the British as reserved and unfriendly, while the British complacently considered all Americans to be vulgar. This was much less true after Argyll House became the one address to which all prominent Americans were summoned as soon as they arrived in England, or at which they eagerly announced themselves. As a result of Sibyl's contacts, friendships were formed which endured, and a deeper understanding between the two countries was forged. It is always difficult to assess the influence of a hostess, and, by a neat contrast, easy to exaggerate it. Influence on this level is oblique, tangential. It must be allowed that Lady Colefax's greatest contribution, deserving of a firm place in the social history of the twentieth century, was to bring Americans to an English drawing-room. Whatever her motives, she considered it her duty to narrow the Atlantic. Her own influence may have been small; she permitted men of influence and power to meet at her table, and exchange views in private after the ladies had left.

Another result of the American connection was much less welcome, yet led indirectly to Lady Colefax's second major contribution to English life. Her elder son Peter invested what little money she had, choosing the American stock market in preference to the English, and was one of the victims of the great Crash of 1929. Peter had been advised by one of his mother's friends on Wall Street. Every penny she possessed vanished overnight, depriving her of all security for the future. At the same time, Sir Arthur's deafness grew so acute that he was forced to give up his practice as a patent lawyer with its £20,000 a year income. Suddenly, Lady Colefax was not just poor, but a pauper. 'There they were with a beggarly thousand in what's to provide all London with vermouth', wrote Virginia Woolf to Ethel Smyth.

Sibyl's response to disaster was heroic. Her taste in interior

decoration had always been faultless, even her denigrators joining
the chorus to praise her impeccable talent for combining harmo-
nious colours with comfortable furnishings. Argyll House was a
treat for anyone with an eye for taste. This was the one ability which
she could turn to good use. Without pause for complaint, she set up
her own interior decoration business, beginning with nothing but
determination to commend her. And, naturally, a ready-made army
of potential customers. She took one room on the first floor of Lady
Islington's house in Bruton Street, and opened for business. At
first, she was virtually a one-man operation, undertaking all the
visiting, the measuring, on her hands and knees running a tape
along skirting-boards, climbing ladders, supervising plumbing,
designing sinks, from nine in the morning until seven at night.
Virginia Woolf thought it tragic that she should be reduced to a
hardhearted shopkeeper after thirty-five years of being in society,
but Sibyl gave no sign of martyrdom. She was brave, she was
persevering, and she would not be beaten. The very qualities of
obduracy and tenacity which allowed her to bully her way to a
position as one of London's leading hostesses were now turned to
quite different effect. She discovered that she was an excellent
businesswoman. In her first year, she made a profit of £2,000
entirely by her own work.

As the business grew, Lady Colefax took on help and moved
premises. To employ Mrs Ronald Tree as her buyer was an inspired
choice. Mrs Tree (now Nancy Lancaster) was a compulsive buyer
anyway, and her husband resolved that the only way to prevent her
keeping everything she bought was to turn the illness to an
employment. She proved to be brilliant, though erratic as far as
money was concerned. Countess (Peggy) Münster joined the firm
as a procurer of customers, and Baron Radowitz was taken on to
fold up samples initially, then to sell. The new shop in Grosvenor
Street duly opened. Business boomed in such proportions that
there was hardly a flat or house, in the upper and middle reaches of
London society, that was not decorated, at least in part, by Lady
Colefax.

From adversity arose one of the great interior decorating styles of
England. Sibyl was in every sense a pioneer of what has become a

widespread and fashionable habit, adopted even by the large department stores which cater in more modest prices, of ordering design and materials, furnishings, fabrics, wallpapers, all from one source, and buying, in fact, the opinion and taste of one person.

The entertaining did not abate. On the contrary, Lady Colefax used the shop for her social affairs. Illegible invitation cards were scribbled out on the counter and posted from the shop, telephone bills were run up to confirm or cajole. Lady Colefax the hostess and Lady Colefax the businesswoman overlapped and complemented each other. Thus it was that Sibyl was the only hostess operating on any scale who was also a working woman. Paradoxically, her list of friends and lions was longer than that of Lady Cunard, Mrs Greville, Mrs Corrigan, Lady Londonderry, Lady Astor, Lady Oxford, and in the United States Mrs Stuyvesant Fish, Mrs Potter Palmer and Mrs Vanderbilt (from an earlier generation), none of whom had to earn a living.

A few years later, Countess Münster discovered a young man called John Fowler, and persuaded Sibyl to take him into the business. Now universally recognized as a genius of interior design, Fowler's work was soon in such demand that the name of the business was amended to pay tribute to his part in it. 'Colefax and Fowler' was born, and continues under that name to the present day.

As the thirties progressed, entertaining at Argyll House flourished as never before. To enumerate the evenings on which distinguished guests were received would itself fill an entire book. A selection must be permitted to give the flavour and suggest the scope. On 6 May 1931, there was a dinner for H.G. Wells, Maynard Keynes, J.L. Garvin, Oswald Mosley and Harold Nicolson, at which a 'fierce political discussion' took place after the ladies' departure. Given such company, it comes as no surprise. On 1 October of the same year, Mosley and Wells were there again, with Diana Cooper and Charlie Chaplin, who said he never realized he was famous until he visited New York for the first time and found chocolates, soap and hoardings everywhere bearing his image; yet no one knew him in the street, so he went to have his photograph taken as he really was. Also that evening Mosley revealed the substance of a secret meeting he had had with Neville Chamberlain. In 1933 we find Robert Bruce Lockhart, Somerset Maugham, John Gielgud, Edward Lutyens, Gerald Berners, Roger Fry, Lady Cunard, Lady Weymouth, André Maurois, Alfred Beit, Desmond MacCarthy, Gertrude Lawrence, ambassadors, first secretaries, and Rothschilds. Others appear in profusion towards the end of George V's reign—Austen Chamberlain, Brendan Bracken, Mrs Churchill, Alexander Korda, Beaverbrook, the Duke of Buccleuch, Vincent Massey, R.A. Butler, Thelma Cazalet, Gerry Wellesley (later Duke of Wellington), the Mountbattens, the Dufferins, the Jebbs. The greatest catch of all, which would eventually lead to Sibyl's footnote in the constitutional history of England, was the heir to the throne himself, the Prince of Wales. In the spring of 1935 the way was being prepared. The Prince's friend, Mrs Ernest Simpson, of whose existence the British public was still quite unaware, enjoyed parties and gay social evenings. She was herself an excellent hostess. It was inevitable that she should bring the Prince into the relaxed convivial surroundings where his glamour was an asset and his tenseness subsided. Equally understandable was it that Mrs Simpson had not the smallest appreciation that such outings were an indiscretion on the part of the heir to the throne. In the drama which ensued every party was innocent, save the Prince of Wales himself. Mrs Simpson's first mention at Argyll House is on 2 April 1935*; a month later, on 2 May, she is there again, dining with Somerset Maugham, H.G. Wells, Brendan Bracken, and Lady Cunard. Wells made a fool of himself by claiming that he would have too much pride to accept the Order of Merit (were it offered), because it had been given to such people as Galsworthy and Hardy. While this absurdity was passing over the port, Lady Colefax and Mrs Simpson discussed the possibility of an invitation to the Prince of Wales. Mrs Simpson would arrange it. Just over three weeks later, on 27 May, the Prince of Wales dined for the first time at Argyll House.

Sibyl made very careful preparations. The dining-room was divided to make room for two round tables. Her guests included

---

* She was taken there by Mr & Mrs Paul Bonner.

Lord and Lady Dalkeith (soon to be Duke and Duchess of Buccleuch, and among the weekend guests at the only Balmoral party the future Edward VIII was to give as King); Alexander Korda; an American journalist called Macmullen, working for *Vogue*; Robert Bruce Lockhart; Brendan Bracken; and Elsie Mendl, the Parisian hostess with blue hair, who was standing on her head long before Laura Corrigan assumed the habit. The party was a huge success, with the Prince very relaxed and joking a great deal, and making it quite obvious that he listened to, and expected everyone else to listen to, each word uttered by Mrs Simpson.

After dinner, Lockhart, Bracken and the Prince of Wales became involved in a long discussion on foreign policy. Bracken was expounding strong anti-German views which the Prince did not care for. Bracken was thought to be an 'extremist' in his dislike of Hitler, whereas the Prince made no secret that he advocated firm ties of friendship with Hitler's Reich. Bruce Lockhart tactfully took the Prince's side to temper Bracken's violence, but since he recorded that the Prince spoke more 'definitely' than on any other subject, perhaps there was vehemence on both sides. The episode is interesting for it illustrates yet again the indirect influence wielded by a society hostess. For days afterwards it was suggested that Lockhart had levered the Prince into his pro-German position, a position which was to cause growing embarrassment before the Abdication, and afterwards, the comforting satisfaction that the country was better off without a King who might have compromised its credibility in war. All this came from Lady Colefax's dinner party. Society hostesses in the short reign of Edward VIII brought the monarch to the dining-table as none had been able to do in the reigns of George V and Queen Victoria. Not since the Prince Regent had there been such easy access, and no one could remember an heir to the throne at a private dinner party in King's Road, Chelsea.

Whispers had already been heard that the Prince of Wales entertained strong views about Germany. Why, then, did Lady Colefax invite Bracken to sit at his table? It is much to her credit that she was the only one among the hostesses who was against Hitler from the very beginning. She saw the danger, and assembled at her parties Conservative MPs who also saw it and were constantly warning the country of its possible consequences. That the Prince should hear unpalatable views at Argyll House was a brave attempt on her part to exercise influence for the good. It was not her fault that it failed.

Similarly, she sometimes invited Hitler's Ambassador, Herr von Ribbentrop, and brought him into contact with a number of people whose opinion mattered. Though she detested Ribbentrop's policy, she never compromised the rules of courtesy, but allowed him to talk as much as he liked so that others present would see him as he was. Gradually Ribbentrop's nature revealed itself without provocation. Lady Colefax was extremely astute.

Another dinner party was given at Argyll House on 13 December that year. On this occasion Sibyl invited Diana Cooper, the Garvins, Harold Nicolson and Bruce Lockhart, as well as the Prince and both Simpsons. Again foreign policy was discussed, and again the Prince spoke out firmly for a deal with Germany.

On 13 January of the new and crucial year of 1936, Lady Colefax and Harold Nicolson accompanied the Prince and Mrs Simpson to the first night of Noël Coward's new play, *Tonight at Eight-thirty*, dining at the Savoy Grill afterwards. Nicolson noticed that Mrs Simpson forbade the Prince to smoke in the interval, and he obeyed, but Nicolson also confessed that the frivolity of the evening disturbed him. He suspected that Sibyl thought she was bringing the heir into touch with Young England, and that Mrs Simpson was making it harder for him to associate with the right people. There was little need for force. The Prince of Wales enjoyed unstuffy company, and much preferred Noël Coward to Chopin, as a later evening at Argyll House would all too graphically demonstrate.

By this time, George V was known to be seriously ill, and the country was anticipating the transformation of dashing young prince into glamorous king. One week after the Coward evening, Sibyl went with Robert Bruce Lockhart and Lady Hudson (Northcliffe's widow) to see *Mutiny on the Bounty* at the Empire Cinema. When they came out, the crowds in the streets were subdued, thoughtful. Evening newspapers prepared for the worst. 'The King's life is drawing to a close' proclaimed the headlines and the placards. Sibyl and her friends drove to Buckingham Palace and walked over to the railings, where a small crowd had gathered in the cold night. Two men emerged from the palace and walked across the courtyard. As one pinned the final bulletin, the other, a policeman, announced to those waiting, 'It is the end'. The King had died at 11.55 p.m. on 20 January. Sibyl's new friend was now King Edward VIII.

This was only the beginning of a very eventful year for Sibyl Colefax. One month later, on 19 February, Sir Arthur Colefax died after one day's illness. The shock genuinely overwhelmed Sibyl, who had had no time to accustom herself to this earthquake in her life. She had been blessed with a good and happy marriage which had taken like a skin graft and was fundamental to her existence. Now the skin was suddenly ripped off. Virginia Woolf was the first to hear. She delivered some flowers to Argyll House with a note sending love from Virginia and Leonard. In response Sibyl wrote a heart-broken letter which touched Mrs Woolf until she discovered (she says not how) that Sibyl had written in more or less the same terms to people she hardly knew. The discovery appears to have horrified Mrs Woolf, with very little cause, for such letters can only really be written in one manner, and grief does not give one pause to construct literary variations. With greater justification, Mrs Woolf observed that the loss did nothing to interrupt Sibyl's frenetic list of social engagements. 'Was she so tanned and leathered by society that the only thing she could not face was solitude?' Yes, perhaps. After all, a woman who prefers to be alone would make a very poor hostess. Mrs Woolf found her plucky, but arid, dust-strewn. 'I don't feel at my ease with people who take the death of husbands so heroically,' she said.

There is no doubt Sibyl felt her husband's loss deeply. She had slept every night in the crook of his arm, she told Cynthia Jebb. There is also no doubt that she dealt with this loss, both at work and at leisure, by crowding her hours with even more occupations than before.

This was hardly difficult, as she was now very close to the centre of the threatening crisis involving the King and Mrs Simpson. Those 'in the know' watched the Court Circular in *The Times* with

Emerald Cunard as a young woman, drawn by the Marchioness of Anglesey

Emerald Cunard in old age, in a photograph by Cecil Beaton (*right*)

Emerald Cunard and George Moore in the sitting-room of Lady Cunard's house in Grosvenor Square, painted by Lavery (*below*)

more interest than that column had ever received, for hidden behind the names mentioned, and the names omitted, lay the unfolding drama of the King's private life. At the first dinner party given by Edward VIII, to which Mr Ernest Simpson was pointedly *not* invited, there among the guests was the name of Lady Colefax; others were David Margesson (Chief Whip), Sir Samuel Hoare and his wife, the Duke and Duchess of York (later George VI and his consort), Winston Churchill and his wife, Lady Diana Cooper, and Mrs Simpson. By keeping Mr Simpson away, two things were made apparent: that the King was in earnest about his affair, and that a select group of people were potentially privy to his intentions. Winston Churchill was one, and Sibyl Colefax another.

As one would expect, Churchill was a friend of the King, while Sibyl was more in the confidence of Wallis Simpson. Not that the King disliked her; on the contrary, he applauded Sibyl's easy domesticity and simple manners. But it was poor beleaguered Mrs Simpson who sought a quiet word with Sibyl as she tottered unknowingly towards catastrophe.

The Visitors' Book at Argyll House reveals that Mrs Simpson was often a guest without the King during the Spring of 1936, and the considerable correspondence between the two women, preserved on both sides but yet to be published, contains further evidence that Wallis trusted Sibyl for her native good sense and her discretion. Lady Cunard, whom Wallis also knew socially, was anything but discreet, and was the last person to protect a confidence. Besides, she was herself American. Sibyl, with her middle-class ancestry, her Anglo-Indian upbringing and her ordinary family virtues, understood those nebulous qualities of English life which were so mysterious to Mrs Simpson and made it impossible for her to understand why the King could not cavort about as much as he pleased. Sibyl was on the side of circumspection. On at least one occasion, the King met Mrs Simpson clandestinely at Sibyl Colefax's shop. Wallis came in by the front door, as if to buy something or seek Sibyl's professional advice, while the King, wearing a boater, entered by the tradesman's door at the back.

On 2 April, Wallis Simpson gave an 'intimate' party for the King at her flat in Bryanston Court. Apart from Harold Nicolson, Alexander Woollcott, a couple from the US Embassy in Buenos Aires, and Ernest Simpson himself, Wallis asked three of London's hostesses—the Ladies Cunard, Colefax and Oxford (Margot Asquith)—each of whom was furious at finding the other two present. They smouldered with ill-disguised resentment at the implicit revelation they were considered equally deserving of the special honour. Sibyl unluckily told a funny story which, as usual with her, fell flat.

Amidst all the growing excitement engendered by the King's private life, Sibyl's own was subjected to considerable upheaval. Since her husband's death in February, she had decided that her limited means, notwithstanding the success of her business, would no longer allow her to live in her beloved Argyll House. Once the decision had been taken, characteristically she did not prevaricate. The house was put on the market, a buyer was found, and by June Lady Colefax was already packing her bags ready for the move into a far smaller house in North Street, Westminster. But first, there would be dinner parties to the very end, and one more grand party to surpass them all. It would be the swan song of Argyll House. Sibyl set the date for 10 June 1936.

The customary scribbled notes went out to a chosen sixteen for dinner, with up to another ten guests for drinks afterwards. The King and Mrs Simpson would be Guests of Honour, with Diana Cooper, Lady Brownlow, Mr and Mrs Kenneth Clark, Sir Robert Bruce Lockhart, Harold Nicolson, the Lamonts, the Duchess of Buccleuch and others. Sibyl persuaded Artur Rubinstein to play the piano after dinner, a rare honour which he did not accord easily. He disliked playing for 'society' company, more interested in food, drink and gossip than in music, but he was fond of Sibyl and agreed to make an exception.

One of the guests invited to come after dinner was Lord Berners. He did not respond immediately, so she telephoned him. 'I especially want you to come, Gerald, to meet Arthur.'

'But I thought Arthur was dead,' said Berners.

'Oh, not my Arthur—Arthur Rubinstein.'

The party went well enough during dinner, with the King very relaxed and happy, completely without A.D.C. or official attendance of any kind. When the ladies left, all the gentlemen moved to the King's table (there had been two seatings of eight) until about eleven. What happened next is not too clear. Various accounts of the latter part of the evening found their way into diaries (at least three of the men guests recorded the event), and others still alive have vivid recollections. They all agree that it hovered on the edge of disaster for poor Sibyl.

The men joined the ladies in the drawing-room to hear Artur Rubinstein play. After-dinner guests were by now making their appearance, including Berners, Princesse de Polignac (Winaretta Singer, the sewing-machine heiress), Mr and Mrs Winston Churchill, Daisy Fellowes, and Noël Coward. Churchill and the politicians had just come from a meeting at which Neville Chamberlain had announced the suspension of sanctions against Mussolini's Italy, so there was much political gossip in the air, encouraged by the amount of wine that had been consumed and by the King's declared inclination to be well informed. The hubbub took some time to subside, while Rubinstein became increasingly restless. Finally, the King sat on a stool near the piano, next to Mrs Simpson, and the Princesse de Polignac, a true connoisseur of music, took the next best position by the piano and bristled with keen expectation of the glories to come from Rubinstein's fingers. Lady Colefax and Lady Diana Cooper sprawled inelegantly on the floor, presumably to give an air of informality to the occasion. Harold Nicolson remarked that Sibyl on the floor was an incongruity, 'as if someone had laid an inkstand there'.

Rubinstein played three Chopin pieces, including a Barcarolle and a Prelude, to the accompaniment of intermittent chat from the King. When he wasn't talking, His Majesty looked very bored, and made no attempt to hide the fact. Mme de Polignac was clearly irritated by this unabashed example of the philistinism of the British (such a misfortune could not have happened in Paris), and Kenneth Clark was embarrassed. The King was not the only one to interrupt with chatter. Lady Colefax was near to tears, as much at the affront to Rubinstein as at the manifest irritation of her most honoured guest. Rubinstein was about to play a fourth piece, when the proceedings came to an abrupt stop. The King walked over to him and said, 'We enjoyed that very much, Mr Rubinstein', which was a clear enough command not to play any more. Some say that the pianist replied, 'I am afraid that you do not like my playing, Your Majesty', but all agree he walked out of the room, with the Kenneth Clarks, in some dudgeon. Clark was angry at the humiliation. The King had had enough, and prepared to leave. It was still early for him, and Sibyl clearly saw that what she intended as her finest party was something of a flop. Then someone suggested that Noël Coward should play. Without more ado, Coward sat at the piano and sang 'Mad Dogs and Englishmen', 'Don't put your daughter on the stage, Mrs Worthington', and other choice pieces. The atmosphere re-charged. All those who failed to be enthused by Chopin gave their rapt attention to the trivia which followed it, and they included an unrepentant Churchill. The King resumed his seat, stayed another hour, and thanked Mr Coward fulsomely. Sibyl's evening had been rescued, but Mme de Polignac admitted she had been shocked by the rudeness towards Rubinstein.

Sibyl was no stranger to this kind of awkward moment. There had been the time when Olga Lynn was singing and grew so furious at the ceaseless chatter in the room that she threw down her music in disgust. Balfour had then been recruited to placate her. But this was different. You cannot tell the King of England to shut up.

Not long afterwards, Virginia Woolf went to tea, while the packing cases were being loaded and the odd bits of furniture labelled for sale. The house bore an acute sadness about it, which Mrs Woolf, with her unerring antennae, felt keenly. 'We were sitting in the ruins of that magnificent structure which had borne so lately the royal crown on top,' she said. Mrs Woolf admired Sibyl's achievement and applauded her courage, her determination to carry on. She said so. Tears came into Sibyl's eyes (but did not fall, observed Mrs Woolf) as she looked around the room. 'I've always had a passion for this house,' she said. 'I've felt about it as a lover feels.' Mrs Woolf placed her hand on Sibyl's and commiserated.

The telephone rang several times during their colloquy of confidence. Sibyl professed to be irritated by the interruptions, but always got up to attend to them, sighing. She sighed again when she returned, to speak of the past, and of those terrible women who were mere climbers and should be avoided like the plague. Virginia Woolf began to feel uneasy, as if her attempt at womanly closeness were still-born. In a letter to Vita Sackville-West years before, she had said as much: 'Friendship, let alone intimacy, is impossible. Yet I respect, even admire . . . one never speaks the truth to her. She skated over everything, evaded, palliated, compromised; yet is fundamentally kind and good. It's odd for me, who have some gift for intimacy, to be nonplussed entirely.'

Mrs Woolf tried no longer. She recalled the many evenings she had spent at Argyll House, on that very sofa, how she had met Arnold Bennett there, and Max Beerbohm, and George Moore . . . Sibyl's demeanour underwent a magical transformation as the list of names clattered out. So even Virginia Woolf had been impressed! She smiled, relaxed, warmed to her companion. 'That's what I like you to say,' she remarked guilelessly. Never was it clearer than at that moment of sadness that Lady Colefax, in her innocence, really had lived entirely for other people, and for other people's enjoyment at her house.

The crisis in the King's affairs reached its peak in November, when at last the newspapers revealed to an unsuspecting public that their monarch threatened a constitutional catastrophe such as they had never known, by refusing to part with Mrs Simpson. Lady Colefax, though not at the centre, was within the small circle of intimates throughout. The night before the Bishop of Bradford's sermon, which had signalled the press to break its silence, she had been to the cinema with the King, Wallis, and Edward Stanley. Edward VIII had been in fine form that evening, asking Sibyl to give a dinner for himself and Wallis at Christmas.

It is hard to be fair to Sibyl at this moment. Was she genuinely fond of the couple, as friends are? She was very proud of being 'in the know' and told all details of the crisis to anyone who would listen. It was, in a sense, her hour of glory. She said she thought 'H.M.' a genius, but had little time for the Duke of Kent. She confirmed she had personally advised them, if the worst came to the worst, to live in South America. She told Virginia Woolf, in a lapse from her usual high standards of discretion, that H.M. and Wallis had never been to bed together. Many formed the impression that Sibyl seriously expected to be called upon to liaise between Queen Mary and Mrs Simpson.

One Sunday in November Sibyl spent the entire day alone with Mrs Simpson at Fòrt Belvedere. Wallis was desperately miserable, and frightened. People were exhorting her to leave the country, but she assured Sibyl that the King would only follow her wherever she went, which would damage his prestige even further. He had gone so far as to threaten suicide if she left him. But she never thought he could be serious about marriage, and had never understood that abdication was a real possibility. Had he actually proposed marriage? asked Sibyl. Of course not! Mrs Simpson authorized Lady Colefax to convey this intelligence to the Government through Mrs Chamberlain, which she duly did, but by this time the King had told Baldwin that he intended to marry his lady come what might. Three weeks later the reign of Edward VIII was over.

The changes effected by the Abdication Crisis of 1936 are now part of history. The smaller outcome which concerns us here was the consternation caused in the drawing-rooms of London's society hostesses. Many had courted Mrs Simpson, encouraged her, pushed her on, only to find that their prize evaporated in a matter of hours. Some then turned and disparaged the woman whose friendship they had laboured hard to gain, and Lady Colefax was quite unfairly included in their number. As one versifier put it,

> The ladies Colefax and Cunard
> Took it very, very hard.

Osbert Sitwell wrote a cruel satirical poem suggesting that 'Coalbox' and her kind were uniform hypocrites:

> What do they say, that jolly crew?
> Oh . . . her they hardly knew,
> They never found her really *nice*
> (And here the sickened cock crew thrice):
> Him they had never thought quite sane,
> But weak and obstinate and vain.

The poem was entitled 'Rat Week' and proposed that Lady Colefax 'in her iron cage of curls' had been one of the rats to desert the sinking ship.

This was untrue and unworthy. Hypocrisy was not one of Lady Colefax's sins, and loyalty she valued even above lion-hunting. In the months and years to come she would always defend the Duchess of Windsor against spiteful attacks, and would visit her whenever she could. She hurried to see her in France, making a detour from her holiday simply to give pleasure; there were, after all, no advantages in being known as the friend of a disgraced ex-King's wife. The Duchess returned the friendship. They spent Christmas Day together, two weeks after the Abdication, at Somerset Maugham's Villa Mauresque, and Sibyl was even included in the Windsors' honeymoon at Wasserleonberg, the house in Austria which the Münsters lent them; Sibyl spent one week there. On a discreet visit by the Duchess to London after the war, Sibyl was in hospital. The Duchess of Windsor visited her sick-bed, announced by a flustered nurse as 'Mrs Simpson'. There was sufficient trust between the two women not to be threatened by the malice of an Osbert Sitwell or the gossip of the ill-informed. Wallis and Sibyl were basically simple women, and they responded to each other's ingenuousness. The Lady Colefax that Wallis knew was not the same creature observed by the hypercritical Virginia Woolf. Both impressions of Sibyl were true, but whereas Wallis was not bright enough to look beneath the surface, Mrs Woolf was too bright to look anywhere else. The Sibyl known to Wallis (and to Cynthia Jebb, Rebecca West and many others) was quite the nicer.*

Meanwhile, there was much else to occupy Sibyl's attentions apart from the abdication affair. She was struck down by a serious illness in the autumn and had to spend part of September in the Empire Nursing Home, at a time when she ought to have been busy preparing the new house for habitation. The North Street house was significantly smaller than Argyll House, and had been left in a deplorable state by the previous owner, whom she thought a

---

* It is also significant that it was Sibyl Colefax who advised the Windsors not to go to Germany. They took her advice.

'madman'. It would need all Sibyl's decorating and designing skills to make it agreeable. Though these terms are relative, North Street in those days was almost a slum, and Sibyl's change of abode was certainly a retreat into a more modest style of living.

Coming out of hospital, she still had a few weeks to entertain in a depleted Argyll House. Her last dinner there, a kind of epilogue to the 'swan song' in June, was given on 28 October, when the guests included the Winston Churchills, the Duff Coopers, the Mountbattens, Philip Sassoon, Somerset Maugham, Rubinstein, Harold Nicolson and the Duchess of Rutland. Mrs Simpson had by then obtained her divorce, but the ultimate drama had yet to be enacted. Churchill, who knew much, gave away little. Two days later, on 30 October, Lady Colefax closed the door into King's Road for the last time.

Her strength had been sapped by the operation she had undergone, but she was undaunted. With both health and finances in a fragile state, she would not countenance an abridgement of her social activities. North Street, renamed 'Lord North Street' shortly after Lady Colefax's arrival (which was, of course, a coincidence), was transformed into a house of beguiling charm and not much space. The drawing-room was upstairs, with the large basket of recently published books overflowing on to the carpet, placed at the top of the stairs before the drawing-room door. Black lacquered furniture dominated the décor. These tiny eighteenth-century houses, with two rooms on each floor, do not lend themselves to entertaining on a large scale, but Lady Colefax triumphantly overcame the difficulties imposed by lack of space simply by ignoring them. The small dining-room table in the ground-floor room, surrounded by gilt chairs, continued to receive the great, the famous, and the powerful. It says much for Sibyl's qualities that none of her friends or regular guests abandoned her. They went to Lord North Street as they had gone to King's Road, though they would be frequently so packed together that shoulders collided and eating could only be achieved by agile wrist movements.

The first dinner took place on 4 May 1937, a week before George VI's coronation. Chips Channon confessed he was half dreading it, and he was probably not alone. Yet he and everyone else had to concede that Sibyl had made the little house very cosy. The Churchills were there and the Duff Coopers, Nicolson, Barbie Wallace, and the American journalist H.R. Knickerbocker. It was typical of Sibyl, and demonstrated that her antennae had lost none of their power to pick up the most interesting, that she should capture Knickerbocker for this evening. He had just returned from covering the Spanish Civil War, and had been imprisoned for a while by Franco's troops. A few days earlier Hitler's air force had mercilessly destroyed Guernica as a favour to Franco, causing *The Times* to publish a detailed account which annoyed the Germans. So there could hardly be a more topical or fascinating guest in London than Knickerbocker. Channon found him 'dreadful', because his report on conditions in Spain was severely critical of Franco, but Churchill said that the battle for ideas there had degenerated into 'a mire of blood and ashes'. One cannot dispute that it must have been one of the most spell-binding dinner party conversations in London that evening. As a further tribute to Sibyl's continued power to attract the best, Churchill was expected to go on to Londonderry House, where a far grander reception was taking place, but decided instead to stay on at Sibyl's, so that the Conservative gathering around Lady Londonderry would 'lack the lustre of its most brilliant jewel.' They were joined by Tom Mitford and Daisy Fellowes.

Before long, Lord North Street became as much the pivot of cosy London social life as Argyll House had been. It would almost be a misnomer to call Lady Colefax a 'hostess' in these years, as the word is bound to suggest marble staircases and ballrooms and a large staff. In the little rooms of Lord North Street even half a dozen people seemed a crowd, and the only servants to help Sibyl were the two faithful maids who followed her from Chelsea. The smell of rosemary which hung perpetually about the rooms reminded one that this was not a sumptuous palace, but a widow's private dwelling. But the widow was not ready for retirement, and the hordes of friends continued to eat in her tiny dining-room. The Duke and Duchess of Windsor were there in 1939, again in 1947, and the roll-call of regular visitors continued to reflect Sibyl's alliance with the most interesting people — H.G. Wells, Somerset

Maugham, Victor Cazalet, Jan Masaryk, the Mountbattens, the
U.S. Ambassador John Winant, R.A. Butler, the Master of the
Rolls Lord Greene, Rothermere, Nancy Mitford, Churchill's
personal assistant Desmond Morton, Wavell, T.S. Eliot, Stephen
Spender, Arthur Waley, Edith Sitwell, Cyril Connolly, Sir Ronald
Storrs. Occasionally she overdid it by having jealous giants to share
the attention, as when James Lees-Milne described an evening of a
'pack of lions disconcerted by each other's presence', at which
hardly anyone spoke. The great can be petty. On the whole,
however, Sibyl's evenings were successful and memorable. She no
longer needed to pursue a prey; she simply opened the door and in it
would walk, meekly, gratefully. One felt flattered to be asked to
Lord North Street, with good reason, and the feeling was
experienced by people of power, people of intelligence, people of
discernment.

Nothing could interrupt this gentle flow of social intercourse,
nothing, that is, except the Blitz of London by German bombers in
1940. The Blitz not only disrupted social life, but destroyed all
possibility of planning and keeping rendezvous of almost any kind.
For the first time in thirty years, the stream of illegible postcards
from Lady Colefax ceased. She minded terribly, yet revealed, as did
so many others, that under siege she had her sense of priorities.
Bomb damage in Westminster was severe, and the windows at 19
Lord North Street were blown in, rendering the house intolerably
cold. Sibyl was there alone most evenings, until the time came for
her to walk round to her underground shelter beneath the Institute
for the Blind, where she slept on a straw mattress. In the day, she
was a Red Cross Commandant. Harold Nicolson said she was
perfectly serene.

Naturally, the Blitz also curtailed the activities of Sibyl's
business. It was not until after the war that Colefax and Fowler was
able to renew its pre-eminence in the field of interior decoration.
The result was a further diminution of Sibyl's resources, to the
point where she could be described as very poor indeed.

In addition, her health had never completely recovered after the
operation of 1936, and her age was beginning to tell. James Lees-
Milne described her in the war as 'very tiny, round-shouldered, old

and pathetic', and when she was not busy talking, or was not animated, she collapsed like a wilting tulip, bent over, almost hunch-backed. Unkind gossips referred to her 'hump', and still less attractive individuals in better health would try to lose her in the corridors of a great country house she was visiting by racing on ahead while she, with her stick and her nose pointing to the ground, clop-clopped uneasily some way behind. The inoffensive, well-meaning Lady Colefax, who had given such pleasure to so many, deserved such cruel treatment less than anyone in London.

She was graphically reminded of mortality when, two years after the Blitz and the restoration of her dinner parties, one such terminated in a death. Her guests included James Pope-Hennessy, Ronald Storrs and Winaretta, the Princesse de Polignac. Storrs took Madame de Polignac home in a taxi at 11 p.m., because she complained of feeling unwell. Three hours later she was dead of a heart attack. When Sibyl heard she had been almost the last person on earth to speak to this remarkable woman, she was deeply upset. Not that they were especially close friends, but Sibyl genuinely admired her, and her sudden death immediately following a Colefax evening could not fail to underline her recognition that the lions, and the friends, were disappearing. What would she do without them?

She would not even contemplate the possibility of having to. With tremendous resilience Lady Colefax set about organizing very special gatherings at the Dorchester Hotel, which gradually became a feature of the war years and are remembered by the scores of people in London at the time who attended them. Most significant for her was that the Americans she knew should meet and know the Englishmen she knew at a time when Anglo-American understanding was of cardinal importance. Since her house in Lord North Street was too small to arrange parties on any scale, she would give them at the Dorchester, and since she could not afford to finance them herself, she would make a charge of 10/6d. a head (52½p now). These dinner parties were known as Sibyl's 'Ordinaries'.

Not everybody enjoyed the Ordinaries, probably because they lacked the cosy ambience one had come to expect from Sibyl Colefax. Her friend Harold Nicolson said 'everybody loathes them', which was certainly an exaggeration, though he managed to paint a vivid picture of the 'community of dislike' which bound together people who would not normally seek each other out. It was perhaps a little like the sudden congeniality which occurs in a formerly silent railway compartment when the travellers realize the train has stopped for an hour or so and they share the same frustration. Sibyl 'knows in a way that people hate these ghastly functions', said Nicolson. 'She adopts a mood of will-power. She manages us firmly as if we had all come to the Dorchester to give a blood-transfusion.' Nicolson regarded them as ghastly because he could not bear anything which was, in his eyes, second-rate, and to eat in an hotel and pay for it was like supping with a tradesman as far as he was concerned. But Sibyl had no such pretensions, and most people appreciated the value of her efforts. At an Ordinary one could meet politicians, war correspondents, and Americans. Almost single-handed, Lady Colefax made it her duty to promote Anglo-American relations in wartime.

Once a month, she would send out a bill to the various guests, like a restaurant account. No one complained.

The only danger was that guests of Emerald Cunard, in the same hotel, might collide with guests of Sibyl Colefax. It was understood that if you were invited by one you did not then proceed to catch the tail end of a party *chez* the other. Anyone who risked it might incur the anger of both ladies, though it must be said that Emerald was far more touchy on the subject than Sibyl. Emerald thought the Ordinaries the depth of vulgarity (but still attended some), and Nancy Mitford wickedly admitted that she preferred to go to Lady Cunard, if she had the choice, as her dinner was free.

Nevertheless, that Sibyl should feel able to continue her Ordinaries even after the war, and receive acceptance of her invitations, indicates better than any fluent memoir that her trouble was worthwhile.

In the summer of 1944, the Germans began to send their notorious pilotless aircraft, known as 'doodlebugs', over London. The drone of these machines would increase in strength and menace until suddenly they cut out, sometimes with a splutter, and the thing would fall and explode. It was in fact a flying bomb, but the war cabinet was at first unwilling to make this known to the already battle-weary Londoners. Lady Colefax was among the first, outside government circles, to learn the truth, from private information passed on by one of her friends. The Americans could not believe that anything so devilish was possible. Sibyl herself very nearly made too close an acquaintance with a doodlebug. She and Harold Nicolson were present at a lecture given by a French *député* in Eaton Square when one passed over, then stopped. It was obviously almost overhead. Everyone crouched momentarily, waited for the explosion, then went on listening to the lecture. Coming out to the street afterwards, they found the air thick with dust, proof that the bomb had missed them by a few yards.

After the war, Sibyl's health deteriorated still further, but, doughty as ever, she persevered with her active life. Having sold the decorating business, she still used the shop daily to make her telephone calls and write her notes, a practice to which no one objected, knowing that her need to economize was ever more urgent. Almost the last function there in her time was a coming-out party for Lady Caroline Thynne, Lord Bath's daughter, given above the shop.

By 1950, Lady Colefax was pitifully thin and wasting away. She had cancer. In August Aldous Huxley told Christopher Isherwood that Sibyl was 'bent double with her broken back, but indomitably receiving guests and going out'. At the end of the month she was made reluctantly to accept that she must go into a nursing home. Her frail and shrunken body could no longer carry her to the theatre, nor even give her the strength to write her unique scrawl, but her spirit was fierce to the end.

Of the scores of old friends who visited her in hospital, two recall that majestic determination. Sibyl pleaded with Jimmy Smith and Terence Rattigan to take her to see the latest production at Stratford-upon-Avon. Fully aware that nothing would give her greater pleasure than a little trip to the theatre, and a cosy dinner afterwards, just like the old times, they agreed to get up a party. Rattigan even hired an ambulance and nurse to take Sibyl, as she could not have withstood the rigours of a journey without care. But she never gained sufficient strength to get out of bed, and so the planned excursion never took place. Her friends knew she was happy enough looking forward to it. In a way, she had all her life enjoyed the planning of her evenings and her lunches more than the events themselves, and it was appropriate, touching, that in her last days the diary was still filling up.

The other visitor was Beverley Nichols, who wrote a moving account of Sibyl's behaviour in the *Sunday Chronicle*. 'She was a pair of blazing eyes shining from a body made of tissue paper', he said. 'Her neck was a silken thread, her hands were withered leaves . . . the September breeze through the open window might have carried her away.' No breeze, however, could quench Sibyl Colefax's interest in the topic of the moment. By her side lay a copy of Nancy Mitford's play *The Little Hut*, which had just opened in Shaftesbury Avenue to rapturous notices. Would Beverley kindly arrange tickets for them to see the play together? He gave her the engagement book. She could barely turn the pages. They found a date which could suit them both, but then Sibyl recognized that she had already promised to see *Otello* at Covent Garden that evening. Perhaps she could go to the matinée of *The Little Hut*, if Nichols would not mind. She could then continue to Covent Garden afterwards. Nichols thought this would be quite impossible, but Sibyl would not give up. The most she would concede was that 'in my present state, it might be fatiguing'.

Of course, she attended neither performance. She was allowed home to spend her last days, and died in her sleep at 6.30 on the morning of 22 September. The day before the doctor had arrived to see how she was. When he had rung the doorbell, Sibyl had imagined that it was her husband. 'Oh dear,' she said, 'that's poor Arthur, gone out without his key again.' She thought she was back at Argyll House.

Rumour raced around London that Lady Colefax had died with the telephone in her hand. This was, of course, nonsense, but it would not have been surprising. She was immediately and profoundly missed, even by those who had mocked at her. As Harold Nicolson wrote in his Marginal Comment column in the *Spectator*, her death aroused feelings of 'actual bewilderment . . . the members of her circle, both at home and abroad, feel that they have suddenly been abandoned and dispersed'. Literally hundreds of people suddenly recognized that Lady Colefax had been their common denominator, their link, that she had bothered to keep them in contact with one another when they, most likely, would not have so earnestly taken the trouble. They were now left alone to get on with their friendships without her help.

A vast number of friends turned out for the memorial service, which someone nicknamed 'the last of the Ordinaries', and not a few paused to assess what they owed her. Many of them, now firm friends, had first met as the outcome of an invitation from Lady Colefax. She had a 'respect for the sanctity of personal friendship', wrote R.A. Butler, and she 'held her own and other people's lives together by an exceptional capacity for taking trouble'. She was pre-eminently an organizer, with a gift for bringing people together. It was no mean gift, and should not be underestimated; it was certainly not possessed by other hostesses who were contemporary with her. All Laura Corrigan's guests knew each other before, and would continue to know each other whether or not Laura existed. Had she never come to London, the effect on London social life would not have been noticed. Mrs Greville was too self-important, and Lady Cunard too whimsical to take seriously the business of bringing people together. Had Sibyl Colefax not existed, or more to the point had not bothered, London life would have been measurably the poorer. At her oval table there were many who were 'privileged to meet the eminent on confidential terms', and no one has been able to match Lady Colefax's achievement in bringing this privilege to such a vast number. It takes work and application. There was no one with the energy to take her place.

Lady Salter said in *The Times* that Sibyl's contribution to international relations was 'beyond all estimate'. Kenneth Clark has since written in his autobiography that she genuinely loved people, and made it her life's work to bring them together. All seem to recognize the sincerity which underlay Sibyl Colefax's lion-hunting, and most still feel gratitude towards her.

Why, then, has she been so remorselessly teased, mocked, even by those who were beholden to her? ('When I die, scatter my ashes

over Sibyl Colefax,' said Lord Berners.) Rebecca West would go so
far as to say Lady Colefax had been 'libelled' by the many unkind
references to her in memoirs. Even allowing for the concealed
motives of her obsession, the *Geltungsbedürfnis* we have mentioned,
and the fear of solitude which Virginia Woolf thought she saw, all
this is harmless enough. Name-dropping is not a sin, after all, and at
least she could back it up. Sibyl did not drop a name until it was hers
to drop; she was not a liar. Kenneth Clark probably found the
answer when he said that there was something dehumanising about
any addiction. Because she entertained so much, one thought of her
as a giver of dinner parties rather than a woman. Because she
collected so many people, one thought of her as a collector rather
than a person. She always added, never discarded or eliminated.
Had she turned against someone who behaved badly, no matter
how famous he might be, she would have appeared more natural. As
it was, the simple, good, kindly middle-class woman that she was
found herself submerged in the estimation of some of her friends
beneath the professional hostess she became. It is a paradox, but a
perfectly understandable one, that the more successful she was the
more she laid herself open to the barbs of witty people-watchers. If
one may except the awful Bloomsbury people, and the over-
sensitive, slightly mad Sitwells, Lady Colefax had no real enemies.

Ultimately, the lion-hunting was no more harmful than a child's
game. Sibyl's desire to know everyone was the product of
simplicity, child-like *naïveté* and frank excitement. She gave far
more than this excitement gave her. Indeed, she was the only one to
suffer from it, when the hectic collecting induced an obsessive
terror of solitude.

In his diary, Sir Ronald Storrs paid just tribute to his
sometimes infuriating friend: 'I admired her real pertinacity in
getting out of life what she wanted, which was to have in her house
every man or woman of the moment and to know what they had last
done, written, said or thought. She was at her best in total company
of two, when she was not peering round fearing she might be
missing somebody or something else. She was not malicious and she
was reasonably honest in her opinions and judgements though
forced to sacrifice a good deal to the exigencies of the "business",

keeping in with us . . . as hostess she was a convener rather than a chairman . . . I still think character consists in resolute pursuit of that for which one is most suited, thus Sibyl was one of the strongest characters I have ever known.'

Max Beerbohm said, three years after her death, 'Yes, Sibyl was a reliable, helpful friend, and she seldom missed a year without making a pilgrimage to visit me here [Rapallo, Italy]. She will certainly go down to posterity through countless memoirs. No one could have imagined, herself least of all, that she would figure so largely in the history of her time.'

CHAPTER SEVEN

Laura Corrigan

When Laura Corrigan first arrived in London in 1921, by way of Cleveland, Ohio, New York, and Paris, she knew absolutely no one, and no one had the remotest idea who she was. Yet within less than two years she was giving the most popular and lavish parties in London, and twenty-five years after that her memorial service was attended by royalty, ambassadors, peers and peeresses of the highest rank, a church-full of people who had been fond of her and amused by her, but still did not know who she was. By any standards, Mrs Corrigan's success, achieved by stark determination in the face of mockery, was spectacular.

Not knowing what to make of her, London society initially dubbed her 'Mrs Cory-again', which was neither flattering nor accurate. Mrs Cory was a rich American hostess who lived in a château (or 'shaa-too' as she called it) near Paris, a former star of operetta who had married a steel millionaire and dedicated the remainder of her life to being fashionable. To this purpose, Mrs Cory had undergone an operation to make her mouth the tiny closed rose-bud considered becoming. It was literally sewn up at the corners, so that she could barely speak through it, and was once asked not to whistle in church. Famous for her bizarre choice of words, Mrs Cory would not use transport if she could save money by going on foot, and would announce that she had 'been street-walking'. Though she unwittingly gave much amusement, she never made it to the top as a hostess, because she was so unattractively mean. Guests claimed that they starved at her house, and the wine-glasses were always turned upside down owing to her disapproval of alcohol. A hostess may be forgiven any gaucherie provided she is generous, a basic truth which Mrs Corrigan would soon put to the test. When Mabel Cory left to return to America, she gave her address as 'Mrs Cory, Rocky Mountains'.

Mrs Corrigan was also the wife of a steel magnate, she also made delightfully daft remarks and ecstatic malapropisms, she also tried to improve her looks with facial surgery (not by stitching up her mouth until it disappeared, but by opening her eyes to such an extent that even when she slept the eyelids could never quite meet). There, however, the resemblance ends, for she was incredibly generous, and warm-hearted to such a degree that her kindness soon toppled all barriers and earned her many genuine friends. And she possessed other endearing eccentricities which served to make her an object of some curiosity: she stood on her head every morning for five minutes, and could even be persuaded to do so in august company; and she wore a wig, which nobody was supposed to know about, and everybody commented upon. Add to this her blatant unrepentant chasing after royalty, and the mystery of her origins, and it is easy to see why this frolicsome girl of uncertain age, with unlimited money, should be of interest to those sections of London society bent on having fun. Had they known anything of her life before she married Jimmy Corrigan, they would have been even more intrigued.

The problem was, where to begin? Unheralded and unconnected, Laura passionately yearned to be a successful hostess. She had tried before, and failed in the most humiliating manner. The Corrigan-McKinney Steel Company was situated in Cleveland, Ohio. There, fashionable society ruled over Euclid Avenue, and fashionable society spurned all Laura Corrigan's efforts to wriggle in, despite the fact that she was probably more wealthy than any of the established families who turned their backs upon her. Euclid Avenue did not like the Corrigans because Jimmy Corrigan was an unworthy heir to his father, the esteemed Captain James Corrigan;

he had a nasty reputation as a selfish playboy, and had once been sued for breach of promise by a Pittsburg girl of whom he had taken the usual advantage. He had, moreover, worked as a barman, and Cleveland society would not sip champagne with a man who had once washed the glasses. Jimmy was too much the maverick for their taste. As for his wife, well, she came from somewhere in the midwest, had neither antecedents nor class, and had the impertinence to think she could assume her place without the weight of generations. It was even rumoured that she had been a waitress in Chicago. This would never do.

Laura then dragged Jimmy to New York, where she went to extraordinary lengths to install herself in the highest circles. Week after week, she spent a fortune of her husband's money announcing parties and sending invitations to all the right people, engaging the best chefs, employing twice as many servants as anyone else, erecting lavish decorations, all to no avail. Scarcely anyone turned up, and certainly not one of the grand Fifth Avenue families even deigned to answer. Undeterred, Laura went so far as to set up private telephones for each of her guests, so that anyone wishing to contact a Corrigan guest could discover from the operator what ex-directory number he or she was using, at Mrs Corrigan's expense, that evening. New York had never encountered such an absurd kind of extravagance, but far from being impressed by Laura's determination, society derided her cheek. One reluctant recipient of her invitations, tired of the constant stream of cards which came through his door, had a card printed at Tiffany's declining Mrs Corrigan's kind invitation, and sent one from his plentiful stock every time a card of hers was delivered.

If Laura had ever believed the myth that America boasted a classless society, her experience in Cleveland and New York in the years following her marriage in 1916 was a rude shock. She learned that money was not, after all, the passport to acceptance, and that the highest échelons of privileged society protect themselves fiercely from upstarts, however rich. The Fifth Avenue set had not even bothered to discover that Mrs Corrigan was in fact an amiable and decent woman. And so she turned to Europe, where, in spite of titles and inherited land, in spite of genes passed down through hundreds of years, Society with a big S is paradoxically more open to adventure, because it has confidence bred of long practice. New Yorkers were still *arrivistes*, still insecure.

And so, after a brief sortie in Paris (where she made friends who would play a large role in her story, and will be introduced later), Laura came naked to London. She had first to find a house in which to give her parties, then to find people she could invite to them. She solved both problems in one masterly stroke.

Laura was invited to dinner at Chandos House, leased by another American who had 'made it' and did not look disdainfully upon others who might try. This was Cora, Countess of Strafford, who had been widowed three times. Her first husband was Mr Colgate, the toothpaste millionaire, followed by the 4th Earl of Strafford, whom she married in 1898. He died five months later, and Cora married Martyn Kennard, who died in 1920, enabling Mrs Kennard, somewhat irregularly, to revert to her former name of Lady Strafford. Cora invited half a dozen interesting and important people to meet Mrs Corrigan, among them William Cavendish-Bentinck (later British Ambassador to Poland and now Duke of Portland), and during the course of the evening Laura learned that the celebrated Mrs Keppel, Edward VII's friend, planned to live abroad and was ready to let her magnificent house at 16 Grosvenor Street.

An appointment was swiftly made for Mrs Keppel to meet Laura and discuss the possibility of her taking the Keppel mansion for the season. It was a splendid and unusual house, for it had once been a piano shop with eighteenth-century flats on the upper floors. The Keppels had used the whole building as it stood, with the spacious rooms designed to display pianos now serving as impressive reception rooms, and the flats as private apartments, one for George Keppel, another for his wife Alice, one for each daughter, and so on. The whole was decorated in the most exquisite taste, Mrs Keppel having collected china and porcelain for years, as well as the finest cut-glass chandeliers. None of this, alas, held much significance for Laura, who on being told that the Persian carpets must be cared for with the greatest respect, replied, 'Why, they're not even new!' Nor, at this first interview, did Laura like what she saw of the sleeping arrangements, with flats dividing husband and wife. 'That's no use,' she told Mrs Keppel, 'Mr Corrigan and I live intimate.' Mrs Keppel persuaded her that Corrigan could doubtless come down a little back staircase from his apartment to hers when the impulse arose. As for the rental, it was quite clear that money was no impediment to a satisfactory arrangement as far as Laura was concerned, but the price should include the services of Mr Rolfe, the glorious Edwardian butler, Mrs Rolfe the cook, and the full staff of twenty indoor servants. Moreover, could Mrs Corrigan lease Mrs Keppel's Visitors' Book as well? This was negotiated at supplementary cost, and Laura was now ready to take up residence. Her greatest asset would turn out to be Rolfe. 'Mr and Mrs Rolfe will look after you,' said Mrs Keppel, 'so you will have nothing to worry about.'

Rolfe did more than look after Laura in her first weeks at 16 Grosvenor Street—he procured for her. He would stand on the doorstep and whenever he saw a friend of the Keppels approach, he would accost him gently and say, 'Good morning! I'm sure Madam would like you to come in for a drink.' Thus Laura's very first guests were literally picked up off the street, and she made initial acquaintance with some of her dearest friends in this manner. Rolfe's next, and most telling, contribution was to advise Laura to contact Charlie Stirling. No one in London was better connected than he, the nephew of Lord Rossmore and cousin to almost every other aristocratic family. Unmarried, intensely social and unfailingly popular, Charlie Stirling hopped from one party to the next the whole year round, even turning his enjoyment into a profession: he was social secretary to the powerful Marchioness of Londonderry, the most prominent political hostess of her day. If Mrs Corrigan wished to meet the right people, perhaps Mr Stirling could suggest a way?

Stirling proved immediately receptive to Laura's approach, presumably because the financial inducement was outrageously high. Yes, he would undertake to organize Mrs Corrigan's social life for her, but she must be ready to place herself entirely in his hands. Not only would he tell her whom to invite, and when, but how to behave, what to say, what to wear, how to arrange the *placement*, what to offer. Laura readily agreed, and the two of them sat at a card-table in 16 Grosvenor Street every morning to plan the coming events. At first, it was an embarrassing exercise, for Laura's first question of the day was invariably, 'How many invitations are there?' As there were none, it was not easy to know how to spend the rest of their time together. But Stirling soon managed to secure an invitation for Laura to dine at Londonderry House, and from that moment the ascent to vertiginous heights was assured, for Laura was indeed beginning very near the top.

Londonderry House was socially the most important venue in London, proudly placed on Park Lane with a magnificent staircase at the head of which Lady Londonderry would stand to receive her guests, a sparkling tiara as if growing from her hair, her body ablaze with the incomparable Londonderry jewels, including an un-believable stomacher. It was indeed an honour for anyone to find himself at Londonderry House, and for Mrs Corrigan, the unknown wife of a steel millionaire, it was an honour a hundred times more amazing. Charlie Stirling made it clear that Laura should contribute handsomely to one of Lady Londonderry's favourite charities and her path would not be strewn with potholes. For anyone but Laura, the idea of climbing the stairs at Londonderry House would have been frightening. But this was precisely what she had come for, and it would not be easy to frighten her.

The two women got on so well together that even Charlie Stirling was astonished at the success. Lady Londonderry admired pluck, and recognized in Laura a woman of courage. What did it matter if she came from nowhere and was not allied to a family one knew? Lady Londonderry likewise had a justifiable respect for money, and the uses to which it could be put. She did not need it, but she would gladly help Laura to spend it in furtherance of the right causes.

The Marquess and Marchioness of Londonderry were the first in society to accept an invitation from the American lady. In no time at all the news had buzzed around London, and soon everyone was hoping to find himself on the list. Curiosity and loyalty were the prime motives—curiosity to see and hear what this Mrs Corrigan was like (rumours of her malapropisms had already been spread, and the wig was an object of fascination); loyalty to Charlie Stirling. To help him, friends rallied round, and in helping him they helped Laura. On his instructions, the visit of Lord and Lady Londonderry was announced in *The Times*. Then, on May 17, barely six weeks after taking up residence, Laura was able to announce in that same grave journal (of which, incidentally, she had never heard mention until she arrived in London), that she was giving a small dinner-party at which Princess Marie Louise, the King's cousin, was to be guest of honour. For this occasion, Laura wore a gown of white crêpe embroidered with opalescent pearls. Thanks to Mrs Rolfe, whose cooking was supreme, the evening was a delight, and Laura was now ready to launch a larger party. She sat down for the ritual examination with Charlie Stirling after everyone had left, heard what she had done correctly, what she could improve, and they decided together that cards would be sent the next day to all the best houses.

It seemed to those receiving the invitations that Laura was hopelessly indiscriminate. She simply invited everybody. But the choice was not hers, and Stirling was clever enough to make sure that all those invited would confer with each other and discover that it would be a party of friends. They all knew each other already, and if they could have dinner, a dance and fun at the expense of a wealthy American whom nobody knew but Charlie seemed to approve of, there was no reason on earth why they should refuse. Other American ladies from the grand New York families, who happened to be in London, were not invited. They would have refused anyway, for they still regarded Mrs Corrigan as an impertinent upstart. (To the very end, the likes of Astors and Vanderbilts refused to countenance her, preferring to pretend she did not exist.) Nor was any attempt made to conquer the intellectual set—writers, philosophers, musicians, painters—who would require more than a good meal and a semi-royal guest to entice them. Laura Corrigan's circle was to be strictly confined to the gay young things, mostly titled, who enjoyed social chat, an evening of games, and the intense diversion of seeing each other constantly. They stuck together. Once Laura had captured one, she had captured them all.

A few yards away in Grosvenor Square, the one woman in London who was both American and intellectual viewed the antics at 16 Grosvenor Street with displeasure. Lady Cunard thought Mrs Corrigan was a joke, and not one, moreover, to be encouraged. Those who regularly accepted her invitations did not dispute that Laura was a joke, but saw no harm in encouraging her. Regular names to appear on her list from 1921 onwards were, apart from the Londonderrys and their son Lord Castlereagh: Lady Blandford, Lord and Lady Dalkeith (later Duke and Duchess of Buccleuch), the Duchess of Rutland ('Kakoo'), Lord and Lady Louis Mountbatten, the Duchess of Westminster, Miss Peggy Ward (now Countess Münster), Mr Michael Hornby (of W.H. Smith & Son), the Aga Khan, Lord Weymouth (later Marquess of Bath), Daphne Vivian (later Lady Weymouth and Marchioness of Bath), Lord Herbert (later Earl of Pembroke), Lord Charles Cavendish, the Duke of Devonshire, Chips Channon, Lord Brecknock, Lady Lettice Lygon, and so on for a very long time. At her third season in 1923 she gave a dinner dance for 140 guests, including a clutch of foreign royalties passing through; at another the previous year for 123 people, over a hundred carried titles, and Laura was described wearing 'draped silver lace caught up at the side with a large green bow'. Also in 1923 there was a small dinner party for fourteen persons, of whom thirteen were titled.

By 1924, her fourth season in London, Laura was so well established that she was virtually the social arbiter of the smart set. She no longer needed Charlie Stirling's assistance to survive, but only occasionally, to rescue her from one of her amazing gaffes. For example, in her desire to be friendly with the aristocracy, she took to using the dizzy pattern of nicknames which the best families use among themselves, and which are bewildering to an outsider. The Duchess of Devonshire was known as 'Moucher', the Duchess of Rutland as 'Kakoo'. (They are both now dowagers, and retain their nicknames.) Laura called them 'Moocher' and 'Coco', and everyone giggled uncontrollably. The Duke of Westminster, called 'Bend Or' after a horse he owned, became 'Bend Up' to Laura. At one dinner she had sat Jubie Lancaster next to a Duchess, believing him to be announced as Duke of Lancaster. When Charlie pointed out her error, she waved her hands frantically at the other guests and cried out 'Hands up the next ranking dook!' All this was of course harmless and endearing, and nobody was frank enough to tell Laura how funny she was. It became a matter of huge amusement to wait for her next malapropism. She said Mrs Keppel's Chippendale chairs at 16 Grosvenor Street were very nice, but were spoiled by the '*petits pois*' all over them. A King of England she referred to as 'Richard Gare de Lyon', and her London house as her '*ventre-à-terre*'. She employed a conjurer at one of her entertainments, and finding it difficult to cope with his posh appellation of '*presti-digitateur*' (as who would not!), called him her 'press agitator'. On a visit to Blenheim Palace she asked the Duke of Marlborough ('Mahlboroo') to point out the spot where the Battle of Blenheim took place, and to his shame, he told her the column in the park marked the exact location. Lord Londonderry, she said, had 'three balls on his cuisse'. She told the Aga Khan that she knew his brother Otto. There were other, yet richer, examples to follow in the coming years, which her frequent residence in Paris did nothing to correct, but these were sufficient to promise the delicious antici-pation of a gaffe by 'poor Laura'.

Where she really came into her own was in the organization of her parties, which were planned like a military operation. She would spend £6000 on a single evening, and not blench (already her rent at Grosvenor Street was approaching £500 a week). Laura's three innovations were to offer 'surprise' parties, to provide the atmos-phere of a night-club, with cabaret, and to install a tombola ('Tom Bowler', she said) at the dinner table, so that everyone went away with a grotesquely expensive gift.

The 'surprise' at a Corrigan party could take many forms. Sometimes the invitations were not made until a quarter of an hour before the event, though this was somewhat spurious as most people knew something was afoot, and had cancelled everything else in readiness. The menu might be a surprise, and frequently exotic. 'You never know if you will find singing-birds in your soup,' said a guest. The décor would be breathtaking—curtains sprayed with powdered glass, or a special ballroom built for the occasion in the garden, performers hired to disguise or conceal themselves as trees and statues which would suddenly burst into song, the waiters dressed as old English yokels, or as gardeners in smocks. Mr Rolfe, elegant and rotund, with a great English moustache, was inveigled into joining these pranks, and magically contrived to retain his unsmiling dignity when dressed up as Pulcinello.

'Her ingenuity is only equalled by her assiduity', wrote a gossip columnist as Mrs Corrigan's parties rapidly gained a reputation as the most spectacular in London. She was the first hostess to bring professional entertainment to a private house—singers, dancers, cabaret artistes—and thereby invest the proceedings with the atmosphere of a highly exclusive theatre. Lady Cunard thought it vulgar, Lady Colefax could not have afforded it, but Laura was impervious to critical barbs from her rivals. With Lady Cunard and Lady Colefax, conversation provided the entertainment required, whereas Laura Corrigan well knew that the kind of guest she attracted would soon be bored if intelligent talk were the only amusement. Besides, Laura's conversation was jolly, effervescent, and trivial in the extreme; she would have been out of her depth in the company of people who used their brains. She knew this, and made no apology for it. Her function was to amuse the giddy-headed, and this she did with increasing panache. The cabarets varied with each of her *soirées*, and she was always busy finding new ideas. When she hired some ballet dancers, and it was suggested that they should perform *L'Après-midi d'un Faune*, Laura was horrified. 'Oh my,' she said, 'what do I want with a ballet about a *telephone?*'

She once employed a team of three acrobats, two half-naked men and a girl. The men threw the girl in the air, where she somersaulted and was caught on the way down. Unfortunately, the men dropped her on the second throw, she skidded across the entire ballroom floor and landed at the feet of a startled Lady Cunard, who nearly fell over with the impact.

Some impression that there was more to Laura than met the eye might have been gathered by the extraordinary business acumen she brought to the organization of these evenings. She would decide first what sum she would spend, then work out very carefully a balance sheet with all the expenditure itemized and justified. At one party she had the hall and stairs covered with trellis-work, bunches of grapes and vine leaves hanging everywhere, a profusion of orange trees, rambling roses, and palm trees. She knew perfectly well that her titled guests, or some of them, would scramble to tear down whatever goodies they could walk away with once the party was over, and this cost was anticipated. Financial organization was entirely in her hands, she needing no advice on that score, and the result was 'a work of art that shows no signs of the artist's creative toil', in the words of an appreciative newspaper reporter. Certainly she was indefatigable, planning the next party as soon as the stains were removed from Mrs Keppel's Persian carpet after the last.

The culmination in cabaret came on 21 July 1926, when Laura announced that the entertainment would be provided by the guests themselves. This was a novel idea, bound to appeal both to the young and to those who wished they were younger, and it was the talk of London for weeks afterwards. A bicycling act was performed by Lord Weymouth, Daphne Vivian, Lady Lettice Lygon and Lord Brecknock, scudding around the room on two tandem vehicles, singing the while, 'Daisy, Daisy, give me your answer, do, I'm half crazy over my love for you!' A plantation number was sung rather hesitatingly by Lady Louis Mountbatten, Lady Brecknock, Mrs Richard Norton and Lord Ashley, while Lady Loughborough and Miss Poppy Baring did a satire of sorts. Others played the ukelele, Michael Hornby and Bobby Jenkinson sang a raffish duet, and Dorothy Plunket managed an exhibition dance with aplomb. Lady Maud Warrender intended to break some plates, but cancelled the act when Mr Rolfe indicated that the floor might be damaged. The *pièce de résistance* was, however, the hostess herself dancing the Charleston. Laura had taken lessons weeks in advance in preparation for this event, and rather naughtily she insisted all guests do a Charleston number, which they performed with varying degrees of success and embarrassment, before she donned top hat and red shoes to demonstrate her superiority in the genre. The evening came to an end with much hilarity over a daft game called the 'disappearing aristocrat', in which Lord Weymouth and others of like mind hid behind a curtain and suddenly were no longer there. By 4 a.m. no one worried about making a fool of himself.

For once, Laura did not stand on her head. She was likely to do so with the smallest encouragement, causing some amazement and consternation to Edwardian dowagers like the Duchess of Norfolk and the 'grey, dignified and magnificent' Lady Derby, who were not taught that ladies could be seen upside down. Laura would secure her dress with a belt just below her knees, or around her ankles, and invert herself with no evidence of effort. The small crowd would applaud gleefully, always hoping that, just for once, Laura's wig would stay on the ground when she resumed normal posture, but it never did, and no one ever saw her without it. (Not yet, at least.) Was she bald? How old was she? No one knew.

The trick did not entrance everyone. Baroness Blixen once asked the Governor of Tanganyika after lunch, if he would care to see Laura stand on her head. 'No thank you,' he said with obvious distaste, 'I've got far too much to do.'

By far the most beguiling of Laura's ideas was the raffle, or tombola. It was, of course, rigidly fixed in consultation with Charlie Stirling, the presents won being of descending expense according to rank. Princes and dukes got the best of the pick, untitled young ladies a mere bagatelle. As you thrust your hand into the bowl to bring out a piece of paper with your number on it, Mr Rolfe (now accustomed to his absurd disguise as a moustachioed pierrot) would grab you unseen by the wrist and guide your hand to the paper you were destined to receive. The prizes were astonishingly generous— diamond-studded suspenders, braces with gold buckles, items from Cartier or shipped over especially from Paris. A guest might frequently leave one of Laura's parties several hundred pounds better off than when he arrived, and since even the most elevated peers are not without a trace of venality, they sometimes welcomed an invitation with the warmth of appreciation which derives from the anticipation of some gain.

Sometimes the hierarchy of prizes misfired. The top prize was meant on one occasion to be won by Prince George, the King's son, but Michael Hornby drew the wrong number by mistake and found himself the winner of a gift intended for royalty. Laura was furious, but there was nothing she could do without admitting that the whole game was rigged.

Inevitably, Laura's success caused the envious and the excluded to sneer. The *Sunday Express* voiced the opinion of many when it printed a long article devoted to being Unkind To Laura. Mrs Corrigan, it said, 'collects names like other people collect postage stamps . . . one day, however, she will realize she is barking up the wrong tree. Social success is another word for a waste of time . . . she is being swindled out of the gratitude which should follow free food.' The journalist, Valentine Castlerosse, went on to suggest that Mrs Corrigan might retrieve her reputation by taking an interest in painting or architecture, and encouraging the young in these fields, thus spending her wealth on something more worthwhile than frivolity. 'She would learn something on the way', he added.

These pious exhortations ignored the fact that Laura was quite happy to be frivolous, and nursed no ambitions towards learning. What Lord Castlerosse of the *Sunday Express* did not know, indeed nobody knew, was that Laura had been well used to cruel chastizement from the press, and had suffered far worse sneers in Cleveland, which had armed her with a steely resilience no newspaper could unsettle. Laura was simply not vulnerable. And she was, as everyone was beginning rather guiltily to realize, one of the kindest, most generous, most genuinely warm-hearted people in London. It was possible to be at one and the same time a joke, a snob, and something of a saint.

A snob she certainly was, to an atrocious degree. She chased after royalties with a naïve relish which was almost admirable, and by the end she had accumulated a superb collection. Chips Channon commented that she talked of royalty even when standing on her head, and when she was introduced to John Gielgud backstage after his historic performance of *Hamlet*, she could think of nothing save that Hamlet was a Danish prince. 'Why, I know the Danish royal family *intimately*,' she insisted to the bemused actor. Any minor member of the Bourbon-Parma dynasty (whom she called the 'Berbon Palms') would find a ready welcome at her table, and the Queen of Spain ultimately became a friend. Introducing guests to each other, she once said to a surprised Sir Malcolm Bullock, 'You have the Queen of Spain on the sofa!' She would sometimes entice a luncheon guest with the promise, 'There'll be five of us and eight of them', meaning eight royal personages. The King of Greece was yet another friend. A sensation was caused when Laura was presented to him ahead of a number of titled ladies who ought normally to have preceded her, and when she met his relations, she curtsied to them on both knees.

Nevertheless, it was incidentally due to the favour of royalty that Laura Corrigan reached the ultimate pinnacle of London society. Lady Mountbatten arranged a midnight matinée for charity, at which Laura took the front row of the stalls. Before the performance, Laura gave a large dinner party at 16 Grosvenor Street. Gate-crashing was becoming ever more popular, and increasingly tiresome (the word was coined after a ball given by Lady Ellesmere in 1928 when uninvited guests swelled the numbers uncontrollably: the practice had since spread). Lady Mountbatten's sister, Mary Cunningham-Reid, asked if she could bring some friends to Laura's dinner, which Laura politely refused on the grounds that she had enough people already. However, Mary Cunningham-Reid turned up with the friends, to whom Laura rightly denied admittance, causing Lady Mountbatten and her sister such rage at what they considered an insult, that they determined to take revenge. Laura's next ball promised Prince George of Kent as guest of honour. The Prince had already accepted, when Lady Mountbatten announced a rival ball on the same evening, and she too invited the prince. He thereupon 'chucked' Laura and accepted the new invitation. Cockie Blixen and Charlie Stirling had to break the news to Laura, who collapsed in her armchair with grief. There followed an avalanche of cancellations. Stirling then devised a rescue. He spoke to Lady Londonderry, who had by this time heard what had happened, and she brought the King of Spain to Laura's ball. When society learned that Laura had triumphed, she was finally 'made', and she was understandably pleased with her victory. 'When a prince refuses, a king obliges,' she said. The aftermath of this apparently trivial event was that a host of people who would not normally have gone to Mrs Corrigan's now rallied round to support a woman whom they thought had been unjustly treated; she benefited, in fact, from the English sense of fair play.

Her other triumph, this time over the 'Knickerbocker' set of expatriate New Yorkers, came when the hugely rich Indian prince, Gaekwar of Baroda, turned down an invitation from Mrs Vanderbilt in order to accept one from Laura. He was considered a prize catch, and from that day there was no looking back for the woman formerly despised in Cleveland and ignored in New York.

Lady Londonderry was again the power that opened the doors of Buckingham Palace to Mrs Corrigan. George V and Queen Mary would have nothing to do with her until Lady Londonderry persuaded them. Her one failure was with the Prince of Wales (King Edward VIII) who took against her in the Mountbatten row. Lady Cunard and Lady Colefax, as Laura well knew, were both on terms of easy friendship with the Prince, who never called on Laura. Chips Channon once made the mistake of inviting Laura to drop in after dinner when he was entertaining the King (as he then was), whom he sat next to Lady Cunard. Laura would not be considered second-best in this manner, and to her credit she failed to turn up, though she and Chips were by this time firm friends. She was, he wrote, 'freezingly polite' to him in the following days, but he knew he had hurt her. 'Oh, social rows!' he wailed. 'There is nothing so trivial and yet nothing so wounding and discouraging.' As he should know, social rows as well as social triumphs were all part of the business of being a hostess; one had to be ready for both.

Laura did meet the King once, at a dinner given by Lady Cunard. Chips Channon reported that she was in the seventh heaven of bliss, but Edward VIII never addressed a word to her. Whether Lady Cunard was kind to invite her, or did so knowing she would be ignored, is a matter we can only guess at. Stage-managing the humiliation of a rival was yet another characteristic of the successful hostess. Laura, on the other hand, had too good a heart ever to countenance such guile. It would not have occurred to her, and she could not have carried it off. Edward VIII later stipulated as a condition for his accepting an invitation from the daughter of Lord Iveagh, that Mrs Corrigan should on no account be present. Mercifully, Laura was never informed.

Anyway, when *The Times* Court column thought Laura important enough to announce her arrival in London for the season, and to print the news above that of Mrs Baldwin's visit to the Royal

Sibyl Colefax, the Lion-hunter

Laura Corrigan

Northern Hospital, and in larger type, no one could doubt any longer that Mrs Corrigan was a figure on the London scene.

Throughout this hectic climb towards intimacy with Top People, the husband, Jimmy Corrigan, was scarcely noticed. He rarely spent more than ten days at a time in London, it being supposed that he had pressing business interests in Cleveland. People thought him nice and unobjectionable, a quiet little man with few friends, who tolerated Laura's social success but did not share her hunger for it. He stood like a solid block, shaking hands awkwardly. He was undeniably proud that she had achieved what she most wanted in the world, and quite clearly adored her. They had no children, a fact which her friends found curious, even though they did not know that Laura had told Mrs Keppel on her arrival in London that she and Jimmy lived 'intimate'. She startled an assembly of dinner guests one evening when some one asked her outright why she was childless. 'You see,' she said, without a hint of humour, 'Mr Corrigan's penis isn't virile.' A palpable hush hung over the room and all were happy at least that Mr Corrigan was not present to confirm or deny. Hilarity ensued when Laura was safely out of earshot.

There was never any suggestion that Laura might engage in some amorous intrigue. She seemed completely indifferent to flirtation, even discouraging. A man attacked her in a taxi. 'Oh my,' said Laura, 'I didn't know what to hold on to, my skirt or my wig.' Lord Weymouth mischievously suggested that he would go to bed with her if she would give him a new Rolls-Royce. 'Henry, I'll give you *two* Rolls-Royces *not* to,' she replied. She was said to be very friendly with the Duke of Devonshire, and would on occasion spend days with him at his property near Eastbourne, Compton Place. But her recreation there was no more than chopping wood, which she did with singular skill. Neither the Duke nor anyone else for that matter could imagine why Laura should be such an accomplished lumberwoman. Yet there was a very good reason.

Every indication told that the Corrigans were a happy pair, though perhaps more companions than lovers. Laura had little liking for that sort of thing, and they spent much of their time apart. He certainly kept her well supplied with money, and it was said she felt uncomfortable if there were less than a million dollars in the current account at her London bank. Just how much money she had, no one could guess. A visitor from New York related the tale that she had given a party there at which the dinner service was made of gold, and there was one servant for every guest (more servants than guests of course, as most of the chairs were empty). Curiosity was satisfied at last when, on 24 January 1928, Jimmy Corrigan dropped dead outside his club in Cleveland, leaving a vast fortune to his wife. He was only forty-seven years old. Laura had been with him the night before, and had not suspected he was ripe for a heart attack. The surprise was total. The Cleveland newspapers then rehearsed the local history of Corrigan's millions and what they saw as Laura's snatching of them, details entirely unknown in London. Even today, Laura's surviving friends are quite unaware of the Corrigan saga which had been played out in Ohio.

To understand why Laura Corrigan was so detested in Cleveland, one has to search into the history of the Corrigan family, its pride and achievement, and its downfall. The story is a tragedy of positively Greek dimensions.

Captain James Corrigan, Jimmy's father, had come to the United States in the nineteenth century as an impoverished immigrant boy from Canada and realized the American dream of creating a fortune from guts, hard work, and imagination. He first set up a partnership with Frank Rockefeller, brother of John D., which ended disastrously when John D. redeemed the mortgage on ore lands which his brother and Corrigan wished to develop, sold the land and minerals, and made a handsome profit. Corrigan was ruined. But not for long. He formed another partnership with Judge Stevenson Burke for the mining of iron ore, then expanded into making pig iron, and finally established a steel mill. After a shaky start, the business prospered and developed into one of the dozen richest steel companies in the United States. James Corrigan had the satisfaction of building for himself a vast mansion on the very spot where he had first set foot in the country without a dime in his pocket. Cleveland was proud of him.

The first act of the tragedy occurred on 8 July 1900, at three in the afternoon. Corrigan saw his wife, three daughters, and granddaughter sail out to Lake Erie on his yacht, the *Idler*. A sudden squall overturned the vessel, and the whole family perished beneath the waters. The only member of the family left was James Jr., or 'Jimmy' Corrigan, who had not been on board. Alas, he was not the young man his father would have wished. A spendthrift, ne'er-do-well and playboy, Jimmy was always falling into trouble and being rescued by papa and partners. He showed little promise of the responsibility he would need to manage the huge business empire he stood to inherit, preferring to work as a barman at Goldfield, Nevada, and to saunter in and out of the affections of young women. One such, Miss Georgiana Young, a nineteen-year-old from Pittsburgh, had successfully sued him for breach of promise. With his wayward character and unstable habits, he was clearly not fit to be President of the company. Captain Corrigan had no real alternative but to cut him out. One of the employees was Price McKinney, an energetic and industrious book-keeper, whom Corrigan now made a partner to the exclusion of his own son. The company was henceforth called Corrigan-McKinney Steel Company. Young Jimmy did not give the impression that he cared very much one way or the other.

Another comfort to Captain James was his new acquaintance with a pretty doctor's wife from Chicago, Mrs Laura MacMarten; this was the very same Laura who was later to dominate the giddiest section of London society. She was then talkative and ambitious, still in her twenties, and suffering from the meanness of her husband, a parsimonious Scotsman who had the position of resident doctor at the Northwestern Hotel in Chicago. It was Laura who had pushed him into meeting the 'right people' and had arranged for them to spend some time in a resort frequented by the wealthy. There, James Corrigan Snr. found her company dazzling. He did not know, nor did he care, where she came from before she married MacMarten. (There was even a rumour that Corrigan *père* intended making Laura his wife, and that she had accepted him.) She was working in fact as a waitress to earn enough to stay at the expensive resort.

Captain James Corrigan died in 1908, leaving a will which was a terrible humiliation to young Jimmy. He was left only $15,000 unrestricted, while the millions of his inheritance were left in trust under the control of his father's former accountant, Price McKinney. Laura went to Cleveland for the funeral, and there encountered Jimmy Corrigan, seven years her junior. There arose a friendship which grew and flourished, and finally made Jimmy a more responsible person; some said she 'made a man' of him. He ceased gallivanting, and demonstrated, under Laura's guidance, that he was mature enough to assume some part in his father's company.

But the McKinneys were not about to relinquish control, especially to an outsider. They recognized that Laura MacMarten was the force behind young Jimmy, and determined that she would have to be watched very carefully indeed. McKinney, who made the company ever more prosperous, turned it into a corporation, in which Jimmy Corrigan held by right 40% of the stock; it was an inexplicable move, and it gave Laura the chance she had been hoping for. In 1916 she divorced Dr MacMarten and married young Jimmy. Taking his affairs in hand, she surreptitiously bought a little stock here and a little there, gradually building up the holding without the McKinneys suspecting anything was afoot, until one day Jimmy Corrigan was able to declare at a board meeting that he now held $53\frac{1}{2}\%$ of the company and was therefore President. He and his wife would dictate terms from now on.

Price McKinney, having laboured for years to build his company, and seeing it now pass into the hands of the man he was meant to replace, went home and committed suicide. This was on 13 April 1926. Laura returned immediately to London, where she had to concentrate on the 'stunt' party she was giving two months later, the one in which the guests would perform the cabaret. None of the guests had any notion of her recent victory. She and Jimmy were now worth over sixty million dollars.

When Jimmy collapsed in 1928, the $53\frac{1}{2}\%$ passed to Laura's hands. She shared ownership of the company with three other women, Mrs Price McKinney, Mrs Stevenson Burke (widow of the judge who founded the company with Captain Corrigan), and Mrs

Parthenia Burke Rose (his granddaughter). Control, however, was not in her hands. By the terms of his will, Jimmy had left her the power to sell her shares, but not to vote them; this was in the sole power of the new President, John H. Watson. One cannot help wondering if this was a mistake; Laura would have made an admirable President.

Still, if sell them she could, sell them she would, and in so doing she would again demonstrate that events would march according to her will. She sold her entire stock to William Mather, a deal which resulted in the Republic Steel Corporation into which Corrigan-McKinney was swallowed whole. Mrs Price McKinney was a mere minority share holder in a strange merger, her husband's cherished company having disappeared. Laura's gain from the sale was a tax-free income of $800,000 a year. Price McKinney Junior blew his brains out with a shotgun. It was reported to be accidental.

No wonder Laura's name was poison in Cleveland. The Western Reserve aristocracy did not like her when they first saw her, simply because she was not one of them and had, in their eyes, jostled her way into a formerly exclusive set. She compounded the fault by stealing one of their bright sons, whose inadequacy before she took him in hand they chose to ignore. It was an easy step to regard her as the catalyst which had set in motion the horrid sequence of tragedies which appeared to occur whenever she set foot in Cleveland. Cleveland blamed her for everything. At first the citizens cold-shouldered her, then treated her frigidly, then actively despised her and literally drove her out of the town. Their behaviour was cruel and shabby, and their hatred of her has not abated.

There is even an incredible postscript. Mrs McKinney, having lost husband and son, married again and was soon widowed a second time. When she died, her house was bought by a Corrigan cousin, Margaret Corrigan Williams, and her husband Charles. On 21 March 1960, in the middle of the night, a fire broke out which consumed the whole building and killed both inhabitants.

Laura did not take her usual season in London in 1928, the year Jimmy died, but by 1929 she was once more busy organizing parties with as much acumen as she had arranged her husband's financial affairs. Unfortunately, 16 Grosvenor Street was no longer available, as the Keppels had by now bought a house in Italy and sold the Mayfair mansion. Laura was now more than ever a nomad. For the rest of her life she was 'of no fixed address', taking her mail through her bankers, the Garranty Trust Company, and renting a succession of houses rather than buying any property, the proceeds from which, she well knew, would find their way to the taxman's pocket. She rented at various times Crewe House in Curzon Street, the Duke of Marlborough's house at 11 Kensington Palace Gardens, the Dowager Duchess of Rutland's house in Arlington Street, and Dudley House in Park Lane, which cost her £5,000 for two months at a time when such a sum was enough to buy five large houses. On visits to Paris she had a huge suite on the first floor of the Ritz Hotel, overlooking the Place Vendôme. There was also the Palazzo Mocenigo which she took in Venice.

Still she continued to climb. She was one of the few Americans invited to the Duke of Kent's wedding to Princess Marina in 1934, but those who regarded her as a mere *parvenue* ignored the truth of her very real friendship with Princess Marina. Laura had known the Princess in Paris years before, when as the youngest daughter of Prince Nicholas of Greece she was living modestly in hotels, was uncelebrated and comparatively unknown. In those days there was no anticipation of the eventual alliance with the British royal family, yet Laura, with her usual numbing generosity of spirit, showed uncommon kindness to the Princess and her family, a kindness which Marina never forgot. As the beautiful and popular Duchess of Kent she was loyal to the American lady who had brightened dull days in the past, and would not hear of her being snubbed. The Duke's earlier infelicity in abandoning Laura for a rival party had long been forgotten. Laura presented the Princess with a magnificent full length mink coat as a wedding gift, choosing the mink on a shopping expedition with Marina who, she said, was so excited 'it was most child-like'. (A few years before she had given Lord Weymouth white silk braces when he married Daphne Vivian, and his wife a plentiful supply of the choicest lace-trimmed lingerie.)

Only once was the friendship with Princess Marina threatened momentarily by an indiscretion on the part of Laura. The Princess had naturally drawn the first prize at Laura's tombola, and in her feigned excitement at the surprise, Laura lost her head and screamed 'Marina's won it! Marina's won it!' The next morning an equerry, Ulrick Alexander, arrived from the Palace to point out, as gently as possible, that Mrs Corrigan really must not refer to Her Royal Highness as Marina. Gossips were happy to report that Laura had been ticked off, and for a while the news warmed the hard hearts of the malicious, but in fact it was a matter of protocol only, and people close to the Kents did not suppose for a moment that Laura was seeking the self-aggrandizement which the snobbish clamour for, intimacy with the great. She was already a trusted friend, and had no need to parade it. Laura was mortified to think she had caused embarrassment.

On the other hand, the attractions of name-dropping frequently exposed the ridiculous side of her ambition. She would talk at length about 'Meg' until someone finally answered the need and asked, '*Who*, Laura?' Whereupon, with as much nonchalance as she could muster, she replied, 'Why, Son Altesse Royale the Princesse Rénée de Bourbon-Parme, of course!' Lunching at Holland House, Laura asked if she could use the telephone. Although she was only calling Thomas Cook's, the travel agent, she began the conversation with, 'I'm here at Holland House with Lord and Lady Ilchester, Lord and Lady Stavordale, Lady Mary Herbert and Baron Radowitz.' One can at least understand Mrs Greville's wicked remark that to be known in the United States as an English woman who didn't go to Mrs Corrigan's parties was to be placed on a pedestal, though it would have come better from someone less snobbish than Mrs Greville.

In the summer of 1931 Laura rented the Palazzo Mocenigo in Venice, intending to take a vacation. The palace, in which Byron lived for two years and where he wrote *Don Juan*, stood square on the Grand Canal and contained sumptuous rooms and ornate decorations, not at all to Laura's taste. (She had the pictures which hung in her apartment at the Ritz in Paris doré'd, thus making the decent look vulgar, and the house in Venice she most admired was the one everybody else deplored, an object of beauty swamped under modern white convenience-furniture of the most expensive variety.) Never mind. It was big enough to entertain in, which is what mattered most.

All the local principessas and contessas were enticed to the table of the rich American. They admired her flair for organization, but were astonished to see her so often upside-down, performing her head-standing act. Laura gave dinners almost continuously, with rarely less than seventy-five people seated, at tables of sixteen or so each. A ball she arranged was noted for the tuberoses which festooned the palace (and gave everybody a headache), as all the lady guests were instructed to dress in white and wear flowers in their hair. As Lady Weymouth said, Laura enjoyed 'disciplining pleasure', and her guests were quite prepared to obey her. Her tendency to bossiness was forgivable.

Friends came out from London, including the Weymouths, Diana and Duff Cooper, and Chips Channon, and they all had the most luxurious holiday imaginable. Excursions to the Lido were conducted like a royal progress, with expensive motor-launches, laden with servants, to convey people from palace to beach, private gondoliers, twenty backgammon boards on the scorching sand, food and drink kept permanently available on a yacht a few yards out. Guests could swim out to it, be rowed out to it, driven out to it, or carried on a servant's back to it. Instructions were left at the Lido Bar that none of Mrs Corrigan's guests was to be allowed to pay for anything. Indeed, such was Laura's generosity that it became in the end burdensome. The journey from England was paid for by Laura, every meal, every whisky, every glass of orange juice was paid for. There were strict instructions on cards placed on each bedroom table that no guest was permitted to tip a servant anything at all, must not buy stamps or cigarettes, not pay for washing, laundry, or hairdressing, must sign the bill at the Grand Hotel for anything consumed. It was possible to be with Laura for a month in Venice and never have an opportunity to handle money; even your souvenir shopping was organized by your hostess. Lord Weymouth was once caught short and was obliged to use a public lavatory, which cost him ten *lira*, the first coin he had been able to spend for two weeks. 'It really is too expensive here,' he told Laura. 'I shall have to go back home or I'll be broke.'

On the cruise through the Mediterranean which followed this holiday, for which Laura hired the most lavish yacht she could find, with two crew members to each guest, she gave envelopes to everyone as they came to a port. The envelopes contained a great deal of spending money, in the currency of the country they were visiting. It was all very thoughtful, and had been arranged long in advance with Laura's usual kindness, but it was slightly oppressive. Sam Ashton was delighted with his envelopes; he kept every one of them and banked all the money in England when he got home.

In order to gain some measure of freedom, Laura's friends had to conspire to deceive her. Like children playing truant, they sneaked off to the popular Harry's Bar in Venice, where they could spend their own money without risk of censure; they agreed that no one should tell Laura that Harry's Bar existed, so that they could disport themselves clandestinely. Poor Laura. As Diana Cooper said, 'she really has the world's happiness at heart'.

Prince and Princess Christopher of Greece arrived, and Laura engaged eight extra servants to look after them. She was amazed that they brought no staff of their own, but travelled like 'ordinary' people. The palace had been turned upside down to accommodate the army of personnel she expected. 'I always have two body-maids' she told them, 'and Mr Corrigan never crossed the Atlantic without two body-men.'

On the night of a ball, cards were placed in each room giving instructions. 'Mrs Corrigan requests that all house guests be dressed by 8.45 o'clock this evening, so that the servants may have a chance to put all rooms in order . . . look at the table charts in the main hall to find the place at dinner-tables, to facilitate seating . . . assembly will be in the ballroom at nine o'clock promptly.'

By the end of the summer, Laura was exhausted. 'I don't feel I am getting the vacation I should be getting,' she told Channon.

The reflection did not prevent her organizing another six-week 'vacation' the following year, when she chartered from Vincent Astor his enormous yacht, the *Argosy*, equipped once again with an army of servants and envelopes of foreign notes. She met Mussolini and liked him so much she had a photograph of him in her boudoir, next to those of the Spanish royal family. Also it was on this occasion that she made her most glorious malapropism. Back in London, David Herbert asked her if she had seen the Dardanelles. 'Oh my, no,' said Laura, 'but I did have a letter of introduction to them.' Moreover, anxious to show that she had been well received in Rome, she announced, 'I had Mussolini twice, but unfortunately the Pope doesn't go out.'

The next trip was a safari expedition to Africa, which for once Laura was unable to organize herself. 'Cockie' Blixen, married to a white hunter and familiar with Africa, made all the arrangements, at a cost of $20,000. The explorers, hardly intrepid, were Laura, Count Paul Münster and his wife Peggy, Lord and Lady Ilchester, Baron Blixen-Finecke, and Comte de la Rochefoucauld. Though living in tents, they contrived to bring Parisian food and a chef to cook it, and the main event every two days was the arrival of an aeroplane to take Laura's wigs to Johannesburg for treatment. The pretence was maintained that the plane came solely to bring fresh butter.

Resident at Government House at this time was Sir Ronald Storrs, who in later years painfully recalled Laura's arrival by aeroplane, with maid and luggage in a second, but without any cash. She sent a cry for help to Storrs, who dutifully called upon her that same evening, and was received by Laura in bed, in a night-gown of real Brussels lace. 'A soul-destroying woman,' he reflected, 'a dumpy impossible millionairess. Huge diamond rings with great half-inch black and white pearls protruding from them: a horrible *étalage* of tasteless wealth.'

On her return to London, Laura was greeted by a spiteful remark in the *Sunday Express*, now enjoying its position as her principal enemy. 'When she comes back from the Sahara', wrote the gossip columnist, 'I expect to find her sitting between two pyramids. After all, pyramids were made to climb.'

Laura could afford to ignore the malice; she hardly needed to climb any further as it was. She had a house at Ascot, was admitted to the royal enclosure (this on the intervention of Joe Kennedy, the U.S. Ambassador, whom she entertained regularly), bought horses, which she named Panorama and Hartington (after the Duke of

Devonshire's eldest son, Lord Hartington). Horses had been Jimmy's passion, and Laura kept his memory fresh by racing on his behalf. Not keen on racing herself, she thought it was something she ought to do to maintain his position.

Another idea she had to preserve Jimmy Corrigan's name turned sour. She sent a cheque for $50,000 to William Milliken, director of the Cleveland Museum of Art, instructing him to buy a painting in memory of her husband. Milliken and his curator of paintings, Henry Francis, were ecstatic. They chose a fine Cézanne, hung it in the gallery with a plaque in honour of Corrigan, and informed Laura. To their amazement, she was furious. Cézanne? What an insult! To Laura, 'real' art was a full-length portrait by Romney or Reynolds. Keep the painting, she said, but remove the label mentioning Corrigan. Unfortunately, they failed to comply with the urgency she demanded, so one day she took a plane and flew to Cleveland, flounced into the museum, ripped the label from the wall, tore it in half and handed it to the guard with instructions to deliver the pieces immediately to the Director of the museum. She then strode out again and boarded the next aircraft home.

Nervousness which prevailed in the years preceding the Second World War was not allowed to interrupt Mrs Corrigan's London season. She gave a ball for the Duke and Duchess of Kent, and entertained Herr Ribbentrop. In 1938 there was a party for 137 people, 'all the youth and fashion of London with the Kents enjoying themselves wildly and leading the revels', as Chips Channon reported. Laura, he said, was indefatigable. She was teaching a new dance, the Palais Glide, which smacked of the servants' hall. The degree to which she had entered the affections of many people in England over the years is attested by the number of times she was asked to stand as godmother. She was godmother to Mark Lennox-Boyd, Arthur Boyd-Rochford, and Alexander, Lord Weymouth's eldest son (who is now Lord Weymouth, as his father is the Marquess of Bath). Those who began in the twenties to laugh behind Laura's back had in time grown genuinely fond of her.

Only once did Laura gingerly attempt to entice an intellectual to her circle. She sent a card to George Bernard Shaw proclaiming 'Mrs Corrigan At Home, 6–8 p.m.' Shaw returned the card with a note scribbled on the back, 'G.B.S.—Ditto.' She did not try again.

Lady Cunard is supposed mischievously to have recommended Shaw to Mrs Corrigan. She cannot have forgotten Laura's immortal reply, preserved for us by Daphne Fielding, to a remark of W.G. Moore's. 'I always think, Mrs Corrigan, that of all the sexual perversions chastity is the most incomprehensible,' said Moore. Said Laura, 'I guess I shall have to think that one over, Mr Moore.'

On another occasion she brought conversation to an abrupt halt by her loud declaration that Nijinsky was the greatest exponent of levitation she had ever seen.

The knowledge that Mrs Corrigan wore a wig had spread so far that the *Sunday Express* nicknamed her the Big Wig of London, yet still no acquaintance ventured to refer to the wig in Laura's presence. One should say 'wigs', for she had a collection of them for all occasions; a dishevelled one for waking up in the morning—this was the wig her 'body-maid' saw; a windswept one for visits to the country; a tight, neat one for evening wear; and even an overgrown one, which gave the excuse for her to say 'I really must go visit my "coiffewer"' when what she meant was the wig would have to be sent for its periodic treatment. Peggy Münster is the only person known to have spied Laura without her hair, though some thought they spotted little white wisps peeking beneath it. Ladies would bully young Mairi Vane-Tempest-Stewart, Lady Londonderry's little daughter, to peep inside Laura's room in the hope of finding an array of heads, but she never was able to discover where they were kept, and the maids could not be bribed to reveal their whereabouts. They travelled in a special suitcase, dubbed by her friends 'Laura's wigwam'.

There was a perilous moment when the secret was almost uncovered. Henry Weymouth's pet, a Humbert's woolly monkey, climbed on to Laura's shoulders and began playfully to finger her hair. 'Oh, my *kerls, my kerls*,' the startled lady cried out, darting her hands to her head. The animal was disentangled before any real damage could be done. Again, though she could not swim, she paradoxically adored diving, even diving into the Thames on a visit to the Hornbys at Pusey in Oxfordshire. Her diving was so vigorous that the bathing cap was once dislodged with the hair attached to it. For what seemed an interminable moment, Laura remained underwater and did not emerge until she had retrieved the soggy object and replaced it firmly on her head.

There was usually a sailor in attendance who, after Laura had dived in and disappeared beneath the water, would throw a rope where he thought she would pop up again, and drag her to safety.

The wig matched very appropriately, in fact, the rest of Laura's appearance. She was a small, neat, soignée woman, a fine example of American chic, exquisitely well-dressed, sleek and perfect. Her face, with its enamelled skin, large eyes made larger by surgery, and pencilled eyebrows, looked like a mask. Artificial hair was an adornment rather than an impediment to her face. Lord Weymouth thought, however, that she could have done without it. 'Once you start wearing a wig, you've got to go on with it. She would probably have looked very nice with gray hair—stupid woman!'

The only person who made an oblique remark about Laura's hair was Lady Cunard, who was beginning to warm slightly towards Laura, having at first ignored her. Lady Cunard would occasionally invite Mrs Corrigan, and proffer gratuitous advice, which seemed kind but which served to underline Laura's gaucherie in front of others by suggesting that she was in need of advice. 'Oh no, Laura dear, you really *can't* do that, you know,' she would say, and the company would inwardly snigger. Not Emerald, of course; she was far too clever to snigger. She merely planted the thought which caused sniggers in others. 'Where *is* Lord Blandford,' she said. 'You did say you invited him, didn't you, Laura dear?' At one lunch, Laura was nervous and fluttering as both she and Lady Cunard were to be present at a Court ball. 'Emerald, are you going to wear a tiara?' asked Laura. When she was sure conversation was muted enough for her remarks to be heard, Lady Cunard said, 'Now Laura, dear, princesses wear tiaras, duchesses wear tiaras, but I'm going to wear my *own hair*.' Laura's reaction was not noticed in the general embarrassment around the table.

At least one proposal of marriage came Mrs Corrigan's way, and fell on arid land. She was the most unromantic soul. The Polish Count Alfred Potocki wrote her a letter in which he offered his hand, which she rejected. 'I don't want to bury myself in Poland,' she said, 'I want to stay in London and Paris. Why, I'd be miserable.' So the social climber neglected a genuine opportunity to be a countess. Laura had no desire for a title for herself; she just burned with the fierce need to know everyone who had one.

There was also the bothersome matter of a clumsy blackmail attempt by a young woman in Ohio who claimed that her son was fathered by Jimmy Corrigan, and demanded a great deal of money to support him. Laura was far too astute, and tough, to allow herself to be led down that dangerous path; the would-be blackmailer was trounced in one fell blow, and never heard of again.

Laura frequently talked about 'my sister Mabelle', who lived in San Francisco. From 1925 onwards, Mabelle would pay occasional visits to London, glorying in the fame and position Laura had attained. Unlike her sister, Mabelle was not reluctant to be dragged into a flirtation. William Cavendish-Bentinck had long ago been asked to accompany Laura and Jimmy on a trip to India, but he declined when he realized he was to escort sister Mabelle, who was clearly on the hunt for a husband. Cavendish-Bentinck's mother was Ruth St Maur, granddaughter of the Duke of Somerset; she put her foot down, and Victor Cazalet was recruited to go instead.

Mabelle married an unpretentious and decent man called Dr David Taylor, a member of the University of California Medical Faculty and a distinguished authority on obstetrics. He was completely uninterested in social life, but Mabelle hankered after making herself Queen of San Francisco in emulation of Laura's success across the Atlantic. To this end she first of all changed her name and invented a hyphen—Mabelle Armstrong-Taylor sounded so much better than Mabel Taylor; she then, with Laura's money, thought she should buy some fine art to demonstrate she was a force in the city. Perhaps some Old Masters! She dropped in one day on the dealer Germain Seligman and asked to look at what he had to sell. There were some fine portraits, including a portrait of Rembrandt's Saskia by Ferdinand Bol. She asked the price of the whole lot, was told $70,000 (which was huge before the Second World War) and to Seligman's astonishment paid up immediately without the usual bargaining. 'Send them to San Francisco,' she said imperiously. Seligman informed the museum owners and dealers he knew in San Francisco, who in turn informed the local grandees, and Mabelle's reputation was made. Thereafter, with instructions from Laura on how to go about it, and a constant stream of finance, Mabelle made her way into the world of High Society, and became one of California's notable hostesses. She never lost her naïvety, however, and was even more of a joke than Laura. She acquired more and more art (this was obviously the way to get on in the world), bought many Lawrences and a Gainsborough, including Lawrence's portrait of the Earl and Countess of Plymouth, now hanging in the museum at San Francisco. The Gainsborough, though not one of his best, was recognizable; it was the portrait of a young girl, whom Mabelle proudly announced to be her own great grandmama. When she made these boasts, she always seemed to be winking, and many were the times when she was almost nudged in the ribs in return. Peggy Münster made the mistake of winking back. But Mabelle was in earnest about Gainsborough's picture of her ancestress; the wink was a facial tic left as the result of some surgical embroidery, also in emulation of sister Laura; she winked all the time.

Her pretensions to intimacy with royalty were as keen and as sharp as Laura's. Her greatest coup was to entertain the claimant to the Spanish throne (he is now the King of Spain), her pleasure a little spoiled when she learned that she was referred to as the Old Pretender in company with the Young. In other ways, Mabelle was quite unlike Laura. She drank a deal of alcohol, whereas Laura was not known to touch a drop, making only token gestures to sip a glass of wine at dinner. And Mabelle lacked her sister's panache; she seemed to act the part of a hostess, where Laura positively relished it.

The woman who was initially disparaged when she came to London twenty years earlier now enjoyed a personal reputation which did her credit. It was easy to mock her snobbery, her *faux pas*, the lack of sophistication which made her seriously out of her depth with the kind of guests Emerald Cunard and Sibyl Colefax entertained. Lord Weymouth thought her a 'poor man's Lady Cunard', but she

considered herself a cut above Lady Colefax, whom she looked
upon from on high as a woman who did not really know the right
people. Nor did she have any humour, or any conversation of
substance. David Herbert remarked that Laura never said anything
remotely interesting. She was without subtlety, gave no sign of the
smallest ray of comprehension. She was maddeningly tidy, forever
emptying ashtrays and closing drawers. She would enter a guest's
room and while talking would busily arrange things in their proper
place, leaving the guest to resume a comfortable disarray once she
had left. Her fastidiousness stretched to organizing other people's
wardrobes, throwing out clothes which she thought below standard
and replacing them with lavish items of her own choice. She
discarded the furniture which Cockie Blixen had in South Africa
and refurnished the entire flat at her own expense, from armchairs
and wine cellar even to the pair of scissors. It would not occur to her
that such behaviour was bossy, intrusive, interfering. Her motives
were fine and good; she simply wanted to bring happiness to her
friends, and was glad that they should benefit from her enormous
wealth.

Laura's qualities were more apparent now. Simple and uneducated she might have been, but she had firm resolve, astonishing
determination, and a shrewd head for business, as her amazing coup
in gaining control of Corrigan-McKinney had demonstrated. She
was perfectly honest, and not at all self-deprecating, allowance
made for her appalling taste in décor. Chips Channon said she could
be a colossal bore (so, on occasion, could he), but was a dynamo of
energy. The term 'social climber' is not necessarily pejorative. It
must be applied to Laura Corrigan, but it must equally be said that
she never climbed by treading on the fingers of others. She was
never heard to make a bitchy or uncharitable remark, never seen to
take advantage, never known to be unkind. Her progress was not in
any way built upon hostility towards others.

Laura had more in common with Lady Cunard than with Lady
Colefax. She and Emerald were of course vastly different in
intellect, a matter which made Laura rather afraid of her com-
patriot, who warned James Lees-Milne, for instance, that he might
not like Mrs Corrigan because she was not 'cultivated'. Yet both

women had a certain flamboyance of personality which set them apart from the more commonplace Sibyl Colefax, who had intelligence but little style.

Laura's kind heart would eventually have made her friends wherever she went; her money merely ensured they were friends in high society. As Peter Coats said, 'good nature allied to a vast fortune are two very acceptable qualities'.

The extent and scope of Laura's generosity was truly remarkable. It was easy enough, with her resources, to make sure every guest at a party received an expensive present, but she chose all gifts personally, with some care, and moreover sent further gifts for every imaginable occasion—engagement, marriage, birthday, anniversary; she actually welcomed the excuse to go out and buy another present, whereas so many of us resent the inexorable recurrence of those dates on which we are obliged to buy. She, on the contrary, derived real pleasure from the visible, audible effect of the pleasure she gave others. When Mrs Cavendish-Bentinck gave birth to a son, the infant was presented with an ivory and gold rattle. Daphne Weymouth was given a gold and tortoiseshell comb in a pink leather case from Cartier. She gave Edward Stanley a hugely expensive shaving-brush, which he, disgusted, handed to the taxi-driver on his way home. Quite her most endearing gift was a single pearl every birthday and Christmas to Mairi Vane-Tempest-Stewart. These were carefully kept, accumulated, and eventually passed on to Lady Mairi's daughter, now Lady Sudeley, who to this day wears them regularly. An imaginative gesture was to take the volumes of Castlereagh's Correspondence and have them beautifully bound in leather for his descendant, Lord Londonderry. Knowing that Chips Channon particularly liked a Nattier she possessed, she promised him he would have it, protected it during the war (when she was depleting herself of almost everything she owned), and left it to him in her will.

Thousands of pounds went to the poor and unfortunate who could not possibly have heard of her, and this was always done anonymously, through her secretary Miss Clarke, and never mentioned to the friends who crowded her parties. She sent clothing, for example, to the children of the East End during the worst years of unemployment and paid to educate children of far from wealthy parents, a fact she never mentioned to anyone. To the community of San Francisco she donated the first ever mobile disaster unit to be in service on the Pacific coast. Peter Coats fell ill in New York and had to pass some time in hospital. Medical bills in the United States can bankrupt an Englishman within days, and Coats had no idea how, without a private income, he would be able to settle this awkward debt. As soon as news reached London, through Chips Channon, Laura arranged for the entire account to be paid by her New York bankers.

Laura's generous impulses were not, despite appearances, provoked by a desire to ingratiate or curry favour. They were spontaneous and genuine, and more often than not could hope for no return. Certainly, she was a frequent guest at grand country houses, such as Drumlanrig, Boughton House, Mount Stewart and the rest (though it was frequently a problem to know what to do with her there; she had none of the aristocratic British tradition of leisure, and was always asking what there was to do next. Unless she was planning a social event, she was lost.) These were her rewards, perhaps. Yet much of her kindness was lavished on those who had nothing, and could not reciprocate. Lady Cunard's advice to Elizabeth Leveson-Gower—'You must remember to be kind to the poor. It's only Mrs Corrigan who is kind to the rich'—was not entirely deserved.

Her one fault was a total lack of proportion. She would press five pound notes into the hands of infants, not knowing that they would immediately be confiscated by nanny and banked for the future, with perhaps a shilling allowed for the moment as a treat. Laura had no conception of the meaning of such sums to an English person, nor that it was thought improper in England for a child to be well off; children had to be taught to 'make do', even if they were to come into a vast inheritance one day. Nothing demonstrates better Laura's blindness to the relative difference between American wealth and European impoverishment than her gift to one of the Hesse princesses who was about to be married to George of Hanover. Laura sent hundreds of diaphanous pink underwear items of the very highest quality. The Hesse princess and her sisters were delighted; they set to for the coming weeks to cut up these elegant undies and convert them into the bride's wedding-dress. Laura never knew.

Similarly, when Laura was entertaining the Duchess of Marlborough and Baroness Blixen in Paris, she summoned a gentleman to bring examples of the finest French stockings, which she wished to give the ladies. They must choose what they wanted. They happily chose a fine pair. 'Four?' asked Laura, holding up her fingers. Why not? They nodded. They then had delivery not of four pairs of stockings, but of four dozen pairs each.

With all the people she now knew in London, and every one of them and their children having birthdays, Laura spent more than one or two days a week buying presents. Someone told her after the theatre that it was Sir Humphrey de Trafford's birthday. 'Oh my,' she said, and rushed upstairs. She reappeared bearing a set of solid gold cuff-links and buckles, pressed them into Sir Humphrey's hand and wished him a *very* happy birthday. He accepted graciously, as everyone always did, but with some degree of embarrassment, for it was nowhere near his birthday. Laura had been teased. No one dared tell her. From that day Laura presented Sir Humphrey with a splendid gift on the same date each year, his dilemma growing more delicate as the years passed. Eventually he found a solution. He told Laura that a mistake had been made, that it was not his birthday at all, indeed never had been, but she need not feel foolish, for it was anyway his *name* day. Fortunately Mrs Corrigan did not have the wit to ask who was Saint Humphrey. It was even said that some unscrupulous souls, hearing the story of Sir Humphrey de Trafford, wilfully pretended to a birthday, as if by the way, Laura never failing to respond. As Lord Bath now ruefully confesses, 'We took everything she gave and gave nothing back to the wretched woman.' In its relations with the ridiculous Mrs Corrigan, English society did not present its most attractive face.

There was another aspect to Mrs Corrigan's character which lay unsuspected in all the years of gaiety, and which would have appeared absurdly incongruous had it been even hinted at. She was, at it turned out, a woman of unflinching courage. The approaching war elicited as many varieties of response in people as there are facets in human personality. In Laura, it elicited a brave spirit. Of all the society hostesses, she may have been the least intellectual, the least overtly interesting, but she acquitted herself in the war better than any of them, and terminated her bizarre career in a certain amount of glory.

In the weeks before war broke out, she was journeying through Europe with 'Cockie' Blixen, intending to stay with friends in Rumania. It was while they were in Budapest that they realized a full European war was imminent. They went into a chocolate shop (chocolate was Laura's great weakness), and were told by the shopkeeper, 'You ladies are very brave to stay here. Do you know Hitler has reached Vienna?' They did not know, but they acted immediately. That evening they packed bags and went directly to Lausanne. No sooner had they arrived there than news reached them that Poland had been invaded and war been declared. On the very same day, Laura's two French maids, Marguerite and Marie, took it into their heads to cross the border into France. Being in the service of Mrs Corrigan, they were naturally very smartly dressed, and their passports were stamped with every country in Europe, circumstances which aroused suspicion that they might be spies. The girls were thereupon arrested, and locked up in prison. It fell to Cockie Blixen to explain their innocence and secure their release, with firm instructions from Laura that she must admit to no registered address but make it clear Mrs Corrigan lived only in hotels. The authorities were satisfied, and set free the weeping, bedraggled maids, and all four women, with Rolls-Royce and chauffeur, set off for Paris to resume residence in Laura's suite at the Ritz. The Duchess of Windsor learnt of her presence and took pains to avoid her, as did the Duke's acting equerry, Major 'Fruity' Metcalfe. 'Mrs Corrigan claimed me as almost a prisoner of war', he wrote to his wife. 'I shall escape, believe me.'

Laura's apartment, which occupied almost the whole of the first floor overlooking the Place Vendôme, with three bedrooms, maids' quarters, reception rooms, dining-room, drawing-room, and boudoir ('my bedewer', she said, 'where I have my face and feet done, and rest and think besides'), had seen the last of Mrs Corrigan's lavish entertainments. Now that war was upon her, Laura's energies were immediately directed to more serious purpose. In company with Comte Armand de la Rochefoucauld, she set up a relief organization called 'Bienvenue au Soldat', dedicated to making life more agreeable to the wounded and other victims of hostilities. With the help of two women and one boy, they drove a lorry laden with provisions to and from the firing lines with scarcely a pause for rest and facing the greatest possible danger. At the front Laura herself ran a canteen for the troops, equipped to a luxurious degree with provisions she had chosen and secured. Every soldier who came to her was given hot tea and rum, soft felt slippers to relieve the torture of warfare, a pack of cards, dominoes, film, cigarettes, and a parcel bulging with food. Not only that, but she provided a barber, a chiropodist and a dentist to look after them, had their boots re-soled and mended their clothes before they went off again to fight. Frightened Frenchmen who were hiding in the forest were flushed out by a fearless Laura who went looking for them when nobody else would dare risk his life. As always with Mrs Corrigan, there was a humorous side to her endeavours which amused the less brave. She found the soldiers by shouting out, '*Voici des cigarettes, voici des cigarettes!*', an announcement which worked miracles. She also visited hospitals every day, giving parcels and presents to the wounded, but with an unfortunate benediction which meant the very opposite of her intention. Instead of saying '*Dieu te garde*', she told every soldier, '*Dieu te blesse!*'* No matter. If they laughed, they were none the less grateful for the amazing benevolence of this indefatigable and apparently dauntless stranger.

Laura spent every available other moment, when she was not in the lorry, running the canteen, or visiting a hospital, seeking out poor and frightened citizens to give a moment's comfort. Not always did she bear gifts. She knew in her heart that to the penniless and afflicted an hour of human company was the finest of all bounties. Indeed, she undermined her own health in her frenzied

---

* May God wound you!

efforts to use every moment of the day. Gone were the evenings dining out. Now Laura took a sandwich when she could, and ate alone at the end of the arduous day. 'I never thought this work would get so big and important', she artlessly wrote to Lord Pembroke. 'Sometimes I feel very tired. Maréchal Pétain complimented me on my work.'

One cannot make the abrupt transition from a life of ease to an existence of toil without paying the price. Laura grew weak and careless. One day, on an errand of mercy to a woman dying of pneumonia, she was less alert than she should have been and was knocked down by a lorry. Laura broke both wrists and an ankle. Still she would not surrender to debility. She had herself patched up as best she could, and went on with the work. Weeks later she was still unable to use her right hand, and hobbled uncertainly on one leg.

When the French collapsed and the Germans arrived in Paris, Mrs Corrigan was trapped there. She first sent her secretary, Gertrude Clarke, to the United States by air, barely in time to escape the Occupation. So rushed was the operation, that Miss Clarke did not have time to pack, and Laura went through her belongings with typical thoroughness, throwing out everything she thought unsuitable, and sending on afterwards only those items of Miss Clarke's wardrobe which earned her own approval. (The discarded pieces were naturally replaced with better ones.) The two French maids and the chauffeur, fearing for their lives as the Germans approached, took Laura's car in the middle of the night and sped off to the country. She never saw it or them again.

Bereft of all help, Laura had now to determine how best to deal with the new situation. Her solution was bold and admirable. Never did it enter her head to run away. Understandably, the American government froze all her money in New York, thus limiting her ability to furnish her 'Bienvenue au Soldat' operation. So she set about selling everything she had which could be turned into cash and made useful. The only people in a position to buy were the victorious Germans. Goering took over her apartment at the Ritz (where he stayed throughout the Occupation). She sold Goering her magnificent emerald ring for £50,000, and through him she sold to Hitler her gold dressing-case; this is said to be still in Berlin. With the proceeds she went off to Vichy and continued her work there, ironically using Goering's money to support Goering's enemies. Before she left the Ritz, Laura concealed her minks and sables in a cupboard of her boudoir, dragging a large armoire across to hide the door; they were never discovered by the Germans throughout Goering's residence. She also hid the Nattier she had promised to Chips Channon. Everything else she took to sell as the need arose. Within months, she was reduced to two dresses. 'I have sold everything except my pearls, my two wedding rings and my wristwatch', she wrote to a friend. 'All I possess here could be put in a suitcase.'

At Vichy she lived in a third-rate *pension* sharing a bathroom with six other women. An ordinary bar of soap was a luxury they saw only once every few weeks. Laura was alone and weary. Her only close friend was Armand de la Rochefoucauld. The English friends she had dazzled for so long with her parties now seemed to belong to another existence.

For her work in getting supplies for allied prisoners and delivering them herself in a lorry across the occupied zone frontier time and time again, at great personal risk, Laura Corrigan was decorated by the Vichy government. The ceremony at which she had the Croix de Guerre conferred upon her was described in a letter she wrote to Lord Pembroke. 'The soldiers were drawn up in front in formation of a square open on one side, and Colonel Père took me in front of every soldier. The band played the Marseillaise and the Star-spangled Banner, and I took the salute at the presentation of arms. After that I was placed between two men, one a French Adjut and the other a priest, who had been exceedingly brave with the wounded. The Colonel then conferred the Croix de Guerre on us. I was called out as Caporal-Chef Corrigan. After that we stood between the two colonels and the troops marched past with the band . . . The General of the Division and the officers gave a lunch for me of 48 covers. The walls were hung with flags and there was a large U.S. flag at the back of my chair. I sat on the right hand of the General and the Commanding Colonel on my right. At the end of the lunch the General toasted me in champagne and made a wonderful speech; I had really to look at my plate as I felt confused. When the popotier called out the menu or anybody made a speech they addressed Caporal-Chef Corrigan first and the General second.' Laura's forgivable pride in her honour was interrupted in her letter by a languid, lonely note. 'Give my dear love to all my friends', she said, 'You can't think how much I think of you all in these days.'

Rheumatism had infected her fractured wrists and ankle, to the extent that she was working in pain. The American Ambassador informed her that Maréchal Pétain intended to confer the Légion d'Honneur upon her, but that she should then consider returning to London. Mrs Corrigan had the distinction of being the only American woman apart from Josephine Baker to receive this most coveted of French honours, a distinction hardly diminished by de Gaulle's later rather petty annulment of it on the grounds that Pétain did not truly represent the French government. The essential point remained, that those who benefited from Laura's energetic efforts were French soldiers.

The London to which Laura Corrigan returned in 1942 was hardly recognizable. Gone were the shrieks of merriment and the fizz of champagne, and in their place was an austere yet fierce resolve to win. Parties at 16 Grosvenor Street belonged to an age which could never return. Laura took up residence at Claridge's, not far from Lady Cunard, who was at the Dorchester. Here she resumed contact with old friends, and gave tea parties for their children. Money was now once more within her grasp, as the Americans who had not wanted to see millions of dollars go to Nazi-occupied France were more flexible when London was the destination. With the unfreezing of her finances, Laura set about using them with zest. She arranged for a standing order with a New York shop to send, on a regular basis, the most gargantuan and rich food parcels to everyone she knew in England (to the chosen one hundred-and-twenty, as one of them unkindly put it). This was not enough to satisfy her deep hunger to give. She approached the government and asked what she could do to help. She was told there was a need for some sort of meeting-place and accommodation for air force officers. Without a moment's pause, Laura grabbed the task with both hands. 'Some sort of meeting-place' eventually led to the Wings Club, founded, financed, furnished and run by Mrs Corrigan, with Chips Channon and the Duchess of Marlborough on the Committee.

The Wings Club was located in Lord Moyne's house in Grosvenor Place, of which Laura bought the lease for the purpose. There was no entrance fee or subscription, membership being offered to any R.A.F. air-crew officer who produced his identification. Laura converted the house into a magnificent place, decorated and appointed to the highest degree. From a dealer she bought dozens of huge portraits to cover gaps on the walls (and gave them all away when the war ended and the club was closed). Breakfast she provided for a shilling, lunch for half-a-crown, dinner not much more. The average leave period for junior R.A.F. officers was nine days, so beds could be reserved up to that length of time, at five shillings a night. Laura fitted showers and bathrooms, a library (which Michael Hornby helped her to stock), a billiard room, a writing-room, and an information bureau. No other comparable institution could match it for residential comfort, and the inevitable annual deficit, of huge proportions, was met by Mrs Corrigan herself. For this she was awarded the King's Medal. At the end of the war she was supporting 700 club members. (After this she was frequently observed wearing her medals even at lunch at Claridge's.)

Laura would not be Laura without the endearing malapropisms, which cluttered her speech even more after her long period in France. She would not use an English word if a French word sounded better, and would ask children if they wanted some more '*confiture*' when they would have been happier with jam. An American visitor sightseeing in bomb-spattered London, anxious to understand the glories of architecture, asked her about flying buttresses. 'Oh my,' she said, 'you wouldn't believe it, they came over *every night*.'

Though darkened and scarred London was a sombre city, life proceeded as best it could, and Laura made her own contribution towards making it bearable. We find mention of her entertaining in quieter mood, but with as much energy and generosity as ever. A wartime Christmas party she organized, with holly, sherry, champagne, Christmas pudding and a feast of rarities scarcely ever seen in London during this time of desperate privation, was much cosier than her former grandiose entertainments; Laura had been subdued by her recent experiences. Still, the paramount object of her exertions was to give pleasure, and the party turned out to be charming and unpretentious. It was spoilt only by Lady Cunard's tactless remark that she could never find enough to eat in England.

Emerald Cunard and Laura Corrigan were much in each other's company these days. The earlier misgivings which had led them to contemplate one another at a distance had quite disappeared. They were both American, both old, both alone. Emerald did, however, find it necessary on occasion to apologize to her intellectual friends for Laura's shortcomings in the cultural area, and when they went to the theatre she would try hard to resist the temptation to ask Laura's opinion.

One who was bedevilled by Laura's presence whenever he called on Emerald was Ronald Storrs. 'She held down the table with snob items of intolerable boredom', he wrote; and 'her laboured longwinded unpointed anecdotes worse even than Sibyl Colefax's, ruining an otherwise possible meal'. Storrs resolved that if Lady Cunard asked him again, he would telephone first to make sure there would be no Mrs Corrigan. He did not keep his resolution.

In May 1943, Laura was taken by Chips Channon to the Te Deum service at St Paul's Cathedral to give thanks for victory in Africa. The service had originally been planned for eleven in the morning, but was rescheduled at the last minute in order to confuse the Germans, who might have thought it appealing to bomb the place when it contained the King and Queen, the heir to the throne, the Kings of Norway and Yugoslavia, Churchill, de Gaulle, and practically everyone else of note. Laura Corrigan had every right to feel she belonged as a participant and not a spectator in this impeccably English occasion; however mysterious her past, her present was honourable.

Laura even earned a footnote in the history of Europe's royal families, for it was at one of her parties that Michael of Rumania met the woman whom he subsequently married. One might say that

Laura Corrigan had introduced them.

At the end of the war, Laura was tired and ageing. She was approaching seventy, though the wigs still carefully concealed any evidence of falling hair. Her endless babble of social chatter was slower. She dismantled the Wings Club and gave away the furniture and pictures she had bought for it. (One of the largest pictures now hangs in Peter Coats's flat in London.) It was not long before she decided that her failing health and weariness presaged the end of her eventful life. Once she had made up her mind, she began to give away many of her possessions, holding on to the magnificent pearls, of which she once told someone who admired them that there were 'seven yards in my bedewer'. She did not talk about her health, but she thought she knew she would die of cancer.

At the end of 1947, Laura went to New York where her sister Mabelle was waiting for her. She arrived on Christmas Eve, and made an appointment for a medical check-up in the New Year. The two sisters spent Christmas Day quietly together at the Plaza Hotel, but shortly afterwards Laura weakened. Doctors diagnosed that her fears had been justified. She stayed with Mabelle, reminiscing, remembering their childhood together and musing upon the long journey Laura had made into the choicest and most elegant society in the world. On 21 January 1948, Laura was taken seriously ill and rushed to the Post-graduate Hospital in New York for an emergency operation. She did not survive it, and died there the following morning, exactly twenty years to the day after her husband Jimmy. Her dying words, spoken to a surgeon before the operation, may well be apocryphal, but they were almost true whether or not they were uttered. 'I know I have done a lot of foolish things in my life', she is supposed to have said, 'but as a little girl I often dreamed of knowing all the kings and queens in the world. And I've had my wish.'

Chips Channon recorded in his diary that London was 'grief-stricken' at Laura's sudden and unexpected death. It had been neither sudden nor unexpected to Laura, but she typically had told no one, and had simply given her things away. In an access of conscience, all the friends who had so often benefited from Laura's good nature telephoned each other to register their shock. Now she

was gone, they wished they had been kinder towards her; it is a
common enough reaction. Channon wrote, 'good kind Laura will
long live in my memory', and one believed him. He called Mabelle
at the Plaza in New York and listened to her distant sobs. His
epitaph for her was well-judged, as far as it went, yet even he did not
know her truly.

> Laura was an amazing woman [he said]—sexless, devoid of any
> outward physical attractions and never consciously amusing, yet
> she made an international position for herself in the very highest
> society, which she wooed and cajoled. Her wealth and extreme
> kindness as well as her petty snobberies and eccentricities were
> proverbial . . . her death ends an epoch.

Channon, the Duke of Buccleuch and Alan Lennox-Boyd
together arranged a memorial service at St Mark's Church, North
Audley Street, 'in memory of poor Laura Corrigan'. It was a
moving occasion. The congregation would have pleased her,
including as it did a handful of duchesses (among them the Duchess
of Devonshire, whom Laura had persisted in calling 'Moocher'), a
host of Cavendishes, all the Londonderrys, the Herberts, the
Thynnes, Sacheverell Sitwell, and ambassadors from half a dozen
countries. Most significant of all, Her Royal Highness Princess
Marina, Duchess of Kent, attended. It was the first time she had
been present at a non-royal memorial service. How appropriate that
Laura Corrigan, whom everybody laughed at for the idiotic things
she said, should be accorded this special honour by a lady known for
her perception and wisdom.

Meanwhile, in the United States, Laura's body was taken from
New York to Cleveland, where it was interred beside her husband
at Lake View Cemetery. Attention was focused on the contents of
the will, which was drawn up only eight days before Laura died.
Chips Channon had wondered whether he would stand to inherit 'a
cool million'. When the will was revealed on 17 February, there
were a few surprises. Inevitably, there were mocking remarks about
the list of legatees being taken from the pages of Burke's Peerage
and the Almanach de Gotha, but, like it or not, Laura had found

friends among the European aristocracy after the ladies of Cleveland and New York had slammed the door rudely in her face. Charlie Stirling, who had engineered her introduction into London society, and Lady Milbank, who had helped her with the Wings Club, received $10,000 each. Her godson Lord Weymouth was given $5,000, as were Lady Londonderry, Diana Bowes-Daly (sister of the Duchess of Buccleuch), and the two maids who had run off with her car to escape the Germans, Marie Erbin and Marguerite Rousse. Legacies of $3,000 each went to Princess Réné de Bourbon-Parme, Princess Guy de Faucigny-Lucinge, Comte Armand de la Rochefoucauld, Chips Channon, and Laura's secretary Miss Clarke.

The residue of her estate went to her sister Mabelle, who thereby was the richer by about a million and a half dollars. Mabelle also had the life use of Laura's fabulous four strings of pearls, with the instruction that upon Mabelle's death the pearls should be sold and the proceeds given to the St Alexis Hospital in Cleveland. The surprise came with the mention of two more sisters, of whom Laura had never once spoken in her twenty-five years of party-giving in Europe. A sister Clara, living in Los Angeles, received $50,000, and another half-sister, Grace, was named without a specific legacy.

Nobody, in 1948, was curious enough to investigate the identity of these 'unknown' sisters and thereby discover exactly who was Laura Corrigan and where she had come from. Now it is possible to trace back to her origins; her early life and her subsequent career form such a contrast that it is scarcely believable that they describe the same woman.

In England she was always known as Laura. In her home town of Stevens Point, Wisconsin, she had been born Laura Mae Whitrock, and was called by the full appellation, 'Laura Mae'. Laura Mae was the second of three daughters born to Charles and Emma Whitrock, in 1879. Charles and Emma were desperately poor, with scarcely enough income to keep their little family comfortable or even nourished. Charles's wages were paltry.

Stevens Point lies in the heart of the pine forests (or 'pineries') of Wisconsin. In the nineteenth century there was little employment outside the industry which relied upon the pine trees, so Charles Whitrock was a humble lumberjack. He had come from Canada, of English stock, and may well have learnt his trade as a lumberman there. When first Clara, then Laura, then Mabel were born, Emma had to supplement their income by working as a domestic servant; she had been born in Wales, of a family well used to such service, and had no reason to regard her lot as degrading. On the contrary, Emma Whitrock worked even harder than she needed, in order to help her husband, and when she came home from her duties, she set to work baking bread and cakes for Charles and his work-mates. In time she had a small but regular income from her baking, and set up what amounted to a modest 'diner' where lumbermen could repair for a decent, cheap meal, home-cooked. As the girls grew up, they used to help mother in the kitchen, and take food and cookies out to the men.

Charles Whitrock died suddenly while the girls were all still young, and Emma then married the local odd-jobs man, William Parker. At this time, they lived at 1302 Clark Street. Clara, Laura Mae, and Mabel all attended the Stevens Point High School in their turn, but Laura Mae was early distinguished as the most conscious of herself and her appearance. Even poor, she contrived always to look smart, neat, and pretty, and earned the admiration of the town boys for her feminine graces. Laura Mae and Mabel were virtually inseparable; they looked alike, and went everywhere together.

It was a happy family, but Laura Mae was already showing signs of ambition. By the time she was sixteen, she had seen enough of poverty and was determined her mother and stepfather should escape the arduous life they had known. She would be the agent of their release. She had more intelligence than the rest of the family, and knew that her cleverness could one day be put to use. At no time was she tempted to make similar use of her prettiness. There is no evidence that Laura Mae was ever immoral or 'loose'. Then, as later, the question of sex played little or no role in her imaginings.

Laura Mae's only formal education was the rather limited grounding offered by a small-town high school in the nineteenth century. She afterwards went to the Stevens Point Business College where she learnt the functions of a secretary and absorbed all the useful rules and strategies which go to make a successful business, and would later be put to spectacular practical effect when she wrested control of the mighty Corrigan–McKinney Steel Company. Quietly and securely, Laura Mae accumulated the knowledge to serve her ambitions.

Her first job was as a stenographer in the office of William Wheelan, attorney, in Wisconsin Rapids, graduating to legal secretary. There she naturally learnt the subtle distinctions between what may be lawfully achieved and what is improper. Shortly afterwards, she left home to make a life in Chicago, the nearest large international city. Stevens Point did not castigate her for leaving her parents. It was recognized that she had been a kind and dutiful daughter, had devoted her young life to helping her impoverished parents in every way, and deserved the right to exploit her potential.

When she arrived in Chicago she was described as 'slim, young, blonde and clever' (the wigs which were a feature of her London life were generally dark, and the wisps spied beneath them may have been fair rather than grey). Her employment there was a modest publicity job at the office of Sam Gerson. More to the point, she found her way into the lower reaches of Chicago society; there had been nothing like this hierarchy or sophistication in the pine forests, and Laura Mae found it much to her liking. She wrote her own poems, impressing the city ladies with her provincial talents, and was frequently invited to read them aloud to the Illinois Women's Press Association. (Years later, Laura would write a poem on her husband Jimmy's birthday, every year without fail. These were donated to a museum in New York; Lady Cunard wickedly suggested they could be found under the pseudonym 'Duchess of Few Wits'.) She also edited an amateur magazine called 'School Days'.

In Chicago Laura Mae Whitrock met the Scottish resident doctor at the Great Northern Hotel, Dr Duncan B. MacMarten. They fell in love and married at the church in Stevens Point. It is at this stage that Laura Mae becomes Laura and assumes the personality which was to become so well-known in London. As Mrs MacMarten she met the Corrigan family, divorced, remarried, bought her strings of pearls and came with her millions and her determination to Paris and London. The rest we know.

Meanwhile, Emma and William Parker had two daughters, half-sisters to Laura. The younger one, Veda, died of the 'flu epidemic in the First World War. Grace Parker, the elder sister, survived to spend her life in Wisconsin. Sister Mabel married the boy from the local drug-store, Dave Taylor (they would later be metamorphosed into David and Mabelle Armstrong-Taylor).

It was easy to sneer at the generosity of Laura Corrigan, to note that dukes received ducal presents and baronesses took the dregs, to observe how Laura's eyes lit up when she thought there was somebody in the room worth knowing, to be deflected elsewhere as soon as she realized he was not. It is, however, a jaundiced, unfair assessment. Her true kindness to everyone back home in Wisconsin was totally without guile and heedless of anticipated reward. She paid to educate her brother-in-law David Taylor and transform him from a small-town druggist to an eminent San Francisco surgeon and Professor of obstetrics. Likewise, she provided the means to educate Ed Bassett, whom her half-sister Grace married. For her mother and stepfather she wanted nothing less than the total annihilation of all memories of penury. Laura bought them a house on Main Street, Stevens Point, equipped it, and paid for it to be run with cook, housekeeper, maid and chauffeur for the rest of their lives. Her financial agent in the town was the Baptist pastor, Rev. James Blake, who was instructed by Laura to handle all the expenses incurred by her mother's household so that Emma and William would never have to worry about anything. The house eventually cost $10,000 a year to keep going, a handsome sum in 1930. Every few years, Laura would send a new car to keep her mother up-to-date.

Emma died in 1935, but Laura's flow of funds did not stop. She sent her nephew and niece (Grace's children) through college, exhorting them to improve themselves, write properly, watch their grammar, and so on. The boy, Ronald Bassett, spent two worthwhile years at Harvard at Laura's expense, and persuaded his room-mate to write the thank-you letters which were always demanded from Aunt Laura for any bounty. She commented that his grammar had certainly improved since he went to Harvard.

Her mother's closest friend, Mrs MacNish, received a regular amount of money from Laura for the rest of her life, in gratitude for her friendship towards Mama. In addition, she would receive boxes of clothes, and all kinds of unlooked-for gifts which, for the most part, she did not know what to do with. An expensive leather hand-bag, for example, quite incongruous in Stevens Point, arrived out of the blue one day. It was said that Laura Mae never wore underclothes twice; every month, a huge box of the most exquisite lingerie (similar to that which was ripped apart to provide a wedding-dress for the Hesse princess) arrived on Mrs MacNish's doorstep, until she eventually had accumulated vast quantities. Naturally, since she was an old woman for whom lace knickers held no especial attraction, none of this was ever worn. It was characteristic of Laura Corrigan to be kind yet undiscerning; to overwhelm an elderly mid-west lady with Paris lingerie was akin to offering £5 to a Scottish labourer's daughter on the Buccleuch estates.

By far the most lavish attention was bestowed upon 'my sister Mabelle'. It mattered deeply to Laura that her sister should dominate the San Francisco social scene, so she met all her sister's bills in her attempt to establish herself. It worked, of course. Mrs Armstrong-Taylor's *soirées* were very soon a major subject of gossip in the city and a frequent source of newspaper material, her incessant winking a constant trap to the uninformed, and her pretensions to grand ancestry as much a source of fun as Laura's malapropisms. David Armstrong-Taylor bore all this with heavy patience. He was not interested in social climbing; when Mabelle was having a party, David would find cause not to attend. He would leave the house, buy all the newspapers and magazines he could lay his hands on, drive to his office, and shut himself in for a good long read, having pinned an 'ENGAGED WITH PATIENT' sign on his door. He would not go home until he knew his wife's party was over.

The Taylors had one son, Duncan, educated by Aunt Laura in Paris and Switzerland. It was *peine perdue*; Duncan was neither bright nor attractive, an obese, vapid individual whom no amount of attention could bring to blossom. As Laura herself had no children, Duncan's total lack of promise proved a disappointment. It was extremely difficult to find a girl who would sacrifice her life to become his consort. When he did marry the former Mrs Christin, it was only for a few months, for he died suddenly at the age of thirty-five. Those few months were highly remunerative for Mrs Christin/Taylor; they enabled her to inherit the Corrigan wealth which passed from Jimmy to Laura to Mabelle to Duncan and to Duncan's widow.

Professor David Armstrong-Taylor died in 1944. Mabelle married a property developer, Donald McLeod Lewis in 1949. It was, to say the least, fortunate that Mr Lewis was more society-conscious than Dave Taylor, for Mabelle took him to Paris and rented Laura's old suite on the first floor of the Ritz. So desperate were they to entertain that they were reduced to leaning out of the window and yelling to passers-by in the Place Vendôme below, 'Come up and have a drink!'

Mabelle herself died in 1953. She had the same fastidious habits as Laura, always putting things in their proper place, closing drawers, and arranging lines parallel or symmetrical. The habit was indirectly responsible for her death. She leaned over to pick up an ashtray, slipped on the too highly polished floor, fell and broke a shoulder and hip. She underwent an operation, but developed pneumonia, from which she died. The pearls then went to assist the funds of the hospital, as had been Laura's wish. Mabelle had typically been preparing for a party, a grand and expensive gathering in aid of spastic children.

There are relations of Laura Corrigan alive now. The closest is her nephew Ronald Bassett, son of her half-sister Grace. He is now an insurance broker in South Bend, Indiana. Then there is William Metcalf in Wisconsin Rapids, an attorney-at-law, who is the son of Grace's daughter. Metcalf's office is the historical descendant of the very same law firm which gave Laura Mae Whitrock her first job as a legal secretary—the office of William Wheelan.

A prolific American novelist, Louis Bromfield, was inspired by Laura's story to construct a novel around it. Called *What Became of Anna Bolton?*, the novel portrayed Laura as a misfit from the 'wrong side of the tracks' who made a name for herself as businesswoman and hostess while devoting much energy to the concealment of her origins. 'Money did not mean much to her because there was so much of it', wrote Bromfield. 'Knowing everyone, devouring the whole world was far more important.' Still, Bromfield did not know the details of Laura's early life, and his portrait is only partially identifiable.

The most arresting reflection on Mrs Corrigan, Croix de Guerre, Légion d'Honneur and King's Medal, remains this: the indefatigable hostess and war heroine found her moments of relaxation chopping wood for the Duke of Devonshire, because her father had been a lumberjack.

Sources and Bibliography

A. Manuscript

Desborough Papers, Hertford County Record Office.
Sir Ronald Storrs' Papers, Pembroke College, Cambridge.
Letter from Mrs Greville in Templewood Papers, University
    Library, Cambridge.
Letters from Maurice Baring, privately owned.
Letter from Mrs Corrigan to Lord Pembroke, privately owned.
Letters from Lady Cunard to Nicholas Lawford, privately owned.

B. Newspapers and periodicals

Fortune magazine, December 1935
The Times, 16 Sept. 1942
Vogue (American edition), 15 Nov. 1941 (article by Frank
    Crowninshield)
Spectator, 13 Oct. 1950 (article by Harold Nicolson)
Sunday Times Magazine, 9 Nov. 1975 (article by V.S. Pritchett)
The Times Literary Supplement, 4 January 1980 (article by Alistair
    Forbes)
Newspaper cuttings library, *Daily Express*

C. Books

Harold Acton, *Memoirs of an Aesthete* (1948)
Harold Acton, *More Memoirs of an Aesthete* (1970)
Lady Cynthia Asquith, *Diaries 1915–1918* (1968)
Margot Asquith, *Autobiography* (1920)
Brooke Astor, *Footprints* (1980)
Consuelo Balsan, *The Glitter and the Gold* (1953)
Andrew Barrow, *Gossip* (1978)
Cecil Beaton, *Self-portrait with Friends* (1979)
Max Beerbohm, 'Maltby and Braxton', in *Seven Men*
E.F. Benson, *As We Were* (1930)
Mary Borden, *Four O'Clock and Other Stories* (1926)
Andrew Boyle, *The Climate of Treason*
Ruth Brandon, *The Dollar Princesses* (1980)
Louis Bromfield, *What Became of Anna Bolton?* (1944)
Charles Burkhart, *Herman and Nancy and Ivy: Three lives in art* (1977)
Roderick Cameron, *My Travel's History* (1950)
Boni de Castellane, *Comment J'ai Découvert l'Amérique*
Henry Channon, *Chips*, diaries edited by R. Rhodes James (1967)
Anne Chisholm, *Nancy Cunard* (1979)
Kenneth Clark, *Another Part of the Wood* (1974)
Diana Cooper, *The Rainbow Comes and Goes* (1958)
Diana Cooper, *The Light of Common Day* (1959)
Elizabeth, Lady Decies, *Turn of the World* (1937)
Elizabeth, Lady Decies (under name Elizabeth Drexel Lehr), *King Lehr and the Gilded Age* (1935)
Lady Desborough, *Eyes of Youth* (privately printed, Cambridge)
Lady Desborough, *Pages from a Family Journal* (1916)
Frances Donaldson, *Edward VIII* (1974)
Max Egremont, *Balfour* (1980)
Daphne Fielding, *Emerald and Nancy* (1958)
Daphne Fielding, *Mercury Presides* (1954)
Arthur Gold and Robert Fizdale, *Misia* (1980)
Violet Greville, *Vignettes of Memory* (1911)
Michael Holroyd, *Lytton Strachey*, vol. II (1968)

Edwin P. Hoyt, *The Vanderbilts and Their Fortunes* (1962)
Aldous Huxley, *Letters* (1969)
H. Montgomery Hyde, *Baldwin* (1973)
H. Montgomery Hyde, *The Londonderrys* (1979)
Sonia Keppel, *Edwardian Daughter* (1958)
James Lees-Milne, *Ancestral Voices* (1975)
James Lees-Milne, *Prophesying Peace* (1977)
James Lees-Milne, *Harold Nicolson*, 2 vols. (1981)
John Lehmann, *I Am My Brother* (1960)
Cole Lesley, *Life of Noël Coward* (1976)
Robert Bruce Lockhart, *Diaries*, 2 vols. (1973 and 1980)
Robert Bruce Lockhart, *Your England* (1955)
Robert Bruce Lockhart, *Giants Cast Long Shadows* (1960)
Leslie Mitchell, *Holland House* (1979)
George Moore, *Letters to Lady Cunard* (1957)
Diana Mosley, *A Life of Contrasts* (1977)
Nicholas Mosley, *Julian Grenfell* (1976)
Harold Nicolson, *Diaries* (1966, 1967, 1968)
John Pearson, *Façades* (1978)
Duke of Portland, *Men, Women and Things* (1938)
Peter Quennell, *At The Sign of the Fish* (1960)
Peter Quennell, editor, *Genius in the Drawing-room* (1980)
Osbert Sitwell, *Great Morning* (1948)
Osbert Sitwell, *Laughter in the Next Room* (1949)
Cornelius Vanderbilt, *Farewell to Fifth Avenue* (1935)
Cornelius Vanderbilt, *Queen of the Golden Age* (1956)
Cornelius Vanderbilt, *Man of the World* (1961)
Evelyn Waugh, *Diaries* (1976)
Leonard Woolf, *Downhill all the Way* (1967)
Virginia Woolf, *A Writer's Diary* (1959)
Virginia Woolf, 'Am I a Snob?', in *Collected Essays*
Virginia Woolf, *Letters* (1977)
Philip Ziegler, *Diana Cooper* (1981)

Index